RECLAIMING THE CLASSROOM

Teacher Research as an Agency for Change

RECLAIMING THE CLASSROOM

Teacher Research as an Agency for Change

Edited by

Dixie Goswami and Peter R. Stillman

BOYNTON/COOK PUBLISHERS
HEINEMANN
PORTSMOUTH, NH

Permissions

The editors wish to express their thanks for permission to use the following works:

"A Quiet Form of Research," by James Britton, from *English Journal* (April 1983). Copyright © 1983 by the National Council of Teachers of English. Reprinted by permission of the publisher and the author.

"A Lot of Talk About Nothing," by Shirley Brice Heath, from *Language Arts,* Vol. 60, No. 8. Copyright © by the National Council of Teachers of English. Reprinted by permission of the publisher and the author.

from "Non-Magical Thinking," by Janet Emig, from *Writing: The Nature Development, and Teaching of Written Communication (Vol. II).* Copyright © 1982 by Lawrence Erlbaum Associates. Reprinted by permission of the publisher and the author.

"Diving In: An Introduction to Basic Writing," by Mina P. Shaughnessy, from *College Composition and Communication* (October 1976). Copyright © 1976 by the National Council of Teachers of English. Reprinted by permission of the publisher.

"Class-Based Writing Research: Teachers Learning from Students," by Nancie Atwell, from *English Journal* (January 1982). Copyright © 1982 by the National Council of Teachers of English. Reprinted by permission of the publisher and the author.

"Everyone Sits at a Big Desk: Discovering Topics for Writing," by Nancie Atwell, from *English Journal* (September 1985). Copyright © 1985 by the National Countil of Teachers of English. Reprinted by permission of the publisher and the author.

Library of Congress Cataloging-in-Publication Data

Reclaiming the classroom

1. Action research in education—United States.
2. Teaching.   3. Education—United States—Aims and objectives.   I. Goswami, Dixie.   II. Stillman, Peter.
LB1028.24.R43   1986   371.1   86-21581
ISBN 0-86709-065-0

Printed in the United States of America
89 90 91 92 93 9 8 7 6 5 4 3

Preface

*The hardest bit is making the familiar classroom strange
to yourself.*

Peter Medway

Over the past few years, an alternative research tradition has
been evolving in this country. It goes by various names: "teacher
research," "classroom inquiry," "naturalistic research," "action
research." This notion of teachers as researchers can probably be
traced to the influence of Lawrence Stenhouse and his successors
in the United Kingdom. In a sense, we all have engaged in classroom
inquiry since our earliest experiences as teachers, for we have listened,
observed, questioned, and hypothesized, all to the hoped-for end of
improving the quality of learning in our classrooms.

Most such inquiries have been private, however: daily responses
to the mystifying business of teaching and learning, without system
or specific questions. We are just beginning to find our voices in this
matter, as we develop skills that will allow us to capture what is happening in our classrooms and step back and analyze and interpret
what we have seen and heard—and to go public if we choose. We are
beginning to imagine what would happen if a school or a system
would provide the resources that would let us sustain some of these
inquiries over a period of five—or even ten—years.

Most of us in the classroom have long viewed "research" as the
science of our art: an elaborate, formalistic process best left to experts with special training (and special funding), a view that casts
teachers in the role of consumers rather than producers of knowledge
about learning. We don't question the value of quantitative research
in education, but in this book we take seriously the notion that
teachers and students are able to formulate questions about language
and learning, design and carry out inquiries, reflect on what they
have learned, and tell others about it. In other words, teachers and
students are conducting inquiries that are necessary to provide contexts for, and help us make sense of (and reject or use), the findings
of quantitative, experimental projects. Obviously, teachers who cast
themselves as learners redefine their roles in the classroom: they are

part of classrooms that are "learning communities." This consequence of classroom inquiry is more important to us than findings or publication.

Increasingly, teachers feel the need to ask questions for themselves: to observe, document, and draw conclusions—with the help of their students—and to do so throughout their professional lives. As Nancie Atwell puts it later in this volume, ". . . we teachers are in an ideal position to observe, describe, and learn from the behaviors of our students." We invite those who design in-service programs for professional development to consider the potential of classroom inquiry to improve the quality of education in classrooms and schools and to invent ways to offer teachers opportunities to do this work instead of, or in addition to, participating in traditional in-service programs.

Let's review what many of us have observed about what happens when teachers conduct research as a regular part of their roles as teachers:

1. Their teaching is transformed in important ways: they become theorists, articulating their intentions, testing their assumptions, and finding connections with practice.

2. Their perceptions of themselves as writers and teachers are transformed. They step up their use of resources; they form networks; and they become more active professionally.

3. They become rich resources who can provide the profession with information it simply doesn't have. They can observe closely, over long periods of time, with special insights and knowledge. Teachers know their classrooms and students in ways that outsiders can't.

4. They become critical, responsive readers and users of current research, less apt to accept uncritically others' theories, less vulnerable to fads, and more authoritative in their assessment of curricula, methods, and materials.

5. They can study writing and learning and report their findings without spending large sums of money (although they must have support and recognition). Their studies, while probably not definitive, taken together should help us develop and assess writing curricula in ways that are outside the scope of specialists and external evaluators.

6. They collaborate with their students to answer questions important to both, drawing on community resources in new and unexpected ways. The nature of classroom discourse changes when inquiry begins. Working with teachers to answer real questions provides students with intrinsic motivation for talking, reading, and writing and has the potential for helping them achieve mature language skills.

How does one go about it? Much of *Reclaiming the Classroom* addresses the *how*'s as well as the *why*'s of action research, although it's decidedly not a recipe book; nowhere in it are step-by-step procedures or models meant for replication. Following another's blueprint is inimical to the spirit of classroom research. Instead, it's our hope that *Reclaiming the Classroom* will prove to be a vindication of your deepest professional concerns, for you'll hear from others herein whose need to know moved them to initiate modest but meaningful research projects of their own design. Some of the essays were written by theorist-practitioners central to the development of this alternative research tradition. Their names will be familiar to you. However, many selections are by teacher-researchers who are published here for the first time, documenting their own classroom practices and results.

This is meant to be an encouraging book, whose theme is caught in James Britton's observation, "What the teacher does not achieve in the classroom cannot be achieved by anybody else."

In a true experiment you keep constant every cause you can think of except one, and then see what the effects are of varying that one cause. In the classroom you can never do this.

Robert M. Pirsig
Zen and the Art of Motorcycle Maintenance

Acknowledgments

Nearly a hundred rural teachers from across the country have been part of the classroom inquiry program supported by the Bread Loaf School of English. We owe a great debt to them and their students. They have let us observe them redefine their roles as they worked over several years to learn about the language and learning in their classrooms and communities. They have been generous in sharing all aspects of their inquiries with us. They've considered with us the issues that arise when theory, research, and practice are connected in the laboratories that are their classrooms.

We also wish to acknowledge the part played by Paul Cubeta, Director of the Bread Loaf School of English, whose imagination and practical administrative genius made small grants to Bread Loaf teachers possible, with the generous support of Middlebury College, the Lyndhurst Foundation, the Rockefeller Foundation, the Fund for the Improvement of Postsecondary Education, and other funders. All are partners in this effort.

At every stage, Elizabeth Bailey's help has been vitally important. We cannot list her contributions, but we want to acknowledge her many roles as teaching assistant and friend to the Bread Loaf Program in Writing: she has worked tirelessly with teacher-researchers in all phases of their inquiries, collected manuscripts for this book, pointed out omissions, and helped us understand what we were about.

All members of the Bread Loaf faculty have acted as resources, consultants and, in some cases, co-researchers. All have contributed in substantial ways to this book, especially Nancy Martin, who helped form questions, transcribed interviews, and brought her wit and intelligence to bear on every aspect of the book. James Britton, Donald Graves, Shirley Brice Heath, Tony Burgess, Peter Medway, John Dixon, Boyd Davis, Ken Macrorie, and Jim Moffett have worked with Bread Loaf teacher-researchers and helped us from the beginning. Ann Berthoff gave us more than the book's title: her insistence on observing as a way of engaging the imagination, her deep understanding of *"re*-search," have informed the best parts of the Bread Loaf's classroom inquiry program and our thinking as well.

We are grateful to Robert Boynton for his great patience in particular in bringing this collection to print and in general for his larger role in helping establish the climate which made the work it describes possible.

Contents

PART ONE

Classroom Inquiry: What Is It?

Interview with Cindy Myers

BETTY BAILEY: What happens when you do classroom research?

CINDY MYERS: I think it changes my teaching because I can see better if things are or aren't working.

* * *

Every year when I start research by keeping field notes, I keep thinking that this is an exercise and I'm just writing down what's happening and I'm not getting anything out of it. It seems like a bland kind of thing. But when I keep doing that, all of a sudden I'll hear the kids say something that shows they've changed in some way, and I'll put that down too. And then things start to pull together. It's almost like through the field notes that I keep and through what I see happening—out of those field notes—the classroom becomes more alive. There are things going on that I didn't realize and we're really getting someplace. Just to stand up there and teach every period and not do the classroom research makes the classroom seem boring.

* * *

I guess what I do a lot of times with classroom research is to take special note of things I hear the kids saying. Like at the end of the year when one student turned to another and said, "I've read three more books this year than I've read in my whole life," I wrote that down. My gosh! Now that could have gone right past me, and I could have thought, "Oh, that's nice." But in context with all the other things that happened to that boy during the year, it was such a remarkable change. Sometimes it's just picking up phrases that I hear from the kids and I go ahead and write them down and maybe it doesn't hit me until after I've written it down and looked back at it and looked at what's actually there.

* * *

A student came up to me when we had to do some research papers, and I'd had them doing some informal writing—a thinking log while we were doing the research. And he came running up to me in between classes one day and said that he had just gotten all these *other* ideas while he was writing. The kind of thing I wanted him to be doing! So I wrote down what it was he was telling me. And I was thinking, "Well, my gosh, there's more happening in these kids than I thought." I can look at my classroom and think, "There's not very

3

much going on here," just from the way their faces look sometimes. They act like they're not really too interested. But you can't really tell what's going through their minds. To keep track of what they say really shows a lot of times there's a lot more going on.

*　　*　　*

I felt this past year that being a researcher in the classroom saved me, in a way. I thought most of the year I wasn't getting the kids involved the way I wanted to. I kept thinking, "What is the matter here?" Then in the last three months of school all of a sudden I found all these changes taking place. Because of the questionnaires I gave them, I could see changes taking place there; because of things they were saying to me about the books they read; and because of my notes—the things they were saying to each other while they worked, what they were doing with their writing. All of a sudden I found out it hadn't been a wasted year.

*　　*　　*

If I were a new teacher in my school and I *wasn't* doing classroom research and I went through the whole year like that, I wouldn't have seen all those things happening at the end of the year. I would have thought, "Well, I have to start all over again next year." When I was thinking, "Maybe what I'm doing isn't right," my classroom research showed me I was right, that I was on the right track. Now I can see that what I was trying to do with the kids was putting me on the right track. Now I have to pick up with that and I can do a better job next year.

Addressing the Problem of Elsewhereness

A Case for Action Research in Schools

GARTH BOOMER
The Commonwealth Schools Commission

For Garth Boomer, "To learn deliberately is to research."
Deliberate learning . . . *It's what we ask of our students,*
isn't it? Yet it is easy—even reasonable—for teachers to
leave deliberate learning behind, to become dispensers of
learning rather than its practitioners. As for research, we
know it mostly as an essence emanating from universities
and other outside agencies and exuding an "elsewhere-

*ness"—a bigness and impersonality that may hold gener-
ally useful findings but never quite the ones that fit our
classroom. In fact, we may be so much conditioned by
"big R" Research as to perceive ourselves and our students as being somehow in its service.*

To learn deliberately is to research. The practice of "action
research" for many teachers and students is a reacquainting of themselves with certain parts of their brains; a repossession of the "secrets"
of research with which they were born. This essay makes a case for
developing the school as a "community of thinkers." It is based on
the considered view that, by and large, schools are not presently institutions of learning and thinking and that "big R" Research will
not significantly contribute to educational change until this is so.

If I were to begin with a lament about the struthious behavior
of many "big R" Researchers and the alienating effects of the stirpi-
culture which they have created, I might temporarily turn the more
tenacious and curious of you into researchers. Those of you less curious and tenacious would most likely become alienated because of
the stirpicultural bias of my lexicon and my deliberately adopted
struthiousness with respect to your vocabulary and experience.

Basil Bernstein argued at a conference in Canberra in 1978 that
schools breed citizens with two distinctly different consciousnesses
and world views. One group, those who succeed, tend to believe that
they are capable of seeking, possessing, and banking on knowledge.
The other group, those who fail, tend to believe that knowledge is
"elsewhere," not to be possessed, to be deferred to, rebelled against,
or distrusted. Thus, a kind of knowledge capitalism is reinforced
from generation to generation.

I would be more confident about education if even this were
so. Then teachers, those who have succeeded, would at least teach
that knowledge can be actively sought, possessed, and acted on, if
you agree with me that, enduringly, when all the surfaces of the curriculum are stripped away, teachers teach what they are. It is my
fear, however, that most of those who succeed merely learn the social and economic advantages of "academic" knowledge and how to
show evidence that it has been possessed. Few, I think, learn how to
seek out knowledge and to test it in action; that is, do *research*. I
base this on my own experience of secondary and tertiary education
and the quite remarkably similar tales which generations of gradu-
ates have told me. Research in education is a post-graduate luxury.

I submit that it is a relatively rare teacher who can teach children how to be researchers because it is a relatively rare teacher who
is a self-conscious researcher. The science teacher tends not to be a

scientist; the English teacher tends not to be a writer; the math teacher tends not to be a mathematician. The scientist, the writer, and the mathematician are self-conscious and deliberate learners. They must continually seek out solutions to problems and test their findings to be what they are. Their trades, while differentiated at the surface level, are at base the same. They are professional generators of hypotheses and seekers of solutions.

Now, teachers teach science and mathematics and English. To do this they, too, must generate their hypotheses and test them; hypotheses about how best to teach the next concept, how best to provide materials, how best to control, how best to arrange and order the syllabus, and so on. They are to this extent action researchers in teaching. This is where they have knowledge beyond that of any outside student of education. They are applied educationists. What they are likely to teach students best, then, is what teachers do; how to be taught; how to deal with school; how to be a scholar, and so on. But usually they do not do this *deliberately* and *explicitly.* Unlike the scientist, the writer, and the mathematician, they tend not to be *deliberate* and *self-conscious* applied scientists or artists. If they were, then school staff rooms would be alive with "theories" and the intercollegial hum of reflection on, and surmise about, the ongoing work in the "laboratories."

Three tiers of education have progressively alienated many teachers from their own craft, the craft of teaching and learning. It is as if the medium in and through which they work is invisible to them and therefore inaccessible to theorizing. The established acts of education have become taken for granted. Such teachers tend also to have been alienated from their own heads, having been so constantly challenged in their schooling to accommodate other people's heads. They are, therefore, chronically prone to teach alienation.

I can see, at this point, that I am in danger of confusing the issues through overgeneralization and caricature, through lack of definition (for example, "research") and by leaving the notion of "self-consciousness" unexplored. Let me come at it another way.

Having been invited to a seminar on "action research," I tried to clarify for myself what this term means. If you include "eventual action" research in the definition of "action research," then I contend that you no longer need the term "action research." All research worthy of the label is action research. "Research" is not "research," of course, when it is the onanistic pursuit of academic simulacritude, unless it can be seen as a working hypothesis on how to get a further degree.

What, then, is the special nature of the term "action research"? I think it has something to do with ownership. Most "big R" Research, as I call it, could be defined as institutionally legitimate inquiry into problems which exist in their chronic form elsewhere than with the researcher. The problems become the problems of the researcher, but they usually relate to somewhere or someone else. The researchers are, therefore, to a degree *detached* from the problem. Even though it may be presently a crucial element of their lives, they can usually remain aloof from the central "action" consequences of what they find.

The "action" consequences for them personally are more likely to be in the form of modified strategies for their next piece of research, a refinement of research methodology, rather than a modification of their own lifestyles, belief systems, or behavior related to the problem they have addressed. The required action is usually for others to decide or divine. This is not exactly "disowned" research (although there are many examples where researchers have publicly disowned the consequences of their work), but it is, I think, clearly distinguishable from "owned" research, that which is more commonly differentiated and named as action research.

I must hasten to qualify "owned" because "big R" Research is usually also well and truly "owned" by someone. By "owned," I mean "owned" by the person or the group doing the research. This is their *own* research into their *own* problem so that the consequent action is also "*owned.*" The resultant action will be a modification, however minimal, to their *own* behavior. The research cannot be disowned. "Big R" Research may, in the first instance, be aimed simply at the generation of knowledge. The problem in this case is to find out more. Personally owned research is always oriented towards a solution to the *present* problem with respect to the act, although its effect may be to create new knowledge, new problems, and new questions by the way.

I am nearing a definition of that which I wish to discuss. Only the word "research" remains in my way. We cannot remove the semantic dye into which "research" has been plunged. It is almost impossible to give it the "small r" meaning. It has accumulated connotations of validity, generalizability, objectivity, and control, which get in the way of those of us who want it simply to mean "finding out in order to act more effectively." Therefore, while tempted to cash in on the prestigious ring of the word, I favor putting it aside in order not to complicate things with superficial debate. "Inquiry" or "investigation" will do as a substitute.

One last point and I have a definition of "action research." Teachers, for instance, may unconsciously work on day-to-day problems and incidentally pick up solutions from time to time. I don't include this kind of serendipity problem-solving in my definition.

Thus, "action" research is *deliberate, group or personally owned and conducted, solution-oriented investigation.* And this coincides precisely with what I consider "learning" to be if one omits incidental and accidental learning from the definition. My logic leads me to conclude that research is deliberate learning.

Since schools and universities are institutions for the promotion of deliberate learning, all teaching, if you accept my reasoning, should be directed towards the support of deliberate, personally owned and conducted, solution-oriented investigation. All teachers should be experts in "action research" so that they can show all students how to be "action researchers." That is, all teachers should be experts in learning so that they can remind all students how to learn. Therefore, I don't offer the modest proposal that teachers might bravely encourage a little more small-scale research amongst some of their students; I offer the bold injunction that all students at all levels must be researchers and all teaching should be based on the methods of research, if we are serious about learning.

Whenever people decide to learn, they undertake research. If teachers wish deliberately to learn about their teaching, they must research. If children wish to learn about electricity, they must research. Learning is defined as understanding in such a way that one can say it in one's own words and be understood, or do it and be effective. Quite patently, whether one observes schools casually or examines the growing body of phenomenological studies, classrooms with few exceptions are not places of research, that is, learning, as I have defined it. Learning tends to take place despite the teaching.

The argument so far goes like this: schools promote different attitudes to knowledge according to success and failure, but even those students who succeed may be alienated from knowledge if they have not learnt how to "own" their own investigations; if they still believe, at heart, that knowledge resides "elsewhere." Teachers who have not learnt this will perpetuate and strengthen the belief that knowledge is "elsewhere."

"Action research," as defined, is personally owned learning. It is, if you like, the antithesis of, and antidote to, "elsewhereness." Schools must be institutions of "action research" if children's heads are to come into their own. Now, to make the connection between research and learning clearer, I need to address the workings of the human brain.

With the caveat that we are all capable of rigging our own experiments, I wish to report that 10 years of investigation and reading have confirmed me in the view that human beings are born scientists. We come into this world hypothesizing. The human brain is biologically the same instrument across all but physically brain-impaired humans and it goes about "processing the world" in the same way. When you boil down all the psychologies, including all but the most banal behaviorism, you are left with the basic human processing formula: problem → observation → hypothesis → testing → evaluation. The surface manifestations of this basic formula are infinitely varied, the vehicles and media of learning vary from case to case, "messiness" and nonlinearity may be observable features, but there is always a common underlying "brain strategy."

To write this I must overcome massive educational and social structures. Is it not presumption for a meager individual thus to reduce the massive psychology industry? Is it not almost the holy writ of democracy that we are all different? What is my evidence for such totalitarianism?

In the past five years, hundreds of teachers, students, and parents at conferences throughout South Australia have been asked to tell anecdotes about a recent piece of learning (learning to do, or to "know"). In small groups, they compare and contrast each other's learning, looking for patterns and dissimilarities. Unerringly, the classic scientific method emerges: problem → observation → hypothesis → testing → evaluation. The learner runs back and forth across these "phases," but each and every piece of learning can be accommodated within the model.

I have discovered to my present satisfaction that the human brain is a classic instrument of research. Research is simply institutionalized and formalized thinking. It is doing self-consciously what comes naturally.

I can go for comfort and reassurance to the cognitive psychologists who depict the brain as a kind of aggressive, rule-inducing computer, or to the great educator Dewey who has been rediscovered and reinvented in different ways for 50 years. Perhaps the most powerful illustrations of what I say can be found in the now superbly documented studies of early language acquisition. We may not be born with a "language acquisition device," but we are able to invent rules and try them out. This is what most distinguishes us as humans.

Another way to put it is to say that we are born with the capacity to imagine what it might be like. From observing humans around us reaching and grasping, it seems that we begin to imagine doing it ourselves. Bruner tells us that even before we practice actual reaching out, appropriate muscles at a subliminal level begin "to intend." Within ourselves we are role-playing being a reacher and grasper. Eventually, through trial and error, we come to reach and grasp. And so, throughout life, imagination leads us to reach and grasp. When imagination dies, we are to all intents and purposes dead.

There will be argument and qualification about what I say so simply, but I find my simplification to be powerful, devastating, and liberating when I shine it on the education industry. And therefore, I shall not abandon it lightly.

What happens to intents and purposes in schools? What do teachers intend and purpose? What do children intend and purpose? I find perhaps the greatest enemy of the learners' intents and purposes to be "motivation" as it is understood and practiced in schools. Schools, if you like, tend to have the wrong motives when it comes to learning.

Novick and Waters (1979) show that working-class children come into school firing questions in excess of middle-class children, but within a year they have become alarmingly quiescent. The authors remark tentatively that schools with seemingly the best of motives may work against language development. In pre-school years, the interrogative abounds. Progressively, through school it seems to wither. The work of Barnes (1976) and other observers of classroom interaction confirms that teachers talk at least two-thirds of the time and that child-initiated questions are rare.

Bernstein and many others argue cogently that schools have to become more congruent with the culture of the children who attend them. I want to go further and say that schools must become more congruent with the working of the human brain. To bring this about, I believe that teachers must become students and practitioners of learning. This would lead them to abandon "motivation" (a concept which generally means, in practice, "something that teachers do to get students to learn") in favor of arranging for and ensuring the basic conditions for learning, the most basic of which is that the learner is able to recognize a problem and can imagine what it might be like to have solved it. I submit that there is a world of difference between the classroom based on motivation (where a deficiency model of the human brain is at work—"if I don't they won't") and that based on arousing the learner's intents and purposes (where the teacher assumes an aggressive brain and arranges problematic matter for it to attack).

Between the pre-school child and the adult researcher, there is schooling where teachers traditionally tend to pose the problems and set the tests. Schooling is, therefore, likely to result in some atrophying or retardation of the learner's brain power because most of the school answers are already known and known to be already known.

Fortunately, it is almost impossible to stop the human brain from learning. "Action research" still abounds in classrooms as students investigate such problems as how to get an "A," how to get away with the minimum labor, how to disrupt the teacher, how to be a good student, or how to think of other things while appearing to attend. The challenge for teachers is how to harness this rampant brainpower and get it to engage with those problems which society looks to schools to address—such things as how to read and write. This is unlikely to occur consistently unless teachers are prepared to negotiate the curriculum with their students.

I have now reached the point where I can be a little more practical, where I can consider what happens when teachers believe that their task is to arrange for deliberate, group or personally owned and conducted, solution-oriented investigation amongst their students. You may have rejected some of my supporting arguments, but my conclusions about ideal practice may still be valid. It is simply, or rather profoundly, a matter of doing deliberately and formally what comes naturally.

Looking back on this essay so far I am aware that I have painted a bleak picture of schooling. Of course, there have always been some brilliant teachers who socratically or by sheer exuberant example inspire students to intend and to inquire. Of course, there are lessons, or at least moments, in the daily life of almost every teacher where the teacher's and the students' intentions coincide. Ask teachers to reflect on their most memorable and effective teaching sequences and you are almost certain to hear about occasions where teachers, students, and subject matter together produced mutual excitement. I am interested in deliberately planning to make this happen most of the time.

In a paper (Boomer, 1982), I explore in some depth the problem of warring intentions in schools. I argue that depending on such things as charisma, sanction-making ability, and reward systems, teachers will have more or less success in getting their intentions to prevail over the intentions of the students. I believe that enormous energy is expended by teachers in making their intentions stick. My metaphor of "sheep dogging" indicates what I believe so often to be the state of the learner's mind when teacher's intentions are unremittingly pursued.

I propose that any learning sequence should begin with a negotiation of intentions to the point that both teacher and student intend in the same direction and mutually *own* the curriculum as *jointly planned*. Under this model, the unit of curriculum is itself a piece of action research into learning which can be reflected upon and evaluated by both teacher and student. There are then many action-research "plays" within the "play." The whole class may set

11

itself a certain "product" goal, groups within the class may negotiate inquiry options, and individuals may contract to conduct personal investigations. In this scheme, the teacher is a supporter and collaborator with the students with respect to deliberate, class, group or individually owned and conducted, solution-oriented investigation. Time is not wasted on what is already known. This is established before the journey.

The teacher's role is to make sure that the learners have the opportunity to clarify the problem, to make observations in potentially profitable areas, to form and test hypotheses, and to reflect on the results. To omit any of these opportunities would be to jeopardize the learning.

The principle of ownership and personal intention is crucial. This separates what I am saying from much of the pseudo-inquiry which is now in vogue in schools. (Admirable as it is, this material rests on the premise that a remote teacher can organize the material for the students, a serious flaw which Bruner now recognizes.) Current social studies courses in South Australian primary and secondary schools advocate an "inquiry" approach, but they actually list the questions which the learners will investigate. In the name of humanity, a blatant act of cognitive imperialism is perpetrated.

I contend that the curriculum itself must be problematic for the teachers *and* the students. What shall we teach and learn? How shall we teach and learn it? Why is it worth doing or why are we compelled to do it? What is of such minor significance that it can be told? (Facts, information, background.) What is of such major significance that it must be experienced and investigated in order to be owned?

Acting on these principles, teachers are obliged to think aloud about their intentions, their theories and the ideas which they wish to teach, genuinely inviting students to do the same. In such a "community of thinkers," intentions become shared, thinking power is increased, and, through reflection on the learning, teachers and students progressively learn more about how to learn. They increase their knowledge, or their knowing, at the same time as they become more talented in deploying the capacities of the human brain.

Students are protagonists in the created drama. Teachers are both deuteragonists (in the students' drama) and protagonists (in their own ongoing experiments in education). The whole is a recipe for dispelling the mists of metaphysics which cling to education. There is probably no other human endeavor besides religion itself, where there is such a gap between espoused theory (metaphysics) and practice. Action research will bring theory and practice together, here, in the classroom. Answers will be sought here rather than elsewhere.

The "big R" Research which occurs elsewhere will become potentially vital information *here* in the classroom now that the local problem is defined and owned. "Big R" Research will be picked up, as appropriate, by thinking heads. It will, in this way, become a bona fide participant in the quest to improve action in schools.

References

Barnes, D. (1976). *From communication to curriculum.* London: Penguin.
Boomer, G. (Ed.). (1982). *Negotiating the curriculum.* Sydney: Ashton Scholastic.
Novick, D., & Waters, D. (1979). *Talking in school.* South Australia: Education Department.

A Quiet Form of Research

JAMES BRITTON

James Britton posits that inquiry in a classroom context is a discovery process—a matter of looking closely at the stuff of our lessons, our students, and ourselves. We are all in the business of learning by experiment, for effective teaching is grounded in inquiry. "Every lesson," Britton reasons, "should be for the teacher an inquiry, some further discovery, a quiet form of research. . . ."

Yes, I think things are moving, we are making some progress, and there are signs of a widening realization that research methods appropriate to the physical sciences are not the best model for research in the social sciences. The most recent doctoral thesis on an educational topic that has come my way is a case study of a writing course, and the writer, Nancy Jones (1982) of the University of Iowa, outlines her perspective this way.

The validity of laws about natural phenomena—that, for example H_2O freezes at 32 degrees Fahrenheit, or that testosterone has a direct role in maintaining the accessory sex organs in male rats—requires that studies which support them be capable of replication. It is one thing to do that with inanimate objects like water or animate objects like rats whose breeding and environment can be extensively controlled and manipulated so as to minimize differences among them. It is quite another thing, of course, and finally impossible, ethically and politically, to do that with people. (p. 10)

Coming at things from another angle, Cindy Ray of Pioneer Valley Regional School in Massachusetts opens a proposal for a research project in her own classroom, "Research is not primarily a process of proving something, but primarily a process of discovery and learning," and adds, "This view of research is tremendously liberating, for it allows classroom teachers to take seriously the ordinary business of their lives as teachers."

When younger members of our profession give us a lead in this direction, I am optimistic about the future of educational research.

In the physical sciences, routine research may be seen to *accumulate*. As the monographs on a particular topic fill more and more of the shelf, our secure knowledge of the topic grows. Gaps may be revealed, demanding further research, and these are likely in time to be filled. While, as Karl Popper (1976) has shown, proof of these findings is never possible, yet the chance of disproof becomes ever more remote, and at each stage we act on what we believe.

Experience shows that what accrues in the social sciences is not like this. Contradictory findings abound: what is true of one individual or group of individuals in one context proves inapplicable to others in other contexts. Teachers, from their own experience, are very aware of this phenomenon: what works with one group fails with another. Any generalizations we attempt to make must, therefore, be made in the light of *context* in the broadest sense of that word, and in the final analysis we have to recognize that the context of any human action is so complex as to be experimentally uncontrollable. Common sense—the kind that comes from the experience of living in any family—has taught us all to behave in the implicit light of this truth. We come, paradoxically, to expect the unexpected of people.

Once again, we act in the light of what we believe to be the case, but the mode of appraisal, the criteria for believing, will be different from the criteria we apply in the physical sciences. Limiting our concern to what Kuhn (1962) has called "normal" scientific activity, we should expect the criteria for acceptance to change as we move from the physical to the social sciences, from demonstration by empirical evidence to logical reasonableness, and explanatory power and compatibility with experience. In Karl Popper's terms, falsification by empirical procedures gives way to falsification by critical procedures.

The conscious adoption of the critical method becomes the
main instrument of growth. . . . The critical method, though
it will use certain tests wherever possible, and preferably practical tests, can be generalized into what I described as a critical
or rational attitude. . . . I tried to argue that this critical attitude of reasonableness should be extended as far as possible.
(Popper, 1976, pp. 115–116)

It should be clear that there is no argument here for the un-
critical acceptance of findings in the social sciences or for lack of
rigor in the modes of inquiry. As far as educational research is concerned, I think a lack of rigor shows itself most blatantly when experimental programs or procedures that can profitably be *described*
are in fact *prescribed.* I remember one enthusiastic researcher who,
in a prestigious conference, expressed the hope that "by this time
next year" his thoroughly researched social studies program would
be in use in every school in the state. To think in this way is to ignore totally the teaching/learning context—the minutiae of behavior
of a particular teacher in moment-by-moment interaction with a
particular group of students in a particular school and locality on a
particular occasion. However well a program may have been researched, it can achieve its objectives only as a result of the full
participation of both students and teachers.

If research is seen primarily as a process of discovery, then the
day-to-day work of a teacher comes under the term *teachers as researchers.* It cannot be said too often that effective teaching depends
upon the concern of every teacher for the *rationale* by which he or
she works. Teaching consists of interactive behavior, and it is the
teacher's share in this behavior that most concerns us. In the course
of interacting with individuals and classes, a teacher must make a
hundred and one decisions in every session—off-the-cuff decisions
that can only reliably come from inner conviction, that is to say by
consistently applying an ever-developing rationale. This requires
that every lesson should be for the teacher an inquiry, some further
discovery, a quiet form of research, and that time to reflect, draw
inferences, and plan further inquiry is also essential.

I believe the notion that teaching is interactive and not uni-
directional has been with us long enough for us to realize that what
the teacher does not achieve in the classroom cannot be achieved by
anybody else—by a department head, a principal, the writers of
statutory guidelines, or anybody else. It was for this reason that, in
opening the International Conference in Sydney on "English in the
Eighties," I was rash enough to suggest that in moving into the
eighties we were initiating "the decade of the classroom teacher"
(Britton, 1982).

"Teachers as researchers," Yet if this enterprise is not to miscarry, we must be clear what we mean by research. Nancy Jones develops her perspective by saying,

> It becomes easy to forget what a very basic—even mundane—thing research is, at first and at last. To some extent we engage in it every day, and we certainly do whenever we investigate, inquire, or look at something again with the aim of obtaining more information and knowledge, or discovering something about it. Research is not, by and large, an esoteric experience, and empirical research . . . certainly is not. . . . It is not in touch with superhuman spheres but is the product of human thought and activity, therefore subject to misdirection and error. (Jones, 1982, p. 9)

I think it is useful to demystify research in this way—to see what is common to deliberate research projects and our day-to-day judgments, but I think we then need to establish the level of applicability of what we discover, or in George Kelly's terms, "the range of convenience" of the constructs we discern.

Kelly (1963) would certainly support us in the demystification, for he conceives of all of us as essentially scientists in our ordinary mode of operating. Every significant piece of behavior is, for him, an experiment. As human beings, we meet every new situation armed with expectations derived from past experience or, more accurately, derived from our interpretations of past experience. We face the new, therefore, not only with knowledge drawn from the past but also with developed tendencies to interpret in certain ways. It is in submitting these to the test of fresh experience—that is, in having our expectations and modes of interpreting either confirmed or modified—that the learning, the discovery, takes place. It is always open to us, of course, to ignore differences between what we expect and what takes place—and we may have powerful reasons for doing so—and then the learning does not take place. We act and decide on what we believe to be the case, even when those beliefs fly in the face of evidence. And we remain personally responsible for what we know and believe, whether it be a presentiment that something is about to fall on our head or a conviction that a cooperative classroom is more effective than a competitive one.

As researchers, then, and as teachers and as human beings, we are in the business of learning by experiment. Let me pursue the questions of establishing the level of applicability of our findings. In a remarkable collection of classroom investigations carried out by teachers in one inner London Comprehensive school, John Richmond analyzed the speech and writing of a number of Jamaican teenagers. Here are two findings from his analysis:

> Pat is obviously in considerable confusion about the use of speech marks. They appear where they're not wanted, they don't appear where they are wanted. . . . The English speech mark system is tedious and pedantic, of course. . . . However, stuck with our system as we are, the setting-out and marking of speech was the second major area which Pat and I might fruitfully work on in her fourth year. (Vauxhall Manor School Talk Workshop Group, 1982, p. 129)

> I believe the following things to be true: (a) The nature of speech has a major effect on the nature of writing. (b) A great deal of writing is done in school, maybe too much. (c) If children sense confusion and contradiction around their language, they are likely to use it less well than if they sense approval and security around it. (d) On the other hand, crisis sometimes spawns beauty. (e) It is not a coincidence that poverty, non-standard dialects and alienation from school are often to be found in the same area. (pp. 106–107)

The detailed recording and analysis of data in this account lend support to both sets of conclusions, yet clearly the use to be made of what is discovered differs widely from the first example to the second. The finding in the first instance is one I can make no direct use of because I am not Pat's teacher.

I think educational inquiry can take three forms in relation to the uses to which the findings may be put. The first is an integral part of *teaching* itself, and provided we recognize the heuristic nature of teaching, its essential grounding in inquiry, we need give it no other name. For the second, I would revive a word that has perhaps fallen into disuse—the word *development* in the special sense it has when partnered with the word *research.* Linked in this way, *research* has been used to describe the discovery of something that might, directly or indirectly, be applied to assist the practitioner, and *development* to describe the process of helping practitioners to discover the research and apply it to their own situations and practice. Whenever researchers in education are tempted to embody their discoveries in *teacher-proof kits* (and some funding agencies seem to see this as cost-effective), a stress on the necessity of the development phase becomes paramount.

The third variety, what I have called *research*, might be distinguished by calling it *basic research.* What is important to point out is that all three varieties may be pursued in schools. If my judgment of the evidence offered by John Richmond for his broad conclusions in the second example above is a just one, all three may be carried out by teachers in the schools.

Teaching is something we *do;* research findings are something we come to *know;* development is the process by which we bring this kind of knowing into relation with this kind of doing. Development uses a research finding as its starting point and proceeds to the formulation of fresh hypotheses, asking new questions and arriving at new ends. The value of a piece of research from a practical point of view lies in supplying starting points for a range and variety of such enterprises, and I have no doubt the most effective way of carrying out such research is by means of a team project involving researchers *and* teachers at all stages from the earliest planning to the interpretation of findings.

But as teachers we have to draw also on research that is not all educational. The legitimate ends of researchers in the social sciences may have nothing to do with schools or education and yet may provide understandings from which we build our rationale for teaching. As Halliday has pointed out,

> A child doesn't need to know any linguistics in order to use language to learn; but a teacher needs to know some linguistics if he wants to understand how the process takes place—or what is going wrong when it doesn't. (Halliday, 1981, p. 11)

He goes on to show how closely linguistic research and *development* may be interlinked:

> Applied linguistics is not a separate domain; it is the principles and practice that come from an understanding of language. Adopting these principles and practices provides, in turn, a way in to understanding language. In this perspective you look for models of language that neutralize the difference between theory and application; in the light of which, research and development in language education become one process rather than two.

"The ordinary business of our lives as teachers" may indeed, as Cindy Ray surmised, "be taken seriously."

I have looked at teaching, development, and research as interrelated modes of inquiry, sources of knowledge on a widening range of applicability. But the implications of my title cover a wider span yet, seeing knowledge itself as a form of inquiry. Here is the title in its setting, a paragraph from Michael Polanyi's *Knowing and Being*:

> Knowledge is an activity which would be better described as a process of knowing. Indeed, as the scientist goes on enquiring into yet uncomprehended experiences, so do those who accept his discoveries as established knowledge keep applying this to ever changing situations, developing it each time a step further. Research is an intensely dynamic enquiring, while knowledge

is a more quiet research. Both are ever on the move, according to similar principles, towards a deeper understanding of what is already known. (Polanyi, 1969, p. 132)

Knowing, then, is to be seen as a form of doing. There is no simple sense in which we *apply* our knowledge in the way we apply a poultice to a swelling. In any confrontation, what we know must be reformulated in the light of what we perceive and our knowledge is thus forever on the move.

The point of maximum effect of the educational system on the child is in the classroom. The nature of the school as a community within a community can enormously help or hinder what goes on in the classroom and have its own effect in other less dominant ways. If the eighties are to be the decade of the classroom teacher and realize the full potential of interactive teaching and learning, teachers will need all the help we can give them, whoever we are—researchers, administrators, trustees, parents—or, of course, schoolchildren.

References

Britton, J. (1982). *Prospect and retrospect: Selected essays of James Britton,* ed. Gordon Pradl. Montclair, NJ: Boynton/Cook.

Halliday, M. A. K. (Summer 1981). *The English Magazine.*

Jones, N. L. (1982). *Design, discovery and development in a freshman writing course.* Dissertation, University of Iowa.

Kelly, G. A. (1963). *A theory of personality.* New York: Norton.

Kuhn, T. S. (1962). *The structure of scientific revolutions.* Chicago: University of Chicago Press.

Polanyi, M. (1969). *Knowing and being.* London: Routledge and Kegan Paul.

Popper, K. (1976). *Unended quest.* London: Fontana.

Vauxhall Manor School Talk Workshop Group. (1982). *Becoming our own experts.* London: Inner London Education Authority English Centre.

On the Move

Teacher-Researchers

NANCY MARTIN

Nancy Martin too perceives the contexts *for learning and teaching to figure vitally in the learning process. Likening schools and classrooms to communities, she would have us become their ethnographers, using descriptive techniques to capture whatever can be observed about the settings in which individual students learn. "That ethnographic research is rooted in the experience of those who were actually there has profound implications for classroom inquiry," she writes. Classroom teachers are in the best position to ask questions about learning, to accumulate data, and to take up teaching directions based on the learning patterns that emerge.*

What are broadly called *ethnographic studies* are giving a new impetus and new directions to research in English teaching and learning. Ethnographic procedures, modeled on the ways anthropologists study communities, have much to offer teachers studying the ways in which students learn. Schools are communities (within larger communities) and classrooms are subsets of schools. Within the culture as a whole (for example, the USA), schools have their distinctive patterns of behavior, attitudes towards literacy, for example, beliefs about education and about the roles of teachers and students. Furthermore, these patterns vary to a considerable extent not only from school to school, but from one classroom to another. Ethnographic research in education sets out to describe not only events in classrooms which occur as students and teachers work, speak, write, interrupt, question, etc., but also describe all that can be observed and reported about the contexts of lessons, that is, events in the school and in the students' home lives which bear on what goes on in the classroom. In short, the contexts for learning and teaching are seen as major elements in the learning process.

The chief characteristic of this kind of data is that the documentation (descriptions and records) are made by people who were present at the time, and who can, therefore, describe experience as it was lived. Firsthand accounts differ in important ways from reports made by people who were not there, or were not part of the community.

A New Impetus and Direction for Research

The fact that ethnographic research is rooted in the experience of those who were actually there has profound implications for classroom inquiry. Teachers and their students are the essential sources of information. They, and only they, were present and engaged—deeply or perfunctorily—in the learning process. They are the people who can best ask the questions (springing from firsthand experience) about learning. They can, and should, be the chief source of both the questions and the data from which the questions may be answered. This means that the potential for classroom inquiries has increased a thousandfold. However, the influence of history can't be ignored. Everyone asks questions about education, but research has generally been initiated by universities, administrators, and politicians. Classroom teachers have been the hewers of wood and drawers of water in education, and it will take time for them to learn that it is they who are in the best position to initiate inquiries into learning and to gain the confidence to develop this potential.

Alternative Philosophies

The focus of educational research for many years has been on attempts to measure the effects of different "treatments" on large numbers. Groups, that is, classes, were studied, not individuals, and the changes, that is, learnings, measured in terms of averages and mean differences. In crude terms, it was like examining the effect of different fertilizers on crops and measuring the yields. It is, of course, possible to measure, say, monthly progress in reading: what is not possible is to account for such "growth" in terms of particular and isolable treatments. Many features in the educational context will play a part in the changes. Varying cultural influences, for instance, will play their part in causing different students to respond differently. It is beginning to be realized that classes of students cannot be researched as if they were strains of wheat or farm animals.

The philosophy this kind of research implies is that learning is an accumulation of skills and knowledge which can be taught and tested separately, and if experimentation is carried out with sufficiently large numbers the results may be generalized for wider application.

Social scientists, on the other hand, have worked in other ways and from a different philosophical standpoint. In ethnographic research, there is no hypothesis with a predicted, measurable result. Every individual's life history may affect how and what is learned, so everything that may be observed is part of the picture. Accumulations of descriptions are needed from all sorts of sources, including the learners themselves. But such "thick" descriptions mean that the researcher needs to find the significant patterns within the wealth of data, and make the necessary selections to exemplify the patterns that are found.

Learning and teaching from this standpoint is seen as a complex, interactive process between many variables, and this implies a change of direction towards the study of individual case histories rather than group responses to planned interventions.

It is, however, difficult to generalize ethnographic studies. Anthropologists have said that ethnographic studies need to contain elements of comparison, one with another, and without such comparisons, generalizations may not be made. In this sense, then, many educational case studies are not true ethnographic studies. Nevertheless, they are useful finger posts pointing to discoveries by individual teachers, and they can suggest directions for other teachers to take up; and, given a group of teachers following agreed patterns of observation over a given period of time, a true ethnographic study could result. Comparison could reveal patterns of learning behavior, or generalizable patterns in the environment which appeared to affect learning, or attitudes to learning.

Observers can observe themselves as well as others. Ethnographers have always made use of interviews and written statements from the people whose way of life they were observing. The journals or other writings of learners may serve a similar purpose.

In this context, the history of Mass Observation in Britain is interesting. In 1936 people—anyone, everyone—were invited by advertisement to keep regular journals and to send them in at regular intervals to a central address. It was thought that such a collection of individual accounts of people's lives in the context of public events would yield many patterns of attitude as well as social information useful to historians and sociologists. The outbreak of war in 1939 put a stop to the development of Mass Observation as such, though some contributors continued their journals throughout the war and afterwards. The archive is kept in the University of Sussex in England, and is now beginning to yield publications. Some adaptation of the notion of an accumulation of journals from school students or teachers in a given area could be a significant archive for ethnographic studies in education.

Implications of Classroom Research for Teachers

Generally, teachers have been trained as doers of other people's directions. They have carried out research directed from university projects, or worked to guidelines set by superintendents, and have seldom seen themselves as initiators. The nature of ethnographic research puts them in the center of a different kind of research. This has profound implications both for them and for their students. In addition to any discoveries they may make about learning, they are developing in action an alternative model for teacher education. This may have a powerful effect on their view of themselves and their capacities for initiating changes in education. The learner-researcher pattern is a powerful dynamic. If I set out to find an answer to some classroom matter, I am a learner; but in engaging in the inquiry, I am initiating a small piece of research: I am both learner and researcher—two sides of the same coin.

There was a teacher of a slow learning class in a high school who asked the question, "How much did the students talk to adults out of school?" Each day as they came in they told her whom they had talked to since leaving school the day before. The pattern that emerged from her accumulated records showed that most had talked to their mothers and sometimes other female adults: few had talked to their fathers or other men. Very few had had anything that could be called conversations. When she looked at the patterns of the adults they had talked to in school, she found a similar poverty of talk. As a result of her inquiry she decided to set up organized talk situations in her classes. This included getting parents in when possible to increase the amount of conversation with adults. The theory behind her inquiry—and of the changes she made in her classroom—was, of course, that sustained talk (formulation of ideas) has a bearing on learning. She thought the students' work improved, but there was no way of measuring it. She had to rely on the theory that had prompted her inquiry, and her judgment as an experienced teacher, in assessing the result.

What emerges from this example is that teachers need not wait for inquiries to be initiated by others. They can ask the questions that arise from their own classrooms, can make their own records, collect their own data, and modify their teaching in accordance with what they find. So much is there at hand.

Resocialization: Changes in Attitudes and Beliefs

Persistent classroom inquiry can create a much bigger change in thinking and working in school than we might expect. The ways of doing things and accompanying attitudes that were learned from colleagues when we began to teach—the ground rules of school—have so shaped our ideas and views of what happens that it is hard to persist in trying new ways. We may find, for instance, that the research we started has ceased to confine its questions to the problem we started with and has expanded into questions touching nearly everything we do. Some of the changed attitudes associated with the research may suddenly seem questionable: we wonder if we were right after all. Any teacher who has tried to develop sustained talk in classes will remember the anxiety questions that crowded in: Is the class too noisy? Are the groups discussing anything worthwhile? What is worthwhile talk? What about the silent ones? Will people think my discipline is poor? Is a quiet class really a good learning situation? Is what the students want to talk about as important for them as what I want them to talk about? and so on. Once a teacher moves out of the traditional position of being the giver of questions and the receiver of right or wrong answers, there is no more certainty.

We all depend for our self-respect and confidence on our sense of how colleagues (and authorities) regard us, so it is hard to strike out in new directions unless these are well regarded. It is here that the old ways may erode the new. There are fashions in education as in clothes, but if one is not to swing like a pendulum, the changes need to be related to something other than fashion. The strength of classroom inquiry is that it anchors change in observation and experiment.

The Need to Create Networks of Support

I have said that initiators need someone to share their ideas and plans. Perhaps the most important stage in their research is to find one person who will be interested to hear the half-discovered ideas and plans and help to develop them by questions and applause. After this the search for further allies begins. Conversation will take things a long way, but soon there will be a need for something written or printed which people can think about more deliberately, and better still if some of them are willing to be drawn into a more formal discussion at a specified time. Allies may be found (or created) in one's own school or in neighborhood schools, or in local or regional teachers' gatherings.

While participating in the work of teachers' organizations is generally thought to be a good thing, it is not generally understood that for innovations to live and grow, teachers' organizations are a major communications channel—or network of contacts for keeping in touch, and keeping in good heart. Without such networks of support, we tend to lose heart and revert to older and easier ways.

Some Examples of Classroom Inquiries

Documentation of classroom inquiries generally involves case studies of some sort. Case studies are not new: what is new is to find observation and detailed records becoming a major instrument in the development of teachers as researchers.

In the past, many teachers have recorded samples of children's writing over a number of years, and what can be seen from these collections of writings is a progress towards mastery, but nothing was shown of the contexts—how the topics arose, or were given, how they related to the students' experience, whether they were linked to readings from literature, etc.—so we can learn little from them. Contrast these early studies with the records kept by Donald Graves and his helpers at the Atkinson Elementary School in New Hampshire, where the teachers have steadily documented their conferences with beginning writers as they talked to their teachers about their revisions and rewrites. Both the interviews and the rewrites were recorded, and from these accounts appears a tapestry of conversation and writing through which both the teachers' influence and the changes in writing may be traced. Not everyone would agree with Donald Graves about the value of multiple revision to such young writers (six to eight years), but this is not the place to discuss pedagogy; the point being made is the value of the documentation which allowed teachers and parents to see the process that had been going on.

The range of possible classroom inquiry is enormous but the conditions for success would seem to be some measure of collaborative support among teachers in the school, and some support from education authorities for at least local dissemination. Some examples of work in progress will illustrate this range.

A teacher believes that familiar contexts (the classroom or the school) anesthetizes students' capacity to observe, respond, and write. His previous experience of taking students on field trips to write suggested that a more systematic study could be developed and documented. He found several other rural teachers willing to try what he is trying and to document it, and, as part of the study, to maintain regular contact with each other.

Another teacher is setting up a communication situation between two schools for the exchange of personal letters. Personal letters, even to unknown recipients, such as students in another school, are a largely unstudied source of writing.

Yet another teacher set out to study students' views of the rules and beliefs about writing operating in the classroom compared with the teacher's views of these.

And another teacher has set up a small network of teacher-researchers who meet regularly, discuss their work, and document subsequent changes in practice. The regular discussion sessions in some relaxed place provide a base for assessing what they are doing and for suggesting next moves. Both the discussion and subsequent class work are documented.

Then there are all the studies concerned with the use of word processors. At present, they consist largely of sets of questions while teachers get used to using them themselves. Such questions as, "How does a word processor facilitate response to literature?" "How does creative writing fare on the processor?" "Can any record of growth be traced as students compose on the word processor over a period of time?" "Are case studies, which include students' own journals of their writing experience, to form part of such studies?" In short, are the new ethnographic directions in research in writing to be called in here?

These are only a few of some 30 proposals funded through the Bread Loaf School of English Teacher Research Projects, but they serve to illustrate the scope of classroom based inquiries.

Some of the Problems

The chief problems in ethnographic studies are concerned with size, subjectivity, and the need to move into ideas that go beyond a single classroom. Let us look at size and subjectivity.

The nature of descriptive research means that the sheer amount of data may confound the researcher. How is it to be dealt with? There has to be selection, and the reasons for the selection clearly stated. There needs to be presentation of accounts from many people because different people see events differently; and there need to be comments by the researcher interpreting the data. By interpretation, I mean the researcher's understanding of the significance of the patterns within the data. We can see something of the nature of interpretation if we look at the example of the researcher who set up the small group of teachers who met regularly to record and discuss what they did in their writing classes. They agreed to keep their own journals of lessons, and they read and discussed these journals in their meetings. The researcher's intention was to try to document and thereby reveal the changes in the teachers' thinking and classroom practice, which she hoped might result from the on-going year-long discussions. To reveal these changes, she reproduced extracts from the teachers' journals from the beginning and end of the year, and these revealed very clearly the changes that had taken place. The discussion of these made the teachers aware of these changes in their thinking and of the way these had been reflected in changed classroom practice. It was the researcher's interpretation of the patterns of change in the various journals which enabled her to make these apparent to the group.

Obviously the point of making such inquiries is to make them available to other people. The rich and voluminous data—detailed observations, interviews, transcripts of talk, journals, letters, reports of all kinds, etc.—need to be analyzed, edited, and written up with interpretive comments; and they need to be presented for discussion to all sorts of audiences—small groups in one school, or larger regional or national meetings. It is this drawing in of other people to listen, discuss, and compare which adjusts the subjective judgments of a single teacher to a wider world. And, in submitting papers to professional journals and seeking publication of their collections of working papers, teachers will be creating the support systems needed to maintain the reality of the *meanings* of their findings for the world of classrooms.

Scholar Research and Teacher Research

Traditionally research is university guided. Certainly, there is need for teacher research to move into ideas beyond the single classroom, and perhaps beyond the classroom itself. For these reasons, it is sometimes said that classroom research is not research in the full sense of the term—that teacher research deals only with immediate applications. I, myself, don't think the distinction can be maintained. Inquiry goes on at all sorts of levels, and I would suggest that the difference is more a matter of degree than of kind. Inquiry is the basis of research, and changes in research procedures have made it possible for teachers to undertake small-scale studies without the backing of time and money which supports professional research. Whether it be small scale or large scale, classroom based or university based, it seems to me to partake of the same essential nature, *inquiry;* and the potential for experiment and discovery is enormous. But since nothing like all teachers can engage in university-directed research, the question has to be faced of where and how teachers can find substitutes for the kind of guidance and direction they would find in university advice and direction.

Development of Research Communities

The answer to the question would seem to lie in the development of research communities in schools and neighborhoods. The start must be in the key position teachers hold at the point of learning in classrooms. The wealth of available data is subjective, so it needs to be linked to theory to take the interpretations beyond the single classroom. Perhaps, an early step may be for teachers to learn from their own writings. Can these illuminate the learnings of students?

Next is to have listeners and critics. Their effect on thinking and writing must be a major influence on what is done next.

Then there is the deliberate study of specific theoretical works; these will be relevant to the current classroom inquiries. The discussion of these by the teachers engaged in the inquiry will be the heart of the learning process. Theory and practice brought together: this is what establishing research communities in school neighborhoods can mean, and research communities need not stop here. Contact can be made with people who have made advances in the field. Networks can be expanded; help sought; people invited to consider and discuss local research projects; reports from national gatherings can be brought back and discussed and specific guidance sought when directions seem obscure. In short, the cooperation of inquiring teachers and the drawing in of expertise from all sorts of sources can be a significant substitute for the overall supervision of traditional research procedures. From here the transition to professional university research studies is only a more comprehensive step in a known direction.

The Teacher as REsearcher

ANN E. BERTHOFF
University of Massachusetts/Boston

"We do not need new information," Ann Berthoff argues. "We need to think about the information we have." We need, in other words, to consider, *and to interpret the things we consider; we need constantly to ask why we are doing what we are doing, to the end that our teaching practices are informed by theory. Thus, our business should be a matter of questions as much as answers—of avoiding predeterminations and the gimmicky methodologies that serve them. For Berthoff, teaching is REsearching—looking and looking again.*

An address delivered at the annual meeting of the California Association of Teachers of English, San Diego, 1979. The conference theme was "Directions for Excellence."

What I want to suggest in these remarks is that real teachers in dialogue with one another can find directions for excellence as they work out their own theory. I will conclude with some observations about a theory of the composing process and how it can guide our teaching of writing.

My favorite text on this notion of an exchange between teachers comes from Sylvia Ashton-Warner. "The educational story," she writes in *Teacher,* "is like the writing of a novel. You can't be sure of your beginning until you have checked it with your ending. What might come of infant teachers visiting the university and professors visiting the infant room?" What can come of it, what has come of such visits is not "research," but useful questions and answers that can provide directions. I want to claim that what we need is not what is called "research," but the kind of theory that is generated in dialogue among teachers. When we real teachers get together, we ask one another real questions: "If language capacities are innate, why is it so hard to teach kids to write sound sentences?" "How can you teach the use of *however* if they don't understand the how-ever relationship?" I don't think real teachers ask questions like "what is the T-unit average among your 010 students?" I promise you I will be polemical for only a few minutes, but I want to rock the boat a little: finding directions always entails rocking the boat, doesn't it? (The way I handle a canoe it does.)

The notion that "research" can provide directions is absurd—I mean the kind of research supported, for instance, by the National Institute of Education. The institute guidelines explicitly state that NIE has no interest whatsoever in practical application: no proposals for curriculum, course design, or sequences of assignments will be entertained; attempts to define implications for the classroom are unwelcome. Instead, the guidelines announce, the institute is concerned with establishing scientific understanding by gathering fresh data on, say, the effects of home environment on literacy. The social scientists who prepared these guidelines argue this way: basic research is essential to the advancement of learning in physics; therefore, basic research is essential to an understanding of education. That analogy is fraudulent because education is not comparable to the natural sciences. Why? Because education profoundly and essentially involves language—and language is not a natural process but a symbolic form and a social process, though it's contingent on natural processes. The people who call language "verbal behavior" are the ones who call literature "literary material," just as they are the ones who call making mud pies "earthplay." They are not our allies.

Let me end my polemic with this assertion: educational research is nothing to our purpose, unless we formulate the questions;

if the procedures by which answers are sought are not dialectic and dialogic, that is to say, if the questions and the answers are not continually REformulated by those who are working in the classroom, educational research is pointless. My spies tell me that it's becoming harder and harder for researchers to get into the schools: I rejoice in that news because I think it might encourage teachers to become researchers themselves, and once that happens, the character of research is bound to change.

It helps to pronounce "research" the way southerners do: REsearch. Research, like REcognition, is a REflexive act. It means looking—and looking again. The new kind of REsearch would not mean going out after new "data," but rather REconsidering what is at hand. REsearch would come to mean looking and looking at what happens in the English classroom. We do not need new information: we need to think about the information we have. We need to interpret what goes on when students respond to one kind of assignment and not to another, or when some respond to an assignment and others do not. We need to interpret things like that—and then to interpret our interpretations. There is nothing in the NIE guidelines to suggest that anybody in Washington has ever heard of the idea of thinking about anything. Maybe they'd listen if we reminded them of what Piaget once observed (Piaget is, of course, a hot item just now). Piaget remarked that "to understand is to invent." What we need is not research designed for us by the National Science Foundation, as Professor Hirsch is suggesting, but questions we can invent about what we think we are doing, questions that will help us, too, in devising the criteria for evaluating what we are getting. Inventing as a way of understanding is a truth known to poets as well as to cognitive psychologists. A version of that dialectic is the one we all know concerning the composing process: you can't really know what you mean until you hear what you say. In my opinion, theory and practice should stand in this same relationship to one another, a dialectical relationship: theory and practice need one another.

The way to get them together is to begin with them together. Only that way will we be able to judge the degree to which what we meant to do is matched by what we did. The primary role of theory is to guide us in defining our purposes and thus in evaluating our efforts, in realizing them. How can we know what we're doing, how can we find out where we're going, if we don't have a conception of what we think we're doing? This is not, however, the same thing as stating behavioral objectives. They can forestall our ideas by constraining us too soon, too rigidly. But to be wary of behavioral objectives is not to settle for the visionary. Of course we must have plans, but they should not be narrowly defined in ways meant to make it easy for the researchers to quantify.

The trouble with behavioral objectives is that they are not meant to be modified by our practice; they control what we do (three sentence patterns by October). Rather, the primary use of theory should be to define what our purposes and aims are and thereby how to evaluate our efforts in reaching them: what and thereby how. I don't think there's anything more important for us to remember than that connector *thereby*: we have to keep the what and the how together—the what are we doing? together with the how do we do it? and the how did it go? and the how did it work? Evaluation, in other words, should be considered an aspect of method. Let me tell you about the experience of a friend of mine, Brenda S. Engel, of Lesley College. The question was how to evaluate the then new program of the Cambridge Alternative Schools by appropriate criteria. If you're doing something new and different, you shouldn't expect to evaluate it in terms appropriate to what it's supposed to supplant. The emphasis was on observation in the classroom so as to determine what was being learned how: Brenda worked out ways of coding kinds and modes of learning so that what was actually going on could be documented. Charts could then be prepared showing, for instance, how much time a particular child spent working by himself and how much with others. Or, one could tell at a glance how much independent work was going on, typically, in a particular teacher's classroom.

Theory can help us judge what's going on, and it can also explain why something works. Suppose you look at a particular exercise that has been very successful and you say, "Terrific! Now I'll do this." And you follow X with Y, which seems appropriate, and it doesn't work. If you don't have a theory about why X worked, you won't have any way of defining the real relationship of X to Y, logically or psychologically. Taking my cue from Sylvia Ashton-Warner, let me tell you about an incident described by Patricia Carini, a teacher and researcher in New England.

She tells of how a teacher in a rural school observed her class of youngsters at the sand table as they filled coffee cans and strawberry boxes with wet sand, inverting them to make, as she thought, towers and houses, sheds and factories. "Aha! They're making cities!" So, as a follow-up, she organized a field trip to a nearby town—but the children were bored, unimpressed, and uninterested. Patricia Carini's analysis was as follows: those kids weren't making towns; they weren't into architecture! They were forming: they were playing with shapes, moulded shapes, and what should have followed that—and what did follow successfully, after consultation with the teacher—was playing in empty packing cases. The children went from compact, thingy shapes to empty, explorable shapes with different

31

kinds of limits; they went from one kind of forming to another, from manipulating a shape to being shaped.

Theory can help us figure out why something works so we can repeat it, inventing variations. A theoretical understanding of cognitive development in this case, of how learning involves forming, can help us figure out our sequences of assignments. The centrally important question in all teaching is, "What comes next?" We must learn continually how to build on what has gone before, how to devise what I. A. Richards calls "the partially parallel task." Of course, we follow something with something else like it, but we can't do that authentically unless we can identify the first something: what is really going on? Theory can help us see what act we're trying to follow.

Theory gives us perspective; just as it allows us to determine sequences, it saves us from too much particularity. Teachers have to be pragmatic; they have to be down to earth, but being down to earth without knowing the theoretical coordinates for the landscape is a good way to lose your sense of direction. We English teachers are given to recipe swapping—and that can be hazardous. In my ideal commonwealth, the first thing that would happen—of course ideal commonwealths are really dictatorships—in my ideal commonwealth, *I* would order the closing down of the Exercise Exchange; the NCTE would not be allowed to operate it unless they instituted a Theory Exchange. And you couldn't get a recipe unless you also went there. I have a friend in the Denver schools who does just that. When her colleagues say, "Oh, that sounds wonderful! Can I have that exercise?" she says, "Sure—but you have to take the theory too." And the exercise comes typed up with a little theoretical statement at the top, an explanation of whatever aspect or function of learning the assignment is meant to exercise. That combination of theory and practice can help prevent what so often happens: you know how it is; it has certainly happened to me. You hear something described that sounds good; it's obviously foolproof; you try it, and it doesn't work. So you feel terrible because this great exercise is a proved success—and you flubbed it. By reminding us that reading and writing happen in contexts—social, political, psychological—that can set up static ruinous to the reception of the very best assignments, theory can save us from wasting time blaming ourselves or our students.

By reminding us of contexts, theory can free us from an over-dependence on preparation, reminding us, too, that the alternative to the immutable lesson plan is not the bull session. Those of you who have taught more than a year—or maybe more than a week—know about this. But there is nothing more typical of the inexperi-

32

enced teacher—is there?—than total preparation in which every five minutes is scheduled. Anxiety overloads the circuit. Overpreparation forecloses the possibility of responding to what John Donne calls "emergent occasions." The publishers and the educational establishment want to allay that anxiety, but their prescription is a medicine that's worse than the trouble it's meant to cure. Tight schedules, leakproof syllabi, the instructor's manual, and the gilt-edged study guide are all agencies by which "extension" supplants "communication": those are Paulo Freire's terms. In *Education for Critical Consciousness,* Freire speaks of the agricultural *extension* service in Brazil as being antithetical to the communication by which learning is truly effected. The peasants don't learn from someone *extending* a service to them. Nor do students. I remember, as a most depressing experience indeed, being shown the way literature is taught in the Boston high schools. The head of the English Department showed me proudly the guide that was provided for every teacher—a loose-leaf notebook designed so it could lie flat unobtrusively in front of the teacher, out of sight of the class, between the teacher and the text: the same principle as reading a comic book with *The Return of the Native* propped up in front. For each poem there was provided a page of questions—all variations on the primeval query: "What is the author trying to say?" And with answers! Nothing can kill a class sooner than to ask a question to which there is a prefabricated answer. Of course, using somebody else's list of questions and answers is worse, but I think asking your own, without being able to accommodate the response you get, is almost as bad. I'm not telling you anything you don't know; I simply want to restate the home truths in the context of remarks on the uses of theory.

But the fear of losing control is very real: having an agenda is, after all, a pretty good defense, if that's what we want. When I first taught, I certainly wanted a defense against the possibility that the class or the text would get out of control, or out of my control. And, of course, there were very important facts about *Beowulf* that I wanted them to have. When somebody would ask a question that got me off the track, I was very upset. But back I would go to the agenda, my security blanket. Within a week I had discovered that what was really interesting was what happened when we talked with one another about emergent questions. I learned to come to class, not thinking of a territory to be covered, but with a compass—a metaphor, or a juxtaposition, or a question from the class before. In my experience, that's a lesson that is never finally learned: I have to learn it all over again every time I design a new course. I want to say, "*Listen* to all this fascinating stuff I've just learned about linguistics—" and I proceed with my own order. Only when I really

33

start hearing the questions or eliciting the real ones does the class take on direction—whether towards excellence or not is problematic, but the point is that the show is on the road.

You probably know the story of the first years of Bruner's curriculum, *Man: A Course of Study.* Teachers were prepared to teach the new course by studying the scientific background implicit in the lessons. The course was enormously interesting to students who raised dozens of questions, the answers to which the teachers did not have. They complained to the course designers who then offered a refresher course (*"Do* flies have muscles?"). They returned to their classrooms—and to dozens of new questions! And finally everyone saw that what we needed was to learn a stance, a way of handling any question in dialogue.

That's a good example, I think, of how theory and practice and evaluation can all work together, can all be brought together: unless this happens, practice gets gimmicky and theory becomes dogmatic and evaluation stays in the hands of the Board of Education. The initiation of the teacher as REsearcher could be the ritual burning of all instructors' manuals, and the students could ceremoniously toss on the bonfire their study guides and their yellow felt marking pens. I tell my students that my course is an anti-Evelyn Wood course in how to slow down your reading in order to speed it up eventually.

I've reached the point now at which Cicero suggests that the orator should begin to say *in conclusion:* I'm two-thirds through. I want to spend the rest of my time suggesting how theory can help us teach composition.

The theory we need in that endeavor is a theory of the imagination. Imagination is the conceptual bridge from English to the real world because it is, in Coleridge's resonant phrase, "the prime agent of all human perception." Constructing and construing, writing and reading and perceiving are all acts of interpretation. In my textbook I have experimented with ways in which we might reclaim the imagination as a concept to help us get the affective and the cognitive together, not partitioned in their separate domains or in their separate brain halves. Educators tend to associate imagination with Friday afternoon projects and courses not in the core, with the unintellectual, the noncognitive, the merely personal expression of merely personal experience. But imagination is properly a name for the active mind, the mind of the child making forms in sand, the artist making forms in granite: Dame Barbara Hepworth, the British sculptor, speaks of her left hand as her "thinking" hand; the right is only the motor hand, the hand that holds the mallet. Her thinking hand finds the form in the stone—not her "inspirational" or her genius hand or her "creative" hand: her *thinking* hand. Thinking is not the province of the logician alone. If we can keep thinking and creating together, I don't think there will be any difficulty finding directions. A theory of imagination could guide us in teaching critical and creative writing together, reading and writing together; and most important, it could help us understand what it really means to speak of the composing *process.*

Composing is forming: it is a continuum; it goes on all the time. Composing is what the mind does by nature: composing is the function of the active mind. Composing is the way we make sense of the world: it's our way of learning.

Here's what Gordon Allport has to say about learning: "Whatever else learning may be, it is surely a disposition to form structures." Our chief resource as teachers of composition is right there: it is the mind's disposition to form structures, to compose.

Now what are the pedagogical implications? If composing begins with birth, if composing is making sense of the world and that's what the mind does, and if this composing is a continuum, then whatever is fundamental to perception is also fundamental to conception, to concept formation: a theory of imagination would remind us to provide occasions for lots of perception, for lots of looking at things, for observation. Perception is the other side of concept formation. We don't have to teach that, thank the Lord: thank the Lord for that, because the human mind is created as a composer: by means of language we construe each particular thing as a symbol for that kind of thing. When we see a lamb, we simultaneously see *that* lamb and that lamb as a *kind* of thing. That's what it means to say that man is the *animal symbolicum,* the symbol-making animal. When we teach perception—but of course we don't do that: when we encourage observation, looking and looking again, we're not teaching some merely preliminary thing. (When do we get to "real" writing?) When we offer what I call, after I. A. Richards, "assisted invitations" to students to use their minds in looking at things, we're also exercising the capacity to form concepts. Perception is not something that comes first and then we get to ideas; perception is itself a construing, an interpretation, a making of meaning, a composing.

We let students of composition do a lot of looking—not because we want detail for detail's sake, not because we are committed to "show, don't tell," but because *looking, seeing, turns on the mind.* When we encourage our students to look and look again, we are not differentiating creative and critical writing, which should be kept together, just as composing and editing should be kept apart. In practicing close observation and critical response, students of composition can raise their consciousness of themselves as composers—that process, which Paulo Freire calls "conscientization," a process involving a community of observer-critics, of responsive audiences and purposeful writers. Students of composition who do a lot of looking will learn that perspective and context are essential to interpretation. In short, they will learn habits of mind essential to critical and creative thinking. I do not think these habits should be labeled "cognitive skills"; they have an importance which that label of the educationists cannot suggest.

A theory of imagination helps us invent assignments appropriate to one or another phase of the composing process. It can do that by reminding us that composing is forming and that forms don't come out of the air. Now English teachers have recently rediscovered that fact. In the past seven or eight years, with the help of Peter Elbow and Ken Macrorie especially, we have learned to recognize the role of free writing in the forming that is composing. But I've been noticing recently that as this fundamental idea becomes accepted more widely, it becomes less well-defined; as it is institutionalized, free writing is often just a faddish name for the old method it was meant to replace. In the preface to a writing lab manual for tutors we read that the chief purpose of pre-writing is for the student to get his thesis statement and to learn to outline! Quote from the section called "Pre-writing": "The standard outline is still the best method to help students overcome organizational problems." Of course, if students knew how to outline, they wouldn't have any organizational problems to overcome! And if they can outline right off the bat, then they don't need pre-writing because they will already know what they have to say. Someone who knows exactly what he wants to say without any preliminary forming: that's a fair definition of a *hack.*

The concept of pre-writing as a necessary phase in the composing process is disappearing before our very eyes because there has been no theoretical understanding of the role it plays; I mean any philosophical understanding. The psychological rationale is obvious: it relaxes you; it gives you something other than the blank page to confront and thus can allay anxiety; it can explode one kind of writer's block. The philosophical rationale for pre-writing is not often articulated. Let me try:

Learning to make pre-writing a phase of the composing process and not just a five-finger exercise, a warm-up—though it is that too—means learning the uses of chaos. The reason that free writing, listing, and other modes of pre-writing can lead to something else is that the seemingly shapeless, seemingly random words, the images

36

and phrases and fragments are stand-ins for fuller statements, for
relationships, for assertions and questions. They are protosentences
and paragraphs-in-utero. The conventional wisdom of most schools
of psychology cannot explain that: no theory of verbal behavior can
account for that power of words, but a philosophy of language as
symbolic form can, and so can a theory of imagination as the forming power.

Our students, because they are language animals, because they
have the power of naming, can generate chaos; they can find ways
out of chaos because language creates them. Language is itself the
great heuristic: words come into being as verbal generalization: any
name implies generalization; and as students look again at chaos they
can see it happen. Words cluster because they belong together—and
sentences can be composed that name that relationship. Clusters of
words turn into syntax: it is the discursive character of language, its
tendency to "run along"—and that's what discourse means—language's tendency to be syntactical brings thought along with it. It
is the discursive, generalizing, forming power of language that makes
meanings from chaos, which makes pre-writing not *just* preliminary.

Jean Pumphrey's scatter poems demonstrate this power of language to shape meanings. Kenneth Koch's syntactic structures and
"poetry ideas," as he calls his rhetorical forms, are what generate
the poetry he gets from his youngsters. Any transforming exercise
can demonstrate the power of language to make new meanings.
Here's a passage from a report written for the Materials and Soils
Program of the Division of Highways in Pierre, South Dakota. It's
written as a poem called "Observations":

> Some areas of the upper depositions
> of Pierre Shale are fractured
> and lie in jointed platy layers.
> Surface water tends
> to accumulate
> and build up perched water tables in the roadbeds.
> The platy layers are dyked off
> by impervious shale beds
> and have no free drainage outlets.
> A large water-fed slide
> on old U.S. 16
> required many thousands of yards of material
> to hold the toe of a berm.
> On the interstate near Wasta, South Dakota
> water problems developed which caused
> much differential heaving.

I think this represents something of what I. A. Richards meant when he spoke once of poetry as "an instrument of research."

Students can learn to write by learning the uses of chaos, which is to say, rediscovering the power of language to generate meanings. Our job is to design sequences of assignments that let them discover what language can do, what they can do with language.

Our students can learn to write only if we give them back their language, and that means playing with it, working with it, using it instrumentally, making many starts. We want them to learn the truth of Gaston Bachelard's observation that "in the realm of the mind, to begin is to know you have the right to begin again." If our students are to learn the uses of chaos, we will have to learn ways of teaching them to tolerate ambiguity and to be patient with their beginnings— which should never be graded: identifying mistakes is irrelevant. when we are teaching how to begin the process of making meanings. And when we do come to respond to compositions, our comments should continue the dialogue that has been formed in the writer's mind, transformed in his dialogue on paper. As Josephine Miles has suggested, our comments can most usefully take the form of a question: "The main point seems to be X; your supporting statements are here, here, and here; if this is so, why is that paragraph where it is?" "The main idea of this paper is X; the main steps of its development are here, and here, and here: how then does paragraph 4 fit in, and what transitional connective term would be helpful?"

A theory of the imagination, I've been arguing, can guide us in teaching composition as a dialectical *process*—not a linear, one-way street. In my book, I compare the composer to a sheep dog: a colleague who's using the book told me that nobody knew what a sheep dog was like, but the fact that it was *not* like a tractor got across! Our assignments should be appropriate to all that running about, that hithering and thithering of the sheep dog: short papers, long papers, throw away papers, one sentence written 10 different ways— 10 different intentions written in one sentence pattern; papers written out of class, papers in class, papers to be forgotten, papers to be revised and edited. Surely, teaching from the perspective of a theory of imagination could help us separate composing and editing. Keats couldn't spell for a hot egg!

In conclusion, I want you to hear a paragraph written by a seventh-grader in a remedial class. His teacher, my student, Mrs. Paula Girouard-McCann, who'd been reading George Hillocks' little NCTE pamphlet, *Observing and Writing,* brought in a bag of marbles and told her class that they could write whatever they wanted about how the marble looked to them, and that they were not to worry about grammar and spelling.

A marble is round and made out of glass. When you drop it, it makes a trickle sound. Inside there are little marbles that look like bubbles from a splash in the water. If you think hard enough while your looking in, you can see what you are thinking. Most marbles are see-through. If you whip it down on the ground, it might smash into tiny little pieces. When you put a marble up to a window, you can see your image upside down instead of right side up. It is like an eye whithout a mirror or diaphragm. It looks like there are tiny scratches all over it, but when you feel it, it feels like there are none at all. When you think of it in science terms, you can see parameciums and many other different microrganisms. If you think of it in social science terms, you think of who invented glass and who thought of marbles. If you think of it in math terms, you notice how perfectly round it is. If you think of it in English terms, you can write about it and tell of all the ways it was made, the roundness of it, the science about it, and how you can tell all the ways about a little marble and all the wonders.

I had planned to end with a long passage from Coleridge on the imagination, but I think the seventh-grader looking at the marble is better: everything we need to know about composing as a continuum of forming, thinking, and writing is in the boy's sentence:

If you think hard enough while your looking in, you can see what you are thinking.

A Lot of Talk About Nothing

SHIRLEY BRICE HEATH
Stanford University

Shirley Brice Heath brings to this part of the book a description of her work with teacher-researchers who planned a wealth of language experiences for youngsters based on the distinctive uses of language in the children's homes and communities. This is a classical example of interactive research in which ethnographers, teachers, and children discover together. Like Nancy Martin's piece, it is persuasive about the need to move past generalized commonplaces into close observations of the immediate settings in which our students' learning actually occurs.

Inside a third-grade classroom described by the principal as a class of "low achievers," several pairs of children are working over tape recorders in dialogues with each other. One small group of children is dressed in costumes performing "Curious George" scenes for a few kindergarteners who are visiting. Yet another group is preparing illustrations for a story told by one of their classmates and now being heard on tape as they talk about why their drawings illustrate the words they hear. A lot of talk about nothing? Why are these children who presumably lack basic skills in language arts not spending their time with obvious instruction from the teacher in reading, writing and listening?

These are students in the classroom of a teacher-researcher who has adapted information about the oral and written language experiences of these children at home into a new language arts curriculum for school. She has developed for her children a program in which they spend as much of the day as possible talking—to each other and the teacher, and to fifth- and sixth-graders who come into the class one-half hour each day to read to small groups. This teacher has 30 children and no aides; she enlisted the help of fifth- and sixth-grade teachers who were willing to have some of their students write stories for the younger children and read to them several days of each week. The kindergarten teacher helps out by sending a few of her children for the third-graders to read to each week.

Talk in the classroom is about personal experiences, stories, expository textbook materials and, perhaps most important, about their own and others' talk. Their teacher gives no reading or writing task which is not surrounded by talk about the content knowledge behind the task and the kinds of language skills—oral and written— needed to tackle the task.

Since the beginning of the year, the teacher has asked visitors from the community into her class to talk about their ways of talking and to explain what they read and write at home and at work. The children have come to think of themselves as language "detectives," listening and learning to describe the talk of others. Grocery clerks have to use many politeness terms, and the questions they ask most often of customers require only a yes or no answer. On the other hand, guides at the local nature museum talk in "long paragraphs," describing what is around them and usually asking questions only at the end of one of their descriptions. The children have also learned to analyze their talk at home, beginning early in the year with a simple record of the types of questions they hear asked at home, and moving later in the year to interviews with their parents about the kinds of talking, reading and writing they do at their jobs.

The teacher in this classroom comments on her own talk and the language of textbooks, of older students, and of the third-graders themselves during each day. "Show and tell" time, usually reserved for only first-graders, occurs each day in this class, under the supervision of a committee of students who decide each week whether those who participate in this special time of the day will: (1) narrate about an experience they or someone else has had, (2) describe an event or object without including themselves or another animate being, or (3) read from their diary or journal for a particular day. The children use terms such as *narrative, exposition,* and *diary* or *journal* with ease by the end of the year. Increasingly during the year, the children use "show and tell" time to talk, not about their own direct experiences, but about content areas of their classroom. Also by the end of the year, the children are using this special time of the day for presenting skits about a social studies or science unit. They have found that the fifth- and sixth-graders can offer assistance on these topics, and planning such a presentation guarantees the attention of the upper classmen. By the end of the year, most of these children score above grade level on reading tests, and they are able to write stories, as well as paragraphs of exposition on content areas with which they feel comfortable in their knowledge. This is clearly no longer a class of "low achievers."

Teachers as Researchers

All of these ideas sound like pedagogical practices that many good teachers bring intuitively to their instruction. What was different about the motivations of this third-grade teacher for approaching language arts in these ways? The teacher described here was one of a group of teacher-researchers who cooperated with me for several years during the 1970s. I worked as an ethnographer, a daily participant and observer in homes and communities similar to those of the children in their classrooms, studying the ways in which the children learned to use oral and written language. As I studied the children at home, the teachers focused on their own language uses at home and in the classroom. We brought our knowledge together for comparison and as the baseline data from which to consider new methods and approaches in language arts.

We do not need educational research to tell us that different types of attention spans, parental support systems, and peer pressures can create vast differences among children in the same classroom, school, or community. But what of more subtle features of background differences, such as the amount and kind of talk addressed by adults to children and solicited from children? How can teachers and researchers work together to learn more about children's language experiences at home? And what can this knowledge mean for classroom practice?

For nearly a decade, living and working in three communities located within a few miles of each other in the southeastern part of the United States, I collected information on ways in which the children of these communities learned to use language: (1) Roadville is a white working-class community, (2) Trackton is a black working-class community in which many of the older members have only recently left work as sharecroppers on nearby farms, (3) the townspeople, black and white residents of a cluster of mainstream, school-oriented neighborhoods, are school teachers, local business owners, and executives of the textile mills.

Children from the three groups respond differently to school experiences. Roadville children are successful in the first years of the primary grades. Most Trackton children are not successful during this period, and only a few begin in the higher primary grades to move with adequate success through their classes. Most of the mainstream children of the townspeople, black and white, are successful in school and obtain a high school diploma with plans to go on to higher education. Children from backgrounds similar to those of these three groups make up the majority of the students in many regions of the southeastern United States. They bring to their classrooms different patterns of learning and using oral and written language, and their patterns of academic achievement vary greatly.

Intuitively, most teachers are aware of the different language background experiences children bring to school, but few means exist for providing teachers with information about these differences and their implications for classroom practice. Recent development of the notion of "teacher-as-researcher" has begun to help bridge the long-standing gap between researcher and teacher. This approach pairs the roles of teacher and researcher in a cooperative search for answers to questions raised by the teacher about what is happening in the classroom and why. Answering *why* questions more often than not calls for knowledge about the background experiences of both children and teachers. Thus, researcher working with teacher can help bridge yet another gap—that between the classroom and the homes of students.

Throughout most of the decade of the 1970s, I worked in the Piedmont Carolinas with teachers in several districts as research partners. Together, we addressed the questions teachers raised during the sometimes tumultuous early years of desegregation and ensuing shifts of curricular and testing policies. These teachers accepted the fact that language was fundamental to academic achievement, and their primary concerns related to how they could help children learn to use oral and written language in ways that would bring successful classroom experiences. They asked hard questions of language research. Why were some children seemingly unable to answer straightforward questions? Why were some students able to give elaborate directions and tell fantastic stories on the playground, but unable to respond to assignments calling for similar responses about lesson materials? Why did some children who had achieved adequate success in their first two or three years of school begin to fail in the upper primary grades?

In the 1960s, social scientists had described the language habits of groups of youngsters who were consistently failing to achieve academic excellence. The teachers with whom I worked were familiar with these studies, which had been carried out primarily in black urban areas. Most accepted the fact that children who spoke a nonstandard variety of English had learned a rule-governed language system and, moreover, that these students reflected learned patterns of "logic," considerable facility in handling complicated forms of oral discourse, and adeptness in shifting styles. But knowing this information about language learned at home did not answer the kinds of questions noted above about classroom performance. Neither did it provide for development of improved classroom materials and practices.

Ethnography of Communication

Late in the 1970s, as some language researchers tried to describe the contexts in which children of different cultures learned to use language, they turned to ethnographic methods. Participating and observing over many months and even years in the daily lives of the group being studied, these researchers, who were often anthropologists, focused on oral and written language uses. My work in Roadville, Trackton, and among the townspeople centered on the children of these groups as they learned the ways of acting, believing and valuing around them in their homes and communities. Following the suggestions of anthropologist Dell Hymes, who first proposed in 1964 that ethnographers focus on communication, I lived and worked within these three groups to describe where, when, to whom, how, and with what results children were socialized as talkers, readers and writers. The three communities—located only a few miles apart—had radically different ways of using language and of seeing themselves in communication with their children.

Roadville parents believe they have to teach their children to talk, and they begin their task by talking with infants, responding to their initial sounds as words. They respond with full sentences, varying their tone of voice and emphasis, and affectionately urging infants to turn their heads in the direction of the speaker. As they talk to their infants and young children, they label items in the environment, and as children begin to talk, adults ask many teaching questions: "Where's your nose?" "Can you find Daddy's shoes?" Adults fictionalize their youngsters in talk about them: "He's a little cowboy; see those boots? See that cowboy strut?" Parents read to their children and ask them to name items in books, answer questions about the book's contents and, as they get older, to sit quietly listening to stories read to them. Parents buy coloring and follow-the-number books for their children and tutor them in staying within the lines and coloring items appropriately. All of these habits relate to school practices, and they are transferred to the early years of reading and writing in school. Yet, by the fourth grade many of these children seem to find the talking, reading and writing tasks in school foreign, and their academic achievement begins to decline.

In nearby Trackton, adults immerse their children in an ongoing stream of talk from extended family members and a wide circle of friends and neighbors. Children become the responsibility of all members of the community, and from birth they are kept in the center of most adult activities, including eating, sleeping, or playing. Adults talk about infants and young children, and as they do so, they fictionalize them and often exaggerate their behaviors and physical features. They nickname children and play teasing games with them. They ask young children for specific information which is not known to adults: "Where'd that come from?" "You want what?" By the time they are toddlers, these children begin to tell stories, recounting events or describing objects they have seen. Adults stop and listen to their stories occasionally, but such stories are most often addressed to other children who challenge, extend, tease, or build from the youngster's tales. By about 2, children begin to enter ongoing conversations by actively attracting adults' attention with some physical gesture and then making a request, registering a complaint, or reporting an event. Very quickly, these children are accepted as communicating members of the group, and adults respond directly to them as conversational partners.

Most of these children first go to school with enthusiasm, but by the end of the first half of the first grade, many are coming home with reports that their teacher scolds them for talking too much and working too little. By the third grade, many Trackton children have established a record of failures which often they do not break in the rest of their school careers.

After hearing from me how children of these communities learned to use language, some of their teachers agreed to work with me to study either their own uses of language with their pre-schoolers at home or those of their mainstream friends. They found that when talking to very young infants, they asked questions, simplified their sentences, used special words and changed their tone of voice. Moreover, since most of these mainstream mothers did not work outside the home while their children were very young, they spent long hours each day alone with their pre-schoolers as their primary conversational partners. They arranged many outings, usually with other mothers through voluntary associations, such as their church groups or local social memberships.

These teachers' findings about mainstreamers' uses of language with their pre-schoolers indicated that they and the Roadville parents had many language socialization habits in common. Parents in both communities talked to their children and focused their youngsters' attention at an early age on labels, pictures in books, and educational toys. Both groups played with their children and participated in planned outings and family recreation with them. Yet mainstream children and Roadville children fared very differently in their progress through the middle primary grades.

A close look at the home habits of these two groups indicated that a major difference lay in the amount of running narrative or ongoing commentary in which mainstream parents immersed their young children. As these youngsters pass their first birthday, mothers and other adults who are part of their daily network begin to provide a running commentary on events and items surrounding the child. In these commentaries, adults tell the child what is happening: "Mummy's going to get her purse, and then we're going to take a ride. Mummy's got to go to the post office." As soon as the child begins to talk, adults solicit these kinds of running commentaries: they ask children what they are doing with their toys, what they did when they were at someone else's house, and what they had to eat on a trip to the grocery store. These requests for running descriptions and cumulative accounts of past actions provide children in these families with endless hours of practice of all the sentence-level features necessary to produce successful narratives or recounts of experiences.

In using their own experiences as data, children begin their developmental progression of story conventions and narrative structures which they will be asked to replay in school from the first day of school through their college courses. They learn either to use an existing animate being or to create a fantastic one as the central actor in their stories; they take these actors through events in which

45

they may meet obstacles on their way to a goal. The scripts of the stories that the children have heard read to them and the narratives that have surrounded them and storied their own and others' experiences are replayed with different actors and slightly different settings. Gradually, children learn to open and close stories, to give them a setting and movement of time, and occasionally, even to sum up the meaning of the story in a moralistic pronouncement ("He shouldn't have gone without his mother"). Some children move from linking a collection of events related to one another only by their immediacy of experience for the child to tying a story together by incorporating a central point, a constant goal or direction, and a point of view which may not be that of the child as experiencer and narrator.

When children are very young toddlers, parents talk of and ask children about events of the here-and-now: the immediate tasks of eating, getting dressed, and playing with a particular toy or person. Of older toddlers, adults increasingly ask questions about events that occurred in the past—tasks, settings, and events that the child is expected to recount from memory. These recountings are, however, then interpreted by adults or older siblings in a future frame: "Do you want to go again?" "Do you think Billy's mother will be able to fix the broken car?" Questioners ask children to express their views about future events and to link past occurrences with what will come in the future.

In many ways, all of this is "talk about nothing," and adults and older siblings in these mainstream households model and elicit these kinds of narratives without being highly conscious of their having a didactic purpose or a heavily positive transfer value to school activities. Yet when teacher-researchers examined closely the instructional situations of the classrooms into which these children usually go, they found that, from first-grade reading circles to upper-primary social studies group work, the major activity is producing some sort of commentary on events or objects. In the early primary years, teachers usually request commentary in the form of labels or names of attributes of items or events ("What did the boy in our story find on his walk?"). Later, the requests are for descriptive commentary ("Who are some community helpers? What kinds of jobs do they do for us?"). Gradually the requests are mixed and students have to learn when it is appropriate to respond with labels or features (brief names or attributes of events or objects), fantastic stories, straightforward descriptions, or interpretations in which they comment on the outcome of events, the relative merits of objects, or the internal states of characters.

A Closer Look

On the surface, these summaries of the early language socialization of the children from these three communities support a commonly held idea about links between language at home and at school: the more parents talk to their children, the more likely children are to succeed in school. Yet the details of the differences and similarities across these three communities suggest that this correlation is too simple. Trackton children hear and take part in far more talk around them than the children of either Roadville or the townspeople. Yet, for them, more talk does not have a positive transfer value to the current, primary-level practices of the school. Roadville children have less talk addressed to them than the townspeople's children. Yet, from an early age, they are helped to focus on labels and features of items and events. They are given books and they are read to by parents who buy educational toys for their children and spend many hours playing with their toddlers. As the children grow older, these parents involve their children in handicrafts, home building projects, and family recreational activities such as camping and fishing. Both Trackton and Roadville parents have strong faith in schooling as a positive value for their children, and they believe success in school will help their children get jobs better than those they have held as adults. Yet, neither Roadville nor Trackton children manage to achieve the same patterns of sustained academic success children of townspeople achieve with relatively little apparent effort. Why?

A primary difference seems to be the amount of "talk about nothing" with which the townspeople surround their children and into which they socialize their young. Through their running narratives, which begin almost at the birth of the child, they seemingly focus the attention of their young on objects and events while they point out verbally the labels and features of those that the child should perceive and later talk about. It is as though, in the drama of life, these parents freeze scenes and parts of scenes repeatedly throughout each day. Within the frame of a single scene, they focus the child's attention, sort out labels to name, and give the child ordered turns for sharing talk about these labels and the properties of the objects or events to which they refer; adult and child thus jointly narrate descriptions of scenes. Through this consistent focus, adults pull out some of the stimuli in the array surrounding the child and make these stand still for cooperative examination and narration between parent and child. Later occurrences of the same event or object are identified by adults who call the child's attention to similarities and differences. Thus, townspeople's children are not left on their own to see these relations between two events or to explore ways of integrating something in a new context to its old context. These children learn to attend to items both in real life and in books, both in and out of their usual locations, as they practise throughout their pre-school years running narratives with adults.

In much of their talk, mainstream adults ask: "What do you call that?" "Do you remember how to say the name of that?" Thus, children are alerted to attend to the particulars of talk about talk: names, ways of retelling information, and ways of linking what one has told with something that has gone before. Thus, mainstreamers' children hear a lot of talk about talk and are forced to focus on not only the features and names of the world around them, but also on their ways of communicating about that world. From the earliest days of their infancy, these habits are modeled repeatedly for them, and as soon as they learn to talk, they are called upon to practice similar verbal habits. Day in and day out during their pre-school years, they hear and practice the kinds of talk in which they will display successful learning in school.

The teacher in the third-grade classroom described at the beginning of this essay recognized that her students needed intense and frequent occasions to learn and practice those language uses they had not acquired at home. She, therefore, created a classroom that focused on talk—all kinds of talk. The children labeled, learned to name the features of everyday items and events, told stories, described their own and others' experiences, and narrated skits, puppet shows, and slide exhibits.

Many classrooms include such activities for portions of the day or week; others provide some of these activities for some children. A critical difference in the case given here, however, and one driven by a perspective gained from being part of a research team, was the amount of talk about talk in this classroom. School-age children are capable of—and can be quite proficient at—stepping back from and commenting upon their own and others' activities, *if* the necessary skills are modeled and explicated. In this classroom, and in others which drew from ethnographic data on the home life of their students, teachers and visitors to the classroom called attention to the ways they used language: how they asked questions, showed politeness, got what they wanted, settled arguments, and told funny stories. With early and intensive classroom opportunities to surround learning with many different kinds of talk and much talk about talk, children from homes and communities whose uses of language do not match those of the school *can* achieve academic success. A frequently heard comment, "Talk is cheap," is, in these days of bankrupt school districts and economic cutbacks, perhaps worth a closer examination —for more reasons than one.

Research as Odyssey

KEN MACRORIE
Professor Emeritus, Western Michigan University

Ken Macrorie, like all fine teachers, is a researcher by nature. Indeed, his research stance in the college classroom led to some of the best writing about writing in the last quarter century. Here, Macrorie talks about how the need to find out *can swing away from customary, formalistic research practices—about how such practices may in fact inhibit the kind of discovering most useful to teachers.*

Wish I could make this story about a research project sound like a poem. But it would have to be such a long one. I don't think I could maintain the music, the metaphor, and the compression.

One day reading the local newspaper, I came across a page of pictures and a story about a young elementary-school teacher who ran after-class sessions for little kids afraid of gym and embarrassed at their ineptness in sports. This young man said to them, "In our basketball game, if you hit the rim with the ball, that counts two points!"

I could tell by the rapt and happy faces in the pictures that he had delivered these kids from their agony. They were born again. Maybe such a religious frame for my thoughts led me to the term "good works" to describe acts of students that produce writing, objects, taped words, and other things that count for the doers, their classmates, their teacher, and persons beyond the classroom.

Looking at that newspaper page about a man named Randy Werner, I thought, "Wouldn't it be great to search out a number of teachers like him, who help students become genuine learners and change their lives? I wonder how many there are in this country?"

I thought if I could find some, I would interview them. A few weeks later I saw in *The New York Times* a third of a page of pictures of boys in a private school in Pennsylvania making furniture that looked like the work of professionals. Maybe there were quite a few teachers whose students did *good works.* That woodworking teacher reported in the *Times* might turn out to be the second in what I hoped would be a formidable collection of *enablers.*

The week after summer vacation had begun, I called up Randy Werner's school and found he had quit teaching. He was selling fishing rods and golf club shafts in Texas and making four times as much money as he had made teaching. When I reached him by phone he said he'd be glad to talk to me on one of his trips home to Michigan.

Randy met me at the airport while he was waiting for a plane. I asked him to tell me more about his teaching than I had learned from the newspaper article, and he quickly went into high gear. He was so happy remembering how those kids had changed from fearful blunderers to persons in command of their bodies. He was on a roll, laughing and gesturing, imitating the kids, telling and showing me that he was still part kid himself. I had to remind him that he might miss his plane.

That's one thing I learned interviewing people. Get them to tell you about something they're good at, and they become eloquent. You have to wait for that to happen. Don't make it a question-and-answer session. Just get them talking, and let them go. I discovered that from reading interviews by Whitney Balliett in *The New Yorker*. Usually, he presents a brief resumé of a jazz player's life, written beautifully, with all the devices of poetry; and then the jazz musician appears to take over. The rest of the article is just that person talking out of a love for playing jazz, telling the high and low notes of a hard and ecstatic life. Probably, Mr. Balliett asks questions when the musician slows down or stops, but he doesn't print the questions in the article. He's not trying to make *himself* look good, but to present a person telling an exciting, charming tale.

The questions to ask in interviews are easy to construct if the interviewer remembers that the aim is to get people talking excitedly about what they've done well—and for the book I'm writing about, what their students have done well. It is not to pull out answers to specific questions delivered one after another. It's much like enabling a group of people to do something well in a classroom. Once they're curious, once they're thinking and working with a point of concentration, they'll produce valuable statements, constructions, or performances along with the necessary details out of which they arise. They'll cover the ground you want covered and large chunks of territory you never knew existed. The job of the interviewer is to launch the speaker and then sit back and wait for surprises.

The questions have to be open ended. "How did you get into this way of teaching?" "What was the opening day of class like?" "What do the students do at this point?" "What did you say to them?" "Can you give me a sample of a handout you've written for your students?" "How do you have them sit in the room?" None of these questions can be answered with "yes" or "no." If I had asked, "How long a bibliography do you ask for in student term papers?" the answer might be, "Six pages." Or, "I don't ask for bibliographies." And I might never have found that the teacher asks for something beyond and above such traditional documentation—and the students provide spectacular documentation, maybe a TV tape or a 16-mm film they made in their search.

At first I didn't use a tape recorder for these interviews. I wrote down as fast as I could what people said to me, knowing I would miss a lot, but I remembered earlier experiences with tape-recorded material—I had amassed too many words and couldn't find my way around in them. I became mentally fatigued trying to keep up on the typewriter with the fast pace of a recorded speaker. I would type three words, get behind, back up the recorder, type four more, and repeat the process. It was excruciating. Years earlier in writing a doctoral thesis I had watched veteran news reporters at work writing down only what was essential and then returning to the newsroom to bat the story out under pressure. They could never have done that with the voluminous material gained from tape recording. But, I wanted to capture the individual voices of the teachers, and slowly I began to realize that news reporters' working conditions were different from mine. Their deadline was today; mine was in the vague future—for most of the interviews, years away.

Then, overwhelmed with cassette tape after cassette tape piling up in a shoe box, I decided I must conquer the problem mechanically. I set out to buy a court reporter's equipment, a tape recorder with a foot pedal that would back the tape up as well as stop it or move it forward fast. But it turned out to cost about $600 to $1000, and I didn't plan to write interview books the rest of my life. Someone told me that at an electronics store I could buy a foot pedal for my tape recorder for $3.50. It wouldn't back up the tape but it would stop it instantly, and using the pedal left my hands free to stay at the keyboard of the typewriter instead of bouncing back and forth between it and the controls of the tape recorder.

Soon after that I made the decision to buy a word processor, studied the field, and bought a system that cost as much as my car. I said to mayself, "If I were a traveling salesman, I would buy whatever was needed for my job. I'm a writer of books. I'll buy a word processor." That was one of the best decisions of my professional life. Now I could type faster because the key action is quick and there is no returning of a carriage. When I sent the first draft of the interview to the teacher who had talked to me, and asked him for corrections of fact, I got back those and suggested changes of expression. Then I simply made the changes I decided upon. I didn't have to retype the whole text. I was working with disks that projected the words upon the screen and a printer that reproduced the screened letters onto paper at the rate of 55 characters per second, with carbon-ribbon typewriter quality. If all along I had had that setup for writing, I would probably have finished the book in three years instead of seven, although maybe I needed the longer time to let my thoughts brew and the 20 extraordinary teachers to appear in my life.

The last one was added to *Twenty Teachers* after it had been accepted by Oxford University Press. I had talked to her for two summers while teaching at the Bread Loaf School of English in Vermont and we had become friends. I visited her classes there. What she and her students were doing worked their way into my book at the last minute. They didn't know I was considering including them. In fact, I didn't know it. But their good works and the good sense of that class couldn't be ignored.

There were the usual difficulties in interviewing. I got names wrong, couldn't make out some mumbled or garbled words. Technical things related by the teachers confused me at times. On the whole I did pretty well. Some teachers wrote me that they were surprised how clearly I had interpreted their work. Because I had to cut so much, and to rearrange so much, in order to make things clear, there was a large chance of distortion. Years before that, I had learned from newspaper and television reporters that often the reporter has to paraphrase what's said, or make up sentences that are truer to the source's feelings and beliefs than the words she or he delivered at the moment of being interviewed.

Then there's the normal awkward repetition and lack of syntax in common speech that looks awful in print if not edited. Passages like this, for example:

> Geez, those people I met in Hannibal over there on the other side of the river, and it's a big river there, you know, they had an idea, was not exactly the kind of people I would want to sit down and eat a meal with.

You don't want to quote sentences like that unless you're out to attack someone. You might be thinking, "That's pretty bad language. A college professor would never talk like that." A college professor belongs to the human species and that's the way human beings talk. And so you have to doctor a little what people say, trying to stay true to the spirit and intention of their words. That's standard operating procedure in interviewing, but novices are nonplussed when they first encounter the need to do that. When they begin transcribing a tape, they're more conscious of the words than the meaning because they're trying to get them down on paper. When they did the interview, they were listening for meaning and didn't notice all the torn and ragged edges of the speaker's language.

I interviewed 20 teachers whose students were doing good works and found they were about 75 to 80 percent in agreement in methods, beliefs, and principles. That staggered me and I felt wonderful. The warp and woof of what these teachers and students did and said made a rug you could put down on the floor of any classroom. Detail after detail. In fact, so much detail that I worried

52

that my readers would get lost in all that stuff and not see what was woven into the rug. So every few pages I pointed out to readers what the teacher was doing and why. I did that because my habit as a writer—as my wife has reminded me year after year—is to submerge ideas in too much experience. "What's the point?" Joyce asks. Even if she sees the point herself she senses that a reader who hasn't lived with me for 19 years wouldn't get it.

I intended to follow the interviews with a chapter summarizing what these teachers did and believed in common. When later I sent the manuscript to a publisher, my editor told me that several people at the publishing house who had read it thought that I ought to re-move my editorial remarks from the interviews and let the teachers speak for themselves. Then it would be OK, they said, to put my summarizing comments into a chapter by themselves. I recognized that this was a good idea. My comments within the interviews had interrupted excited people telling exciting stories.

Listing the common practices, ideas, and attitudes of these teachers in a chapter provided that rug I mentioned earlier. Some people might want to call it a *theory of education*; I would prefer to call it a way of teaching people to do good works. It was more than a Christmas basket of assorted fruits and sweets because usually one principle or method couldn't work its way without the support of others. This wasn't a formula or a bag of tricks. Deny one princi-ple or violate one attitude and the whole fabric of trust and confi-dence so necessary to good works would begin to ravel and fall apart. Before beginning this project I had suspected that that would be true. I had seen teachers who borrowed a notion like "free writing" they had read about somewhere, tossed it at their students, and got back empty posturings on paper. They hadn't set up a climate of truth-telling in their room; so the students didn't know what to do with their new "freedom." They thought it was another gimmick from a teacher who had never appeared as any more than a collection of gimmicks himself. As I carried out and wrote up interview after in-terview, notions like that became firm beliefs. No possibility of be-lieving anything else. The teachers who were getting good works from their students had woven a fabric that supported everything they wanted done. When unwittingly they introduced a strand that worked against the other strands, they had trouble; and once they identified it, they got rid of it. The beauty of the project was that by the time I was about two-thirds finished, I began to see which strands belonged in that rug and which ones didn't.

I had published books before and knew many of the dangers of making things public. Usually, I sensed the need to change the name and other necessary details about a student if there were possibilities of libel, injury, or embarrassment. Sometimes the teacher and I decided we had to use an incident that showed a student acting badly, but we did that only when we knew the class would be disbanded before publication occurred; and we used pseudonyms, changed a boy to a girl in the account, and did all sorts of things that would lessen chances of identification. In one instance, we printed some writing of students that we knew would upset parents in the community, whether identification of the individuals was made or not. We felt the importance of what was said outweighed possible injury or bad feeling. The anecdote we were publishing stood for many children's experience throughout the country; and so after getting signed permission slips from the students, we took the risk. As I write this, I hear that the teacher involved is going to quit the profession and move elsewhere, and I'm relieved to know my interview with him won't put him in jeopardy. Like several of the fine teachers in my collection of 20, he got no support from administrators, who often, in their ignorance, kept making his magnificent work harder and harder to carry out.

For about five of the eight years that I worked on this project off and on, I insisted on seeing the teachers in person. That was often difficult and expensive, because they worked in places as distant as Connecticut and California. Sometimes, I could visit one of them as part of a trip to a conference or a consultation I was invited to carry out with members of a school district or department. Near the end of my project, I interviewed several teachers by phone, using a thirty-dollar attachment to my tape recorder and phone that I bought. To my surprise, I found that after a somewhat cold beginning, the teachers heated themselves up and produced long passages of eloquence. Once their warmth subsided, I could ask a strategic question or speak my enthusiasm for what they were telling me, and they would become eloquent again. I'm talking about successful professionals now. Had I been interviewing failures—and I believe the majority of us teachers fail more than we succeed—the telephone interviews probably would have been disasters.

I began this tale by saying it was the story of a *research* project, but that word is fraught with so many bad connotations that I need to rescue it. I'm talking about looking for something that one *needs* to find out. Some research is that, and some is pure professional pretension—a bunch of pages and footnotes ground out to get a degree, a promotion, a grade. Or just to look professional. Many such papers make their writers look like professional boobs. I published a book in 1980 called *Searching Writing,* that explained how to do *I-Search* papers instead of the dumb exercises in plagiarism that undergraduate research papers often are. I'm talking here about searching with curiosity, out of need. Doing something that makes a difference in the researcher's life and the lives of others. The story of that search for even the most trivial answer, such as "What brand of skis should I buy given my budget, the skiing possibilities around here, and my skills?" can be a human document that teaches us all.

Too often research gets lost in numbers, charts, and graphs that spell out minute differences in things that don't matter to anyone, the persons who made them, or the rats whose temperature is being recorded. I once talked to a rat used in research who said, "These investigators don't know me. They have no idea of what I can do, of what I care about. They don't realize, for example, how much I've learned from Uncle Joe over there, the one with the gray fur on his ears. They decided what I was before they got me into this cage."

Classical experimental research is finally just one kind of human perception or action. It was once a welcome change from astrology, alchemy, and palmistry. It has its advantages and limitations. Responding to different sized coins presented in isolation in a laboratory is not part of the normal life cycle of either human beings or rats. This remove from real life oversimplifies our behavior. For example, so-called scientific studies have made a lot of counting the words children recognize. Large vocabulary equals good reader. But researchers like Ken and Yetta Goodman of the University of Arizona have for many years now observed children in the act of reading passages aloud and found that reading is a much more complex act than recognizing individual words and knowing their dictionary meanings. It's more a guessing-from-context game, a series of leaps and suppositions and reassessments arising from an inspection of many kinds of cues picked up from large contexts of words—sentences, paragraphs, pages, chapters. And from the total context of experience both outside and inside school that readers bring with them to their reading of any text. Both present and past experiences help people read. Researchers' insistence on the traditional strategy of keeping constant all experimental variables but one is apt to block their entry into an understanding of such a subtle act as reading.

In much the same way, recent research in writing, such as that carried on by Donald Graves and his associates at the University of New Hampshire, has opened up new insights into the process because it has not followed customary experimental research practices. For example, an observer sits facing a child writing or preparing to write at a desk chair in a classroom. When the observer doesn't understand what the child is doing, she or he may say, "What are you doing now?" or "What are you thinking about?"—classically a fatal intrusion into the act being studied. But here it is an intrusion based on Graves's larger view of the process of writing, which begins before the pencil touches paper. He and his associates recognize that the individual attention given a child writing changes the stereotyped notion of the act of writing in school. Children in the act of writing may be asked, "You said you liked your Teddy bear. What do you like about it?" The question may open the children up and start them writing telling sentences about their Teddy bear. These observers are discovering the elements of good writing and good teaching. In the past, many teachers have stayed out of this production of meaning and contented themselves—sometimes exercising sadistic tendencies—with marking the "errors" committed by their student writers. The fear of contaminating an inquiry by touching or interacting with the "subjects" is often out of place in studying an activity as human as the making of meaning.

In my project—finding out the methods, principles, and attitudes of teachers whose students do good works—I located the first teacher, interviewed him, and kept what he did and thought in mind as I interviewed the next one. I was curious to see whether the second one was much like the first, and so I checked that out, but tried to keep myself always open for surprises, for things that the second one did and thought and felt that were different from those I found in the first one.

I knew that some readers and critics would say, "You didn't really *discover* that all these teachers in different subjects at different levels of schooling actually taught the same way. You knew what you wanted to find and you looked around until you found it." To an extent that was true—and true of any research or looking around for anything in a maelstrom of experience. But the matter is complex. Several teachers recommended to me didn't seem right or upon my visiting their classes showed me they didn't belong in my book. One was a science teacher (I'll disguise particulars) in Nebraska. I was told this fellow had a wonderful free spirit—rabbits and parrots in and out of cages, hopping and flying around; frogs, snakes, and mice available for the children to play with and study. And that was true: when I arrived, I fell in love with a bunny hopping down the hall pursued by a child. And I approved of the school principal, who arriving on the scene, admired the rabbit and calmly reminded the kids that one of Mr. Grey's rules was that the animals were not to run in the halls with or without a pass. When Mr. Grey took the group out to a far corner of the school lot in a wooded glen, I was sure I had the right man.

But, instead of getting the kids to explore the region and discover their own questions, he had a dozen up his sleeve and delivered them slambang at the seated circle of kids, who weren't the least interested in them because they hadn't turned on their own curiosities yet. Back inside the building, it got worse. The teacher gave the children a question and told them to find the answer in any of a dozen books on the shelves in the room. Each child had to bring his written answer to the teacher, who usually said, "No, that's not it. Now what other way could you answer this?" He was looking for *his* way, not *a* way, and once again the kids had been prevented from making any choices. Even worse, their "wrong" answers were not discussed. How they got to them was not a matter of interest to the teacher and consequently to them. Another error, another day gone wrong.

Fortunately, before I approached each person I was considering for the book, I had trained myself to say, "Now I'm looking at how teachers get students to do things in the classroom. I'm not sure your work will fit into the purposes of my book, and even if it does, there's always the chance that the publisher at the last minute will insist that some interviews be dropped—because the book is too long, or too many interviews are alike, or whatever." For that disappointing science teacher I never wrote up an interview.

Searchers must always watch out that they are not sliding into the mindless gathering of information that represents bad science, thinking, looking, and use of time. I didn't want to investigate teaching in general. It had been around me for half a century and I knew most of it was terrible. I had talked to hundreds of kids about what they knew as a result of going to school, and it wasn't much. I didn't have to administer competency tests to find that out. And the kids who displayed the most learning seemed often to have picked it up outside school.

Many professionals and laymen are afraid to admit that school is a failure. They have been taught that kids are the failures, not school. Or they give up and say, "School is that way because—it's school. No one could teach these apathetic, ignorant kids anything. Look at their scores in competency tests!" My 20 teachers taught me not to look at scores in competency tests but good works done in their classrooms—so far beyond *competency* that the word has lost all its power.

In this research project, I didn't want to run my train on any of those tracks. I didn't want to arrange a set of tests or devise a questionnaire and give them to hundreds of teachers across the country as a representative sample, you know. I didn't want to study the practices of bad teachers whose students do dumb, meaningless things because neither they nor their teachers know alternatives. I wanted to find out what good teachers do. So I located 20 whose students did good works. Sometimes I found them through newspaper reports. Sometimes they were people who had written me and sent their students' good works along because they and their students were so excited about them. Several of them wrote me because they had read case histories of teaching I had published in a book called *A Vulnerable Teacher* (1974). It was probable that I would like the way they were teaching because they had liked the way I had taught. But one of them who wrote me was a math teacher and one a professor of environmental science—and I was teaching English. The principles that attracted all of us apparently were something that went beyond personal predilection. When I saw that in these highly different classroom enterprises—adult night school students reading Euripides, little kids raising a giant parachute above their heads, math majors doing topology, foreigners writing English as a second language, or inner-city high-school kids composing an imagined pre-Civil War newspaper—the learners were following common principles, I felt that I had found some hard truths about learning.

I know that my predilections entered into this search. I think I wouldn't have found such good teachers and such good student work if they hadn't. So I'm pleased I went along with the drift—the common sense of this project—rather than get snarled in a profitless, impossible quest for the absolute objectivity we call "scientific detachment."

That's what I want to say here. It's much like what other inquisitive people who appear in this book are saying. They're exciting, loving human beings. They're interested in finding out what other human beings do that works—in the sense of improving the quality of our daily lives, as Henry Thoreau put it.

Expect to make mistakes. Use any uncommon, sophisticated sense or method that will help you do your job of searching, or any simple ordinary kitchen sense or method. Go for something you want and that will make a difference to you, your peers, and other people you don't know yet.

I never did understand that *re* in *research.* I think it should be *search,* a journey—maybe some fun in it as well as some pain, as in Odysseus' search, but not a lot of stretching things as he did. The report should be more like Homer's story of Odysseus' travels than Odysseus' story of them, a true record, of all the lies and golden stories told by Odysseus—the object of the study—related clearly and beautifully and entertainingly. These days I'm seeing occasional research reports that seem closer to Homer's account than to the reports I read in the professional journals.

PART TWO

Inquiry as an Agency
for Change

Interview with Ken Jones

DIXIE GOSWAMI: Ken, how long have you been doing whatever classroom research is?

KEN JONES: I guess it was three years ago I said I'd like to do some classroom research.

GOSWAMI: And you're not taking a credit course for this? There's no dissertation or thesis involved?

JONES: Right, there is not.

GOSWAMI: Then why in the world would a successful teacher like yourself do it?

JONES: I think teachers who are in the spot where I am—at middle age, with 20 years teaching experience—are a forgotten group. Rural teachers, inner city teachers, minority teachers have stuff aimed toward them. And all we are—when there's an article about burnout or teachers leaving the profession, then we're mentioned, then we're included. But there are a lot of us who care about teaching. We stay in it not because it's a dead-end job; we stay in not because we can't do anything else; we stay in it because we like it. But when you do anything that's pretty much the same every year, then no matter how good your intentions are, no matter how good a teacher you are, there's a certain amount of stagnation that creeps in. I think that doing research, regardless of the project, having a new focus to what I'm doing, did a tremendous lot to ward off burnout. For me, the teacher research has done a good bit—I think I'd have to stay at it to get "booster shots"—to ward off boredom, or contentment, or whatever it is. With teaching, as soon as you're content or as soon as you drag out the yellowing notes from last year or the quizzes you used last year, you're on the road to disaster. It's not a good thing.

What the research did for me—it didn't make me young again and it didn't make the kids who are forever 14 older. It sort of let me know about what is in their world besides the 50 minutes that I see them in the classroom. I didn't try to become a teen or do teen-talk or wear teen clothes or hang around teen places. But, I became aware that there is more to them. To know what I knew intellec-tually or passively, to know that actively was an enormous help to me. The project I did involved a lot of work, but it was a lot of pleas-ant work, a lot of happy work. Really, it was.

Teachers who are where I am don't begrudge the work. We're not lazy. But a lot of the time we put in the hours in a not particu-larly productive way—the way I did three years ago before I started classroom research. Proofreaders, nitpickers—spending a lot of time finding minor kinds of flaws and missing the major part of what's there. With the journals I got every other day, just to read them the way you'd read a letter, to learn from.

From Non-Magical Thinking

Presenting Writing Developmentally in Schools

JANET EMIG
Rutgers University

Janet Emig's The Composing Processes of Twelfth-Graders *provides dramatic proof that what we teach may often have little to do with how and what children learn. Many teachers and most textbooks, for example, espouse methods for writing instruction that simply don't square with what we've come to know about the process. To Emig, this amounts to "magical thinking"—the uninsightful notion that what is taught is necessarily learned. She urges here that we adopt a developmental view instead, a conversion based in one's own writing, observing, and assessing.*

As Howard Gruber (1973) points out in a remarkable essay comparing children and scientists, notably Darwin, making a paradigm shift requires not only cognitive change but the courage to make the change. To give up one paradigm about the nature of learning and teaching for another requires that teachers undergo a particularly powerful conversion.

The change in thinking means moving away from an established and perhaps hard-won set of relations with other human beings. This may be more important in the case of children than has been realized. When the child, for example, shifts his way of thought so that he restrains himself from making a judgment based on purely perceptual criteria, he is also making a serious change in life style. He is increasing his independence·from the stimulus. In that sense, he is increasing his independence more generally, and any increase in independence carries with it both a promise and a threat. We would probably discover, if we looked a little more closely at those moments when the child's thinking really seems to move, that the child experiences a sense of exhilaration. When we speak of "insight" or the "Aha Experience," it is not just seeing something new. It is feeling. And what the person is feeling is both the promise and the threat of this unknown that is just opening up. When we think new thoughts we really are changing our relations with the world around us, including our social moorings.

Before specifying what in my opinion such a conversion requires, how can the two paradigms be characterized? What, first, are the tenets of the magical thinking paradigm about writing that currently dominates the schools? Here is its credo:

1. Writing is predominantly taught rather than learned.
2. Children must be taught to write atomistically, from parts to wholes. The commonplace is that children must be taught to write sentences before they can be allowed to write paragraphs before they can be permitted to attempt "whole" pieces of discourse.
3. There is essentially one process of writing that serves all writers for all their aims, modes, intents, and audiences.
4. That process is linear: all planning precedes all writing (often described in the paradigm as transcribing), as all writing precedes all revising.
5. The process of writing is also almost exclusively conscious: as evidence, a full plan or outline can be drawn up and adhered to for any piece of writing: the outline also assumes that writing is transcribing, since it can be so totally prefigured; thought exists prior to its linguistic formulation.
6. Perhaps because writing is conscious, it can be done swiftly and on order.
7. There is no community or collaboration in writing: it is exclusively a silent and solitary activity.

What, in contrast, are the findings from the developmental research into writing:

1. Writing is predominantly learned rather than taught.
2. Writers of all ages as frequently work from wholes to parts as from parts to wholes: in writing, there is a complex interplay between focal and global concerns: from an interest in what word should come next, to the shape of the total piece.
3. There is no monolithic process of writing: there are processes of writing that differ because of aim, intent, mode, and audience: although there are shared features in the ways we write, there are as well individual, even idiosyncratic, features in our processes of writing.

4. The processes of writing do not proceed in a linear sequence: rather, they are recursive—we not only plan, then write, then revise; but we also revise, then plan, then write.

5. Writing is as often a pre-conscious or unconscious roaming as it is a planned and conscious rendering of information and events.

6. The rhythms of writing are uneven—more, erratic. The pace of writing can be very slow, particularly if the writing represents significant learning. Writing is also slow since it involves what Vygotsky calls "elaborating the web of meaning," supplying the specific and explicit links to render lexical, syntactic, semantic, and rhetorical pieces into organic wholes.

7. The processes of writing can be enhanced by working in, and with a group of other writers, perhaps especially a teacher, who give vital response, including advice.

What constitutes a conversion experience for those who present writing in schools, from the magical thinking paradigm to a developmental view? Obviously, since the shift is so great, so dramatic (and at times, traumatic), the evidence and the experiences must be powerful and, indeed, they must be developmental.

To undergo such a conversion, teachers of writing, our research strongly suggests, must:

1. write themselves in many modes, poetic and imaginative, as well as transactional and extensive, and introspect upon their own histories and processes as writers;

2. observe directly, and through such media as videotape, female and male writers of many ages and backgrounds engaging in the processes of writing; and speculate systematically with other teacher-writers about these observations and their implications for presenting writing in schools;

3. ascertain attitudes, constructs, and paradigms of those learning to write because the evidence grows stronger that, as with any learning process, set affects, perhaps even determines, both process and performance;

4. assess growth in writing against its developmental dimensions, with perhaps the most important accomplishment a growing ability to distinguish between a mistake and what can be termed a developmental error.

To examine each of these in turn:

1. What is most powerful and persuasive, developmentally of course, is direct, active, personal experience since only personal experience can transform into personal knowledge. And for teachers especially, personal knowledge of any process to be presented to

learners is not an option; it is a requisite. Persons who don't themselves write cannot sensitively, even sensibly, help others learn to
write.

Teachers of writing, then, must themselves write, frequently
and widely. And they must introspect upon their writing, since without reflection there has been no experience, as philosophers from
Socrates to Dewey point out.

2. To inform themselves about how they at once are like, and
different from, their students, teachers of writing need to take an
intensive look at actual students working through extended and systematic observation; interviews with the students, peers, former
teachers, and parents—in other words, by the preparation of writing
of at least two thorough case studies. (Since the emerging research
on writers of all ages suggests sex differences, I would recommend
studying at least one writer of each sex.)

Models for case studies are available from many sources—from
literary biographies to clinical analyses. Within the specific research
on the composing processes, there are available in doctoral disserta-
tions many exemplars. . . .

3. Teachers' own experiences as writers will provide the kinds
of developmental issues they will want to examine in these case
studies; but it is likely that they will formulate variants on some of
the following questions:

- What are the attitudes toward literacy and the educational background of the family?
- When, and under what circumstances, did the child begin to
  write, and to read?
- If the child remembers these experiences, what description does
  she give? With what feeling tones?
- If the learner currently has difficulty writing, can the learner or
  someone else identify specific times and circumstances when
  difficulties began?
- What does the learner think writing is for? What are its functions?
- Does the learner write equally well in all modes? unevenly? In
  which modes, well; in which, less well or badly?
- How can his process(es) of writing be characterized? total
  length? length of given portions? amount and quality of pre-
  writing including planning? amount and kind of revising, recursive and final? Is the writer self-critical, capable of reflection?
- What are the attitudes, constructs, and paradigms the student
  has about school, about English and the language arts, about
  writing?

Recent research suggests that the older the writer, the more likely that such cumulative clusters of belief will affect the processes of writing and their outcomes.

4. How can teachers learn to assess growth in students' abilities to write, with its concomitant question: How can we teach ourselves to discern the difference between mistakes and what can be termed developmental errors?

We can only make accurate assessments of growth if we have accurate characterizations of writing persons, processes, and outcomes; and thus far what we have are pastels or sketches for the whole or Wyeth-like drawings of a few tight particulars, not a fully delineated model of the developmental dimensions of writing.

A few persons have attempted to provide wide views. Perhaps because he has delineated one of the most compelling developmental sequences for modes, James Moffett has, in my opinion, also developed some major strategies as his metaphor "detecting growth" in writing suggests (Moffett and Wagner, 1983). John Holt (1982, 1983) provides useful, readable general introductions to developmental issues.

Crucial to a developmental view of assessment is to learn to distinguish between mistakes and developmental errors. Developmental errors contrast readily with mistakes in that developmental errors forward learning while mistakes impede it. Developmental errors have two characteristics that mistakes do not: (1) they are bold, chance-taking; (2) and they are rational, intelligent.

While the making of mistakes marks a retreat into the familiar, the result of fear and anxiety, developmental errors represent a student's venturing out and taking chances as a writer, from trying a new spelling, or tying together two sentences with a fresh transition, to a first step into a mode previously unexplored.

A second characteristic of developmental errors is that they are rational and logical; unfortunately, they often happen also to be wrong. In the most thorough account of errors among a given segment of writers, those she calls BW writers (Basic Writers), Mina Shaughnessy (1977) notes the "most damaging aspect" of the BW's experiences with writing:

> they have lost all confidence in the very faculties that serve all language learners: their ability to distinguish between essential and redundant features of a language left them logical but wrong; their abilities to draw analogies between what they knew of language when they began school and what they learned produced mistakes; and such was the quality of their instruction that no one saw the intelligence of their mistakes or thought to harness that intelligence in the service of learning. (pp. 10–11)

Examples of invalid analogies include the over-regularizing of lexical, grammatical, or rhetorical features, as well as more globally, the illogicality of proceeding as if writing were talk written down, a belief some students hold perhaps because some of their teachers have told them it is so.

Assessing growth in writing is a far larger, more complex, more individual and more interesting matter than testing. Too many testing programs, particularly those devised and given by state and national agencies, public and private, use evidence divorced from the linguistic and human histories of the students involved, and evidence divorced from the only sensible developmental requirement that students write organic, sustained pieces of discourse, like the students themselves, with histories and with futures.

Presenting writing developmentally in schools will require major transformations: transformations from the traditional school paradigm that promulgates magical thinking; and consequently, transformations of teacher learning and development. It is quite as demanding as the ways of teaching writing traditionally—perhaps more demanding—requiring no less than that adults admit that the only way they can help others learn to write is that they themselves become learners and writers.

References

Gruber, H. (1973). Courage and cognitive growth in children and scientists. In M. Schwebel & J. Raph (Eds.), *Piaget in the classroom* (p. 74). New York: Basic Books.

Holt, J. (1982). *How children fail* (rev. ed.). New York: Dell.

Holt, J. (1983). *How children learn* (rev. ed.). New York: Dell.

Moffett, J., & Wagner, B. J. (1983). *A student-centered language arts curriculum, grades K–13: A handbook for teachers* (3rd ed.). Boston: Houghton-Mifflin.

Shaughnessy, M. (1977). *Errors and expectations: A guide for the teacher of basic writing* (pp. 10–11). New York: Oxford University Press.

Diving In

An Introduction to Basic Writing

MINA P. SHAUGHNESSY

The late Mina Shaughnessy's Errors and Expectations *challenged the comfortable assumption that for matters to improve in open-admissions writing courses, students alone had to change. In this provocative essay, Shaughnessy argues otherwise, positing that "there may in fact be important connections between the changes teachers undergo and the progress of their students." Here, she charts the stages in such a change, concluding with a teacher's "diving in"—determining "to become a student of new disciplines and of his students themselves. . . ."*

Basic writing, alias remedial, developmental, pre-baccalaureate, or even handicapped English, is commonly thought of as a writing course for young men and women who have many things wrong with them. Not only do medical metaphors dominate the pedagogy (*remedial, clinic, lab, diagnosis,* and so on), but teachers and administrators tend to discuss basic-writing (BW) students much as doctors tend to discuss their patients, without being tinged by mortality themselves and with certainly no expectations that questions will be raised about the state of *their* health.

Yet such is the nature of instruction in writing that teachers and students cannot easily escape one another's maladies. Unlike other courses, where exchanges between teacher and student can be reduced to as little as one or two objective tests a semester, the writing course requires students to write things down regularly, usually once a week, and requires teachers to read what is written and then write things back and every so often even talk directly with individual students about the way they write.

This system of exchange between teacher and student has so far yielded much more information about what is wrong with students than about what is wrong with teachers, reinforcing the notion that students, not teachers, are the people in education who must do the changing. The phrase "catching up," so often used to describe the progress of BW students, is illuminating here, suggesting as it does that the only person who must move in the teaching situation is the student. As a result of this view, we are much more likely in talking about teaching to talk about students, to theorize about *their* needs and attitudes or to chart *their* development and ignore the possibility that teachers also change in response to students, that there may in fact be important connections between the changes teachers undergo and the progress of their students.

I would like, at any rate, to suggest that this is so, and since it is common these days to "place" students on developmental scales, saying they are eighth-graders or fifth-graders when they read and even younger when they write or that they are stalled some place on Piaget's scale without formal propositions, I would further like to propose a developmental scale for teachers, admittedly an impressionistic one, but one that fits the observations I have made over the years as I have watched traditionally prepared English teachers, including myself, learning to teach in the open-admissions classroom.

My scale has four stages, each of which I will name with a familiar metaphor intended to suggest what lies at the center of the teacher's emotional energy during that stage. Thus I have chosen to name the first stage of my developmental scale GUARDING THE TOWER, because during this stage the teacher is in one way or another concentrating on protecting the academy (including himself) from the outsiders, those who do not seem to belong in the community of learners. The grounds for exclusion are various. The mores of the times inhibit anyone's openly ascribing the exclusion to genetic inferiority, but a few teachers doubtless still hold to this view.

More often, however, the teacher comes to the basic-writing class with every intention of preparing his students to write for college courses, only to discover, with the first batch of essays, that the students are so alarmingly and incredibly behind any students he has taught before that the idea of their ever learning to write acceptably for college, let alone learning to do so in one or two semesters, seems utterly pretentious. Whatever the sources of their incompetence— whether rooted in the limits they were born with or those that were imposed upon them by the world they grew up in—the fact seems stunningly, depressingly obvious: they will never "make it" in college unless someone radically lowers the standards.

The first pedagogical question the teacher asks at this stage is therefore not "How do I teach these students?" but "What are the consequences of flunking an entire class?" It is a question that threatens to turn the class into a contest, a peculiar and demoralizing contest for both student and teacher, since neither expects to win. The student, already conditioned to the idea that there is something wrong with his English and that writing is a device for magnifying and exposing this deficiency, risks as little as possible on the page, often straining with what he does write to approximate the academic style and producing in the process what might better be called "written Anguish" rather than English—sentences whose subjects are crowded out by such phrases as "it is my conviction that" or "on the contrary to my opinion," inflections that belong to no variety of English, standard or nonstandard, but grow out of the writer's attempt to be correct, or words whose idiosyncratic spellings reveal not simply an increase in the number of conventional misspellings but new orders of difficulty with the correspondences between spoken and written English. Meanwhile, the teacher assumes that he must not only hold out for the same product he held out for in the past but teach unflinchingly in the same way as before, as if any pedagogical adjustment to the needs of students were a kind of cheating. Obliged because of the exigencies brought on by open admissions to serve his time in the defense of the academy, he does if not his best, at least his duty, setting forth the material to be mastered, as if he expected students to learn it, but feeling grateful when a national holiday happens to fall on a basic-writing day and looking always for ways of evading conscription next semester.

But gradually, student and teacher are drawn into closer range. They are obliged, like emissaries from opposing camps, to send messages back and forth. They meet to consider each other's words and separate to study them in private. Slowly, the teacher's preconceptions of his students begin to give way here and there. It now appears that, in some instances at least, their writing, with its rudimentary errors and labored style has belied their intelligence and individuality. Examined at a closer range, the class now appears to have at least some members in it who might with hard work, eventually "catch up." And it is the intent of reaching these students that moves the teacher into the second stage of development—which I will name CONVERTING THE NATIVES.

As the image suggests, the teacher has now admitted at least some to the community of the educable. These learners are perceived, however, as empty vessels, ready to be filled with new knowledge. Learning is thought of not so much as a constant and often troubling reformulation of the world so as to encompass new knowledge but as a steady flow of truth into a void. Whether the truth is delivered in lectures or modules, cassettes or computers, circles or squares, the teacher's purpose is the same: to carry the technology of advanced literacy to the inhabitants of an underdeveloped country. And so confident is he of the reasonableness and allure of what he is presenting, it does not occur to him to consider the competing logics and values and habits that may be influencing his students, often in ways that they themselves are unaware of.

Sensing no need to relate what he is teaching to what his students know, to stop to explore the contexts within which the conventions of academic discourse have developed, and to view these conventions in patterns large enough to encompass what students do know about language already, the teacher becomes a mechanic of the sentence, the paragraph, and the essay. Drawing usually upon the rules and formulas that were part of his training in composition, he conscientiously presents to his students flawless schemes for achieving order and grammaticality and anatomizes model passages of English prose to uncover, beneath brilliant, unique surfaces, the skeletons of ordinary paragraphs.

Yet too often the schemes, however well meant, do not seem to work. Like other simplistic prescriptions, they illuminate for the moment and then disappear in the melee of real situations, where paradigms frequently break down and thoughts will not be regimented. S's keep reappearing or disappearing in the wrong places; regular verbs shed their inflections and irregular verbs acquire them; tenses collide; sentences derail; and whole essays idle at one level of generalization.

Baffled, the teacher asks, "How is it that these young men and women whom I have personally admitted to the community of learners cannot learn these simple things?" Until one day, it occurs to him that perhaps these simple things—so transparent and compelling to him—are not in fact simple at all, that they only appear simple to those who already know them, that the grammar and rhetoric of formal written English have been shaped by the irrationalities of history and habit and by the peculiar restrictions and rituals that come from putting words on paper instead of into the air, that the sense and nonsense of written English must often collide with the spoken English that has been serving students in their negotiations with the world for many years. The insight leads our teacher to the third stage of his development, which I will name SOUNDING THE DEPTHS, for he turns now to the careful observation not only of his students and their writing but of himself as writer and teacher, seeking a deeper understanding of the behavior called writing and of the special difficulties his students have in mastering the skill. Let us imagine, for the sake of illustration, that the teacher now begins to look more carefully at two common problems among basic writers—the problem of grammatical errors and the problem of undeveloped paragraphs.

Should he begin in his exploration of error not only to count and name errors but to search for patterns and pose hypotheses that might explain them, he will begin to see that while his lessons in the past may have been "simple," the sources of the error he was trying to correct were often complex. The insight leads not inevitably or finally to a rejection of all rules and standards, but to a more careful look at error, to the formulation of what might be called a "logic" of errors that serves to mark a pedagogical path for teacher and student to follow.

Let us consider in this connection the "simple" *s* inflection on the verb, the source of a variety of grammatical errors in BW papers. It is, first, an alien form to many students whose mother tongues inflect the verb differently or not at all. Uniformly called for, however, in all verbs in the third person singular present indicative of standard English, it would seem to be a highly predictable or stable form and therefore one easily remembered. But note the grammatical concepts the student must grasp before he can apply the rule: the concepts of person, tense, number, and mood. Note that the *s* inflection is an atypical inflection within the modern English verb system. Note too how often it must seem to the student that he hears the stem form of the verb after third person singular subjects in what sounds like the present, as he does for example whenever he hears questions like "Does *she want* to go?" or "Can the *subway stop*?" In such sentences, the standard language itself reinforces the student's own resistance to the inflection.

An then, beyond these apparent unpredictabilities within the standard system, there is the influence of the student's own language or dialect, which urges him to ignore a troublesome form that brings no commensurate increase in meaning. Indeed, the very *s* he struggles with here may shift in a moment to signify plurality simply by being attached to a noun instead of a verb. No wonder then that students of formal English throughout the world find this inflection difficult, not because they lack intelligence or care but because they think analogically and are linguistically efficient. The issue is not the capacity of students finally to master this and the many other forms of written English that go against the grain of their instincts and experience but the priority this kind of problem ought to have in the larger scheme of learning to write and the willingness of students to mobilize themselves to master such forms at the initial stages of instruction.

Somewhere between the folly of pretending that errors don't matter and the rigidity of insisting that they matter more than anything, the teacher must find his answer, searching always under pressure for shortcuts that will not ultimately restrict the intellectual power of his students. But as yet, we lack models for the maturation of the writing skill among young, native-born adults and can only theorize about the adaptability of other models for these students. We cannot say with certainty just what progress in writing ought to look like for basic-writing students, and more particularly how the elimination of error is related to their overall improvement.

Should the teacher then turn from problems of error to his students' difficulties with the paragraphs of academic essays, new complexities emerge. Why, he wonders, do they reach such instant closure on their ideas, seldom moving into even one subordinate level of qualification but either moving on to a new topic sentence or drifting off into reverie and anecdote until the point of the essay has been dissolved? Where is that attitude of "suspended conclusion" that Dewey called thinking, and what can one infer about their intellectual competence from such behavior?

Before consigning his students to some earlier stage of mental development, the teacher at this stage begins to look more closely at the task he is asking students to perform. Are they aware, for example, after years of right/wrong testing, after the ACT's and the GED's and the SAT's, after straining to memorize what they read but never learning to doubt it, after "psyching out" answers rather than discovering them, are they aware that the rules have changed and that the rewards now go to those who can sustain a play of mind upon ideas—testing out the contradictions and ambiguities and frailties of statements?

Or again, are the students sensitive to the ways in which the conventions of talk differ from those of academic discourse? Committed to extending the boundaries of what is known, the scholar proposes generalizations that cover the greatest possible number of instances and then sets about supporting his case according to the rules of evidence and sound reasoning that govern his subject. The spoken language, looping back and forth between speakers, offering chances for groping and backing up and even hiding, leaving room for the language of hands and faces, of pitch and pauses, is by comparison generous and inviting. The speaker is not responsible for the advancement of formal learning. He is free to assert opinions without a display of evidence or recount experiences without explaining what they "mean." His movements from one level of generality to another are more often brought on by shifts in the winds of conversation rather than by some decision of his to be more specific or to sum things up. For him the injunction to "be more specific" is difficult to carry out because the conditions that lead to specificity are usually missing. He may not have acquired the habit of questioning his propositions, as a listener might, in order to locate the points that require amplification or evidence. Or he may be marooned with a proposition he cannot defend for lack of information or for want of practice in retrieving the history of an idea as it developed in his own mind.

Similarly, the query "What is your point?" may be difficult to answer because the conditions under which the student is writing have not allowed for the slow generation of an orienting conviction, that underlying sense of the direction he wants his thinking to take. Yet without this conviction, he cannot judge the relevance of what comes to his mind, as one sentence branches out into another or one idea engenders another, gradually crowding from his memory the direction he initially set for himself.

Or finally, the writer may lack the vocabulary that would enable him to move more easily up the ladder of abstraction and must instead forge out of a nonanalytical vocabulary a way of discussing thoughts about thoughts, a task so formidable as to discourage him, as travelers in a foreign land are discouraged, from venturing far beyond bread-and-butter matters.

From such soundings, our teacher begins to see that teaching at the remedial level is not a matter of being simpler but of being more profound, of not only starting from "scratch" but also determining where "scratch" is. The experience of studenthood is the experience of being just so far over one's head that it is both realistic and essential to work at surviving. But by underestimating the sophistication of our students and by ignoring the complexity of the tasks we set before them, we have failed to locate in precise ways where to begin and what follows what.

But I have created a fourth stage in my developmental scheme, which I am calling DIVING IN, in order to suggest that the teacher who has come this far must now make a decision that demands professional courage—the decision to remediate himself, to become a student of new disciplines and of his students themselves in order to perceive both their difficulties and their incipient excellence. "Always assume," wrote Leo Strauss to the teacher, "that there is one silent student in your class who is by far superior to you in head and in heart." This assumption, as I have been trying to suggest, does not come easily or naturally when the teacher is a college teacher and the young men and women in his class are labeled remedial. But as we come to know these students better, we begin to see that the greatest barrier to our work with them is our ignorance of them and of the very subject we have contracted to teach. We see that we must grope our ways into the turbulent disciplines of semantics and linguistics for fuller, more accurate data about words and sentences; we must pursue more rigorously the design of developmental models, basing our schemes less upon loose comparisons with children and more upon case studies and developmental research of the sort that produced William Perry's impressive study of the intellectual development of Harvard students; we need finally to examine more closely the nature of speaking and writing and divine the subtle ways in which these forms of language both support and undo each other.

The work is waiting for us. And so irrevocable now is the tide that brings the new students into the nation's college classrooms that it is no longer within our power, as perhaps it once was, to refuse to accept them into the community of the educable. They are here. DIVING IN is simply deciding that teaching them to write well is not only suitable but challenging work for those who would be teachers and scholars in a democracy.

From Dialogue to Dialectic to Dialogue

ANN E. BERTHOFF
University of Massachusetts/Boston

In her preceding piece, Ann Berthoff deals with the need to teach from a theoretical stance. In this essay, she chronicles how and why she "came to see the classroom as a philosophical laboratory." She shares with us as well the genesis of her text, Forming/Thinking/Writing.

I think it's probably true that I learned half of what I may claim to know about teaching composition in the first two weeks I spent in a classroom thirty-five years ago. In no time at all, I concluded that a theoretical knowledge of grammatical rules bore no necessary relationship to a capacity for writing sound sentences and coherent paragraphs and that students who couldn't read carefully were poor writers. I discovered that I. A. Richards was right—that if everybody understood what you meant right away, you'd have taught nobody anything; that he was right, too, about pedagogy and mountain climbing—if people don't feel the tension of the rope, they feel insecure. I learned that neither corrections keyed to the handbook I was required to use nor lengthy comments I was proud to be able to concoct effected any improvement; that things went best when echoes and analogues became apparent. I certainly knew from my own experience in both a newspaper office and graduate school that compositions did not grow from outlines. Nothing unsettled my belief that ideas develop when they are felt to have a significance beyond the context in which they first appear. But the other half of what I think I know about teaching people to write was hard-won.

Some twenty years later, after teaching composition to some of the best students in the country, I took a position at an urban university where my students bore little resemblance to those at Bryn Mawr, Haverford, and Swarthmore (or so I thought), and I discovered that I didn't know how to teach them: I didn't know enough and what I did know didn't seem to help. Learning what I needed to know and reclaiming what I did know has not always been an exhilarating experience, but it has been immensely interesting. It required inventing new procedures (new for me) for discovering what was actually going on in my classroom. To interpret those findings, I turned to philosophy. For one thing, pedagogy is unspeakably boring unless it is conceived in philosophical terms, but the real point is that unless practice is guided by theory it will indeed be aimless and teachers will be increasingly desperate. I sought philosophical guidance to bring theory to bear on practice and to let practice correct theory. What follows is an account of how I came to see the classroom as a philosophical laboratory.

After the first discouraging month as UMass/Boston, I decided that unless I could get people to talk, there was not going to be any learning. But how was I ever to do that, to elicit any response from the bewildered people who faced me in sullen rows? The answer came from a student, the first young man I'd ever seen with shoulder-length hair. In conference I asked him who he was and how he came to be at UMass, since he was clearly not in the mold of my other students. He was from Maryland and the only member of his class not to go to Princeton or Bard. He'd come to UMass because he wanted to be in "the real world." "Why don't these real people talk?" I asked him. "Because," he said, "they've never had a teacher who asked questions she didn't know the answer to. It scares them! And they are contemptuous of you when you demonstrate that you're thinking things out as you talk, that you don't already have the answer." I knew he was right and asked him to help me by talking up in class. He promised he would.

Now, I was dedicated to the principles of the New Criticism and I wanted everybody to have the text in front of them. We were reading *Leaves of Grass* in a beautifully printed version of the first edition, but it had begun to occur to me that the text-and-I was not the model to follow if I wanted conversation to develop, so the first class meeting after my conference with Jonathan the hippy, I wrote the following line from *Leaves of Grass* on the board:

Who goes there? hankering, gross, mystical, nude. . . .

"Okay, please form two groups. Turn your chairs so that you more or less face one another across this midline. Now I want you to talk to one another, to people in the other group, about that line."

When the noise of chair-arranging subsided, there was a dead silence. Realizing that I was not going to be able to resist posing questions, I took off my scarf and tied it around my mouth. A few embarrassed giggles and then silence ensued. Suddenly Jonathan said, "I don't see why *mystical* is in there." Instantly, there was a response: "Well, *that* doesn't bother me! Of *course* he's mystical! He's mystical all the time! But why does he say it's *gross*?" Another comment, instantly: "He doesn't say IT's gross. He means he *feels* gross." "Well, wouldn't *you* feel gross if you took your clothes off in the woods?" "No . . . well, I don't know, but maybe he thinks somebody *else* would think so." They were talking! They were even thinking! I can't remember what followed and, because I hadn't yet learned to log my classes, I have no record to return to, but I will never forget that first time hearing my students talk with one another about a shared text, making sense out of it in the exchange of responses. I reclaimed that morning the knowledge that dialectic and dialogue are consonant and cognate, simultaneous and correlative.

I came to value this kind of exchange however it can be encouraged, whenever it develops, as a sign that the dialogue with the text, which is the point of departure for all critical reading, is being REpresented in a social context and has thus become accessible to critical response and review. I decided that the final paper in this freshman course should somehow involve dialogue, so I asked my students to interview someone over forty (this was 1968) about life in America before World War II. Consternation! "I don't know anybody that old except my parents, and I sure can't talk to them!" "Try it," I said. "They will want to talk about this and you might find what they have to say rather interesting." The one stipulation was that the paper could not be in dialogue form. They could write in the first person or they could transform their notes into a short story; they could write an essay.

Even before I got the papers, I was pretty sure that something interesting was going on from what I overheard in conversations they were having with on another. When the papers came in, I was astonished. They were lively and touching, amusing and full of wonderful stories and scenes and moments, all emblematic of American life in the Great Depression. More than one paper included a postscript noting that the student had never before understood what his parents meant in talking about how things were different in those days—about the change in values. So not only had they learned how narrative and "telling detail" and voice all worked to REpresent feelings and judgments: they also had found it possible to talk to their parents, to listen, and learn. I was proud of having invented this assignment; I had never heard of Studs Terkel or sociolinguistics or oral history. I can remember meeting Lewis Mumford at a party and telling him about it. He congratulated me on doing something about bridging the generation gap, which was the topic of the day.

In subsequent years, I continued the search for ways to get the dialectic going and, as it has turned out, all these heuristics have been analogous to dialogue. As a shorthand term, I call them *oppositions*: they are all ways of REpresenting the inner dialogue, which is the mind in action as we see relationships. An opposition is any relationship—spatial, temporal, causal. The simplest, most flexible, most powerfully generative is a line drawn down the middle of the page. In this instance, the idea came from thinking what I could do in conference that would teach composing not editing. I had decided that conference time was too valuable to be spent on explaining this or that error, that it would be more profitable if I could offer a method, a procedure, something for students to do which might possibly forestall their committing some of the errors in the first place. Most errors result (as Ken Macrorie shortly made abundantly clear) from a mismatch of intention and wherewithal: there was often no purpose, and that emptiness was being camouflaged by tricking out insubstantial assertions in half-remembered conventional expressions, cant phrases, clichés, and periphrastic clouds. I admit that for a time I was so disheartened by the fragments and fractures of "basic writing" that I was tempted to see "Engfish" as a step in the right direction, but I soon found that it was absurd to clear away the thicket to let the undergrowth flourish: there *was* no undergrowth, no healthy stock which needed only the light of rhetorical encouragement. I concluded that teaching writing was better modeled by careful work in the greenhouse and the cold frame than by breaking sod, draining swamps, or irrigating deserts. Engfish was not worth the time it took to correct it; the real solution was to see to it that students didn't write it in the first place.

In conference one afternoon, when I hadn't been able to elicit a single statement about a *tree*, I took a blank piece of paper and (probably) with a degree of exasperation drew a line down the middle, writing TREE on one side and then (probably) shouted at this inert young man to tell me what trees *do*, what they're *for*. And he started naming what trees do and what they're for: *they grow; they look good; they're for shade; they're for building with; you can hang swings and people from them.* "Look what you've done!" I (probably) shouted. "You've got half a dozen sentences!" He saw simultaneously that there were no sentences and that out of what he had set down in those columns he could *make* sentences. The line down the middle of the page taught him—and me—that predication is sometimes easier to generate schematically than syntactically.

I took this idea to class, asking students to categorize the sixty or so words we had listed in the course of going around the room three times recording responses to a photograph of a rice paddy from Steichen's *Family of Man.* What two words from the list could serve to name categories in which we could group the remaining fifty-eight? I then asked that everybody compose a poem in Whitman's manner. (I had again chosen *Leaves of Grass.*) The list provided the lexicon and the category heads, the conceptual armature; we had by then discussed the principal characteristics of Whitman's style. The inert young man wrote a poem which I can't quote, because I had not yet developed the habit of copying significant student papers, but I remember that after a nicely organized catalogue of observations made by the poet as he stood watching the activities of the rice paddy, he ended with this line:

At dusk, I go home refreshed.

I thought then that perhaps he'd learned how to think with the oppositions of *them* and *me, here* and *there, beginnings* and *ends, dawn* and *dusk.*

The following year, my friend and colleague Rosamond Rose-meier suggested that she and I should design a course, to be taught in two sections, called Report Writing, in which we would try to teach what you need to do to write a good report, but to do so *not* by reading or writing "reports" but by recording the close reading of poems and stories carried on in something called "small groups." There were several Jonathans in the class and I made them my allies in a version of "each one teach one." They were responsible for some memorable breakthroughs, as when one of them brought a Vietnam veteran to a new understanding of Sarah Orne Jewett's characters in *The Country of the Pointed Firs.* The veteran had scoffed at "these elderly Shirley Temples," but this young Black man gave him an *ex tempore* lecture on how Elmiry Todd, the herb gatherer, is a shaman, an exemplar of that figure in any community who represents spirit and power. But on the whole, I found the unit of the small group almost as inappropriate for the composition class as that of individual readers, each in communion with his own text.

It was this frustration with trying to teach via small groups that led to the first, deliberate attempt to report to myself what in the world was happening as my class suffered atomization. These logs allowed me to explore the shape and form of the exchanges in these small groups. With the help of an excellent tutor assigned to my section, Jean Parsons, I began to see that whenever students recognized how to use the limits of the readings to their advantage, they wrote in a more purposeful and focused way.

In order to "foreground" those limits so that the thinking they elicited could be REpresented more directly in their writing, I radically changed my reading list. Whereas I had normally assigned one or two novels (*Bread and Wine, Man's Fate*), three or four poems and a tract (*Pacem in Terris*), I began preparing several short passages on a single theme, favoring the unit of the paragraph. I assured that they were tough—hard to read, recalcitrant, perplexing—so that I wouldn't need to plead with the class to spend an hour reading a single page. And I assured that the ideas set forth would seem, once in hand, to have deserved the hard work required to apprehend them. I juxtaposed passages from works by Kierkegaard, John Donne, and D. H. Lawrence, for instance, and asked students to decide which two seemed clearly to have something in common which could then be set over against the third selection. To make this manageable, I taught them to gloss the paragraphs (a procedure described at length in *Forming/Thinking/Writing* (Berthoff, 1978)) which they could follow in order to formulate their understanding of the conceptual armature on which the paragraph had been shaped. The fact that their individually composed glosses could very well differ helped teach the essential dialectic of perspective and context. Whatever struck them as important as they paired paragraphs and set them in opposition to a third was *their* discovery; it wasn't an inert thesis statement prepared according to a sentence pattern offered like a muffin tin, nor was it a matter of finding a topic sentence, waiting like an Easter egg to be uncovered.

This experience convinced me that small groups are effective only when they return the student to a text—not necessarily his own—for the purposes of interpreting interpretations. And this is not a matter of opinion-swapping; I share the impatience many teachers feel about what they often call "relativism," chiefly because it imitates that sense of fallibility which should indeed be cultivated. Interpreting interpretation means conducting an "audit of meaning" (I. A. Richards' definition of dialectic) in order to see how changing words changes meaning and how intentions can be reshaped as language REpresents them. I have argued in *The Making of Meaning* (Berthoff, 1981), that the chief pedagogical value of encouraging an awareness that there can be, logically, no final answer when it comes to interpretation is that it encourages students to make careful arguments to support their interpretations (Southeastern Ohio Council of Teachers of English, 1981). And this is not a matter of debate; as Richards notes, "the disputant is commonly too busy making his points to see what they are" (1955). The debate is only the mirror image of the rap group—which is often the actual form of "peer group" exchanges—so far as their nonheuristic character is concerned: neither fosters the dialectical exploration of meaning.

I was ready, then, in 1974, to compose a composition course dialectically, letting the exercises and assignments grow from one another, encouraging a spiraling by which we could continually return to the fundamental acts of mind which are in operation at all times as we make sense of the world. I began with the premise that composing is what the mind does. Writing, therefore, is of a kind with perception and the agent of writing, as perception is of imagination. My point of departure was the idea that whenever we respond critically to what we see, we apprehend form; forming, thinking, and writing are thus consonant with one another and whatever can be learned about one will strengthen the others.

The armature for *Forming/Thinking/Writing* was provided by a newly devised course offered by the Department of English in recognition of the fact that our freshman English sections were not doing the job we wanted them to do and indeed that no two-semester sequence would be adequate for the majority of our students. The principles were clearly in mind. First, Intermediate Composition would not confuse composing and editing, but it would offer assistance in editing; we would work hard at learning ways to identify and correct syntactical errors. Second, there would be room for experimental and "creative" writing insofar as they could serve heuristically to enlighten the students about the nature of composing. Third, we wanted students to think about thinking, to develop a method of composing which would stand them in good stead in other courses.

I wanted them to see how they could learn to use in writing what they already knew about how to make sense of the world. During the first week, I brought in bits and pieces collected from several workbenches, dressing tables, and kitchen drawers and asked that each student choose something from the array of junk and, observing carefully, write a description which could then be developed as a definition. My shocked discovery was that nobody knew the definition of a definition, much less how to go about formulating one. We established that definition requires the naming of a class but that classification is not enough; definition requires differentiation of one member from others of the same class. ("A table is a piece of furniture" classifies without defining.) The idea of context came instantly into play when we tried to "define" a perfume bottle. If you juxtaposed it to an oil drum, it was clearly a *container*; if you considered its shape, it was just as clearly a member of the class *decorative piece of junk*. I soon saw that definition is concept formation in miniature: the class name was neither the point of departure nor the inevitable end; it emerged from the dialectic of particularizing and generalizing. I learned, too, how the process of defining made dramatically clear the need to question in order to generate names—identifications and generalizations—with which to compose. From logging those questions, I learned another way of teaching the uses of chaos.

From one student, we all learned how definitions grow out of understanding function, which careful observation guided by judicious questioning can identify. This young woman was a ship carpenter and she knew what was what:

A stove bolt is the only kind of bolt that is used without a washer under the head and unlike all other bolts when recessed into wood, it looks like a screw rather than a bolt.

Uneconomical and awkward, ready for editing, but full of *telling* detail, the kind required by definition. *Stovebolt* thus became emblematic of the naming of particulars from which generalizations could be developed to arrive at class names. (Somebody suggested that successful pieces of writing could be published in a weekly newsletter called *The Stovebolt*. Some years later I returned to that idea, and in Advanced Composition, I always begin with the Sentence of the Day, either a splendid bit of syntactical deployment or a tangled mass of fractured idiom.) I sent everybody to the dictionary to study the shape of lexical definitions and we experimented day after day in class with generating a chaos of names on the board which could then yield *genus* and *differentiae*. We came to see naming as *implicit classification* and classifying as *organized comparing* (Berthoff, 1978, pp. 94–111).

John Wilson's *Thinking with Concepts* (1963), a little book written for British high school students and often found useful in graduate seminars in this country, helped us develop our definitions when it came to abstract concepts. Particularizing and generalizing work together in all thinking, but it is harder to get the dialectic going when the point of departure is a general term. (For that reason, assigning topics is an anti-pedagogy if we want to teach the composing process.) Wilson suggests that after conceptual questions are separated from those of fact and value, a procedure which is somewhat more problematic than this linguistic philosopher lets on, the next step in critical analysis should be to lay out an argument by means of developing the model case and contrary, related, and borderline cases—in that order. Pedagogically, it is not an appropriate response sequence because it is not psychologically, or epistemologically, sound. (The same misconception is at work when Wilson admonishes his readers not to begin writing until they know what to say!) That is to say, thinking of counter-examples and logical opposites is much easier than determining right off the bat what an idea IS: the model case is what the writer wants to develop; it can't so easily be his point of departure, unless we are teaching composition as a set of conventions. Setting topics—which were once called common places —yields, precisely, *commonplaces.*

Developing cases—moving from contrary to borderline to related to model cases—was an excellent way for the class to learn how the logical analysis of ideas is comparable to observation and continual questioning in the case of stove bolts and oil valves and nutmeg graters: *What is it for? How does it work? What does it remind you of?* are all questions as appropriate to an understanding of a concept as they are to the description and definition of strange and familiar objects.

Another continually useful way of starting the dialectic of concept formation was Kenneth Burke's notion of thinking of names as titles for situations. It is a real advance to learn to move from *What is it?* to *What is happening? What has happened? What could happen?* Photographs—mostly of figures in a landscape—served as points of departure in practicing transformation as a way of generating new contexts and perspectives. The heuristic value of "reading" images—of interpreting scenes as if they were texts, of converting texts to scenes—came clear when one student, on her own in another course, used a photograph of Bogotá as a point of departure in composing a paper on a modern city. She saw the photograph as an emblem of the kind of place it is. (Berthoff, 1978, p. 132.) This idea of pictures as spatial representations of events or processes, of something ongoing, led to using natural objects in an advanced composition course the following year. Shells and pods and burs are symbolic indicators of process: they point beyond themselves to other times (past and future), emblems of their own history. (Berthoff, 1978, Part I.)

It was essential that class discussion be structured so that the dialectic of dialogue could be apprehended. If the first problem I encountered at UMass was silence, an equally trying one was confused babble. The trick was to encourage a certain direction without seeming to squelch others—and yet squelching is part of composing, of knowing when and how to choose amongst promising lines. I saw my job as that of a conductor who could say, "There! What have you done with that point? What does it suggest? How do you know?" Looking and looking again was matched by saying and saying again. This kind of return provides the best practice a writer can have for the central activity writing entails, which is revision. It is, of course, the very antithesis of the merely repetitive which drill depends on.

Rereading too—reading and reading again—came to be seen as the way to learn to interpret, to learn to paraphrase as a mode of critical reading. Students were mystified by a procedure which was once at the heart of the teaching of reading; I think paraphrase has an especially important role to play, now that foreign language study has virtually disappeared from the school curriculum. A comment of one student brought me to see how to explain it: "You seem to be satisfied with paraphrase: Is that what you mean by *interpretation?*" Well, yes and no: interpretative paraphrase involves more than lexical substitution; it involves asking, "How does it change the meaning if I put it this way?" (I. A. Richards (1938, 1942) used Basic English as a "translation" medium in such exercises.) I don't know of any activity (it is not a "skill" to be developed like a capacity for diving or place kicking) of greater importance for a writer to practice than changing words and observing the consequent shifts in his meaning. Writing as revision means learning to see meanings as dependent on how you use words in responding to your emergent interpretations. Reading in this way is indispensable in the composition classroom, if we want to teach how we construct is how we construe. When we compose, we do what we do when we read: we interpret what we are saying and hearing.

Looking and looking again; saying and saying it again; reading and reading-and-writing it again, watching the "it" change. And listening: the fact that listening, like reading, requires a lively expectation of what might be coming next is what makes it such good practice for the writer; all language use requires the sense of developing meaning. I read a short story aloud and had the class take notes as if it has been a formal lecture. Katherine Mansfield's "Miss Brill" served very well since the point of view holds steady; the descriptions and metaphors are continued throughout the story; it has as neat a shape as a sonata or a formal dance. When I described what I wanted them to do, there was consternation: "But how do we know what to listen for?!" I didn't stop to point out that the question is analogous to "I don't know what to say!" and "I don't know what to writer!" but noted in my log that the question arose from the anxiety caused by years and years of being asked, "What is the author trying to say?"—a favorite of English teachers and not so much a generator as a suffocator. I suggested that they should listen for repetitions; that they should imagine the scene described as a kind of frame which is going to determine the pattern. I read and they listened and noted; they then wrote for ten minutes in response to the question "What does Miss Brill learn?" The question is analogous to "How does it look if you turn it around?" Several were able to see *learn* as a concept that had to be formed, to see that it entailed *change* and that my question was a heuristic. But I learned in the discussions that followed just how little they'd been taught about how to read/listen. Years of symbol-chasing had not taught them such general principles as, for instance, the consonance of season with action (or, of course, the ironic dissonance of seasonal imagery and theme). If an "old maid" is described as sitting by herself in a park in the autumn fantasizing about the theatricality of the lively scene, certain limits have been established, certain structures have been sketched so that images and juxtapositions can be expected. and, as it were, *recognized* when they appear.

I decided that my students could learn to take better notes, that they could train themselves in patterns of recognition, if they could develop a procedure which would allow expectation and recognition to work together dialectically. It occurred to me that law students take notes on paper ruled with wide margins; as they review their lecture notes, they annotate by listing relevant cases and other references. Two columns, one played over against the other, could encourage the idea of generalizing tentatively while the lecture or reading was in progress and could help make note-taking a *dimension* of listening, not something else that somehow had to go on concurrently with listening. Teaching them how to take notes by letting the double entry represent the dialectic helped my students discover that listening is interpreting and that notes can record the progress of their meaning-making.

The following year, I worked out a sequence for my writing assignments, the logic of which was based not on topics, raw or refined, but on that constant movement of thought from generalization to particularization and back which Vygotsky defines as the dynamic of concept formation. I tried to keep this complexity in every assignment as a way of teaching the *allatonceness* of composition. The greatest challenge was to find an order in which each exercise, as it echoed and reflected previous ones, would be seen as "a partially parallel task," as I. A. Richards puts it. Something learned from any one of them would thus be useful and appropriate for the others. Borrowing a phrase from Richards, I called these exercises "assisted invitations" to students to find out what they were doing and *thereby* how to do it. Indeed, I wanted to call the emerging textbook *Assisted Invitations,* but a friend who's a librarian observed that it might be catalogued with Emily Post. Since the assignments invited students to think about what they were doing in writing; to discover the power of an active mind in forming concepts; to reclaim their imagination in this process of composing, I decided to call the book, instead, *Forming/Thinking/Writing: The Composing Imagination.*

References

Berthoff, A. E. (1978). *Forming/thinking/writing: The composing imagination.* Rochelle Park, NJ: Hayden.

Berthoff, A. E. (1981). *The making of meaning.* Montclair, NJ: Boynton/Cook.

Richards, I. A. (1938). *Interpretation in teaching.* London: Routledge and Kegan Paul.

Richards, I. A. (1942). *How to read a page.* Boston: Beacon Press.

Richards, I. A. (1955). *Speculative instruments* (p. 52). New York: Harcourt Brace and World.

Southeastern Ohio Council of Teachers of English and the Department of English, Ohio University. (Winter 1981). A curious triangle and the double-entry notebook; or how theory can help us teach reading and writing. *Focus: Teaching English Language Arts.*

Wilson, J. (1963; reprint 1971). *Thinking with concepts.* Cambridge, England: Cambridge University Press.

The three pieces that follow are as valuable for what they reveal about the dynamics of research as for their useful classroom findings, particularly what happens when teachers become teacher-researchers, working together as agents for inquiry and change.

Class-Based Writing Research

Teachers Learning from Students

NANCIE ATWELL
Boothbay (Maine) Region Elementary School

In review of writing research in the *English Journal,* discussion almost invariably focuses on procedures and findings of experimental design research conducted by professional researchers. These inquiries follow the traditional, scientific model: establishing control groups of teachers and students, assigning instructional strategies and materials as variables, measuring the relative benefits of one or another teaching method through a statistical analysis of the resulting written products, and then explaining and predicting teaching and learning processes based upon this evidence.

Experimental design research has had relatively little effect on classroom practices in the teaching of writing. Investigations that focus on the teacher and the method ignore the broader context of learners' writing behaviors, concepts, and backgrounds, and the often contradictory results simply fail to provide teachers with useful insights into the nature of language and writing processes and their development.

A New Research Direction

The last decade witnessed an important shift in emphasis in the area of writing research. Emig (1971), Graves (1975), Graves, Calkins, and Sowers (1982), Bissex (1980), and others have provided teachers with a new kind of information about students' writing. Rejecting the scientific model of writing research, they turned instead to naturalistic studies of writers' activity, observing writers *in the process* of composing. Their inquiry procedures—case study, documentation, and description—are characterized by extensive, prolonged data-gathering and full attention to and acknowledgment of context: the setting where the writing is produced as well as the writer's choices and behaviors, concepts of writing and of the functions served by writing, background as a reader and writer, and a complete and chronological collection of the writer's texts. Based upon an examination of these data, the naturalistic researcher generates hypotheses concerning writing processes, in contrast to the experimental-design procedure of generating data (written products) to prove *a priori* hypotheses.

Descriptive studies of writers' activity yield information that makes sense to classroom teachers, providing us with new perspectives from which to view our students' development as writers and clear implications for the kinds of writing instruction that will support that development. In addition, this method of investigation is one that classroom teachers can effectively employ to inquire into students' writing processes and practices for ourselves. As guests in our schools, professional researchers such as Emig and Graves have clearly demonstrated the value of gathering data in carefully described, natural settings. As members of that classroom community, we teachers are in an ideal position to observe, describe, and learn from the behaviors of our student writers. As those who will most directly benefit from an increased awareness of children's language learning processes, it is to our advantage to take on the role of researchers of writing.

Boothbay Elementary's Teacher-Researchers

In Boothbay, Maine, fourteen teachers of grades one through eight have done just that. Working together to develop a new writing curriculum, we are writing, studying our writing, reading writing theory and research, and conducting our own class-based, naturalistic, writing research. Using inquiry procedures modeled on those of Goswami (1979), Goswami and Odell (1981), Emig (1971), Graves (1975) and Graves, Calkins, and Sowers (1982), we observe children through the course of the writing process, conduct regular interviews with student writers focusing on their choices and constructs, gather background information on their writing and reading histories, maintain portfolios of and describe their written texts, and keep daily logs in which we record our observations of their activity. Rather than design a writing program based on prior practices and assumptions, publishers' materials or mastery checklists, and then evaluate its effect on students' written products, we are observing and describing our students' writing processes and developing a curriculum based on what we learn from the writers in our classrooms.

Writing teacher and researcher Dixie Goswami speculates about the nature of the transformations that occur in teachers' perceptions, instructional practices, and levels of professional activity when they conduct class-based research. These conjectures have been realized in the experiences of Boothbay teachers. The following describes the changes in fourteen classroom teachers who became writing researchers.

Goswami posits that teachers who study their own writing and the writing of their students undergo transformations in their behavior in the classroom. Six months into our inquiries, every one of us had dramatically altered his or her approach to the teaching of writing. We found that we concur with Graves (1980) in that teachers *slow down* when we engage in looking at and thinking and raising questions about our students' writing. Rather than conforming writing instruction to our timing, we adjust our teaching to attend to individual students' needs, progress and stages in the writing process. We stop focusing on presenting a lesson and evaluating its results and start observing our students in the process of learning, listening to what they can tell us, and responding as they need us. As a result of this shift in focus, a different relationship between teacher and students emerges. The teacher-centered classroom becomes a community of writers and learners in which teacher and students are partners in inquiry.

Joyce Parent, a second-grade teacher, used to devote half of her scheduled hour-and-a-half-per-week writing time to providing lessons to motivate students to write. Now, she allots four and a half hours each week to writing. During that time, her students are writing and she is circulating among them. She listens to what they have written, responds to their questions, asks questions about their drawings and writing, logs her observations, records data about skills she has noticed or introduced in individual writing conferences, writes, and shares her writing with her students. Parent discovered that students can provide their own direction, and she watches children she had previously assumed required her motivation to compose carry clipboards onto the playground so they can continue to write at recess.

In past years, first-grade teacher Pam Hall stood at her chalkboard conducting lessons in the construction of complete sentences, or asked students to fill in or dictate to her the endings to sentences she had started for them. She now holds daily publishing conferences with first-grade authors in which they read to her the books they have written and select the story they would like to have typed and published for the classroom library. Prior to her research, she thought first-grade writers "couldn't do much on their own." Today she states, "They can accomplish a lot on their own. They'll try to get me to do it, but I won't. *They* have to have the control if they're to learn." Before, Hall's firm expectation was that her students should leave the first grade knowing how to write a complete sentence. Now, she refuses to speculate about their June writing skills. "I'm afraid I'll hold them back by limiting expectations. They're doing so much now I think, what will they be doing by the end of the year?"

Seventh-grade teacher Gloria Walter, previously dependent on the security she derived from minutely-detailed lessons, abandoned her planbook. Instead, she records daily descriptions of each of her student writers' topic choices, problems, accomplishments, discoveries, and stages in the writing process. She wonders now—and asks them—what they plan to do next.

Susan Stires is Boothbay's resource room teacher; the students who come to her for instruction in language arts are identified as writing disabled. She "gave up on writing, because the interesting, creative topics I chose went flat" and turned to worksheet exercises in sentence construction and combining. Now, as a researcher in her classroom, she focuses on what her students can do as writers. They choose their own topics, draft, seek and give response in writing conferences, revise, edit, and publish. Stires says of them: "This may sound crazy, but I think they're smarter. They seem livelier; they talk about things more, and in more interesting ways. Maybe it's just that I'm listening to them this year, and attending to and appreciating what they do know about."

Because we are focusing on individual students' learning processes, in the context of their writing, another significant change in our classroom behavior is a growing awareness—and acceptance—of individual differences. Rather than emphasizing mastery or ranking our students, we look for individual writers' growth over time. And because we are engaged in the close observation and documentation of individual growth in writing, we have discovered that there are as many writing processes as there are students in our classrooms. Joyce Parent remarked that as a result of two formal case studies she conducted, she became closer to all her students: "I sometimes felt as if I were doing twenty case studies. Now that I'm really looking and listening, I've discovered that each of my kids is doing something interesting, something of note, something unique."

Finally, regarding the evolution of our classroom behaviors, we have discovered that the teacher who is also a researcher is no longer a victim of "our profession's energy crisis" (Graves, 1978). When we change our role to that of an inquirer, we become learners, too. We no longer feel drained by the demands we impose on ourselves when we view our classrooms as contexts we motivate, orchestrate, and evaluate. Instead, we are energized as our student writers assume new control and responsibility: deciding about topics, modes and audiences, providing response and assistance to each other, keeping track of the conventions they have learned, and teaching their teachers what they know and can do. Third-grade teacher Debbie Matthews remarked of a student, "He's the kind of writer whose papers I would have dreaded correcting last year. He would have been bored with what I'd assigned, and I would have been bored with what he'd written. His mechanics were way below most of my other kids', too. Now, I really look forward to hearing and reading what he has to say and how he'll say it. And the growth I'm seeing in his writing—on every level—is remarkable.

Professional Satisfactions

Goswami theorizes that a second outcome of teachers taking on the role of researchers is a change in our sense of professionalism and status within the teaching profession. On the most basic—and perhaps most important—level, this means a change in the quality of teacher interaction. Talk in our teachers' room has taken on a new dimension as Boothbay teacher-researchers serve each other as resources and consultants, sharing insights, observations, and speculations concerning our own and students' writing. The nature of teacher-talk shifted away from discussions of specific children's problems and attendant teacher frustrations toward excited descriptions of students' resourcefulness and accomplishments, as well as question-raising concerning the logic behind a particular writer's particular behavior.

As researchers, we have discovered a new sense of pride in being classroom teachers. Our roles and functions in the larger community of educators are redefined. No longer the peripheral recipients of others' theories, findings, and programs, we have become professionals essentially active in and central to the improvement of writing instruction. We are more knowledgeable about curriculum design. We are writing descriptions of our research for educators' journals. We are serving as resources to teachers outside of our district and presenting our research findings at state and national conferences. And we are seeing a change in our community's perceptions of our professionalism and expertise.

In addition to increasing our levels of professional activity, we have increased our use of professional resources. Because we are, as researchers, asking questions, we turn to other sources for help with

the answers, seeking out and drawing on—and knowledgeably criticizing—the procedures and findings of other researchers. Susan
Stires, intrigued by the nature of her students' writing disabilities,
looked to the published research. Frustrated by what she perceived
as a misguided emphasis on isolated surface features, she is writing
and publishing papers based on language theory she has read, her
own research, and her insights into the appropriateness of descriptive, nonstatistical research procedures in investigations of children's
writing disabilities.

The final rationale Goswami offers for teacher-conducted, class-
based research is the richness of the data that can be gathered as a
result of the unique position of the classroom teacher. As researchers
in the position of participant-observers, we are able to observe and
describe, daily and minutely, the writing processes of our students.
Because they are our students, we know them better than professional researchers do, we know them differently, we have a natural
access to their learning behaviors, and we have most at stake in studies of their writing development. It only makes sense that we, too,
pose questions and seek answers in the very contexts where those
questions and answers count most. As Berthoff (1981) asserts, it is
time that teachers themselves begin to "look and look again at what
happens in the English classroom. We do not need new information;
we need to think about the information we have."

Professional Needs

How can classroom teachers acquire the background in language
theory and research procedures that will enable us to conduct full,
naturalistic investigations of our students' writing processes? At
Atkinson Academy in New Hampshire, site of Donald Graves's two-
year study of children's writing development, first-grade teacher
Mary Ellen Giacobbe (1981; and Giacobbe and Graves, 1982) designed and conducted her own class-based research using inquiry
methods she developed as a result of her work with Graves. In Boothbay, I am the director of the elementary school's writing project; I
am also a student at the Bread Loaf School of English Program in
Writing, a graduate school unique in encouraging and training
teachers of writing in naturalistic research procedures. Because
Boothbay's teacher-researchers feel strongly that the field of writing
research must be expanded to include inquiries conducted by classroom teachers, we suggest these possibilities:
1. Universities and state departments of education can begin to
   foster teacher research by including teacher-researcher courses
   in their certification programs.

2. Teachers can request that directors of in-service programs provide workshops and seminars in theories and procedures of writing research.
3. Teachers can establish—perhaps through Bread Loaf's Program in Writing or NCTE—nationwide networks of teacher-researchers who can offer each other information, assistance and support.
4. Funding sources which support educational research, such as the National Institute of Education, can begin to look to and finance classroom teachers as researchers.
5. NCTE can demonstrate its commitment to the concept of teacher-conducted, class-based research by seeking out funding sources to support teachers' research endeavors and by publishing the research findings of regular classroom teachers—those working without institutional connections, using naturalistic inquiry procedures which do not result in the statistical data toward which journals of educational research are so heavily biased.

There is a great need for basic research in writing, research that will provide educators with theories and definitions of writing essential to the development of effective teaching methods. And there is an untapped resource for carrying out such research—the classroom teacher. When we acquire the researcher's tool, when we assume responsibility for thoughtfully exploring the real questions we have about our students' writing development, and when we are supported in our efforts by the educational community, the whole profession will benefit from our insights into the writing and learning of the students in our classrooms.

References

Berthoff, A. E. (1981). The teacher as REsearcher. In *The making of meaning.* Montclair, NJ: Boynton/Cook.

Bissex, G. L. (1980). *Gnys at wrk: A child learns to write and read.* Cambridge, MA: Harvard University Press.

Emig, J. (1971). *The composing processes of twelfth graders.* Urbana, IL: National Council of Teachers of English.

Giacobbe, M. E. (1981, September). Kids *can* write the first week of school. *Learning.*

Giacobbe, M. E., & Graves, D. H. (1982, May). Questions for teachers who wonder if their writers change. *Language Arts.*

Goswami, D. (1979, July). Classroom presentation at the Bread Loaf School of English, Middlebury, VT.

Goswami, D., & Odell, L. (1981). *Writing in a social service agency.* Washington, DC: Report to the National Institute of Education.

Graves, D. H. (1975). An examination of the writing processes of seven year old children. *Research in the Teaching of English 9*, 227–241.

Graves, D. H. (1978). We can end the energy crisis. *Language Arts 55*, 795–796.

Graves, D. H. (1980, April 26). *Students write: We listen: A new source of energy*. Paper presented to the New York University Language Arts Conference, New York.

Graves, D. H., Calkins, L., & Sowers, S. (1982). Papers describing their 1978–1980 inquiry into children's writing development, available through the University of New Hampshire Writing Process Laboratory, Durham, NH. (NIE Final Report, NIE-G-78-0174)

Teacher-Researchers and the Study of the Writing Process

MARIAN M. MOHR
Groveton High School, Alexandria, Virginia

After several review sentences, polite nods in the direction of previous researchers, the transition sentence appears: "Little is known, however, about . . . ," after which the researcher takes off into the new territory. This sentence sums up the literature search, the difficult discovery of the topic, and the hope that this little known territory is significant, truly new, and is now, in this research report, to be mapped.

As I read educational research, I look for that sentence as a sign of hope that research is a help. Frequently, however, I think of the repeated Josh Billings comment about people who "know what ain't so." Researchers, particularly those who do quantitative and experimental studies, seem to know a lot that ain't so when their findings are required to survive the context of the classroom. Teachers, on the other hand, work daily without benefit of research knowledge in areas where little is known.

How can a teacher *not* be interested in educational research? And how can an educational researcher *not* be interested in the classroom context? I think the apparent contradiction has several origins. Educational research has traditionally been conducted by outsiders, usually from universities, who conduct their studies and report their findings in their terminology to their readers. They may not see teachers as part of their audience and they usually do not see dissemination of their findings to teachers as part of their responsibility as researchers. They publish for different reasons. Teachers, although frequently the target of criticism concerning their teaching and lack of knowledge about research findings, are usually described as being uninterested in research and caring only for practical classroom suggestions.

Donald Graves, in a series of articles about writing research (1981), describes this background of estrangement and takes issue with experimental and quantitative methodology when used to understand writing. Graves asserts that teachers can and should conduct qualitative research in their classrooms; in fact, that they are in the best possible position to do so because of their understanding of the variables involved.

Previous to Graves's series, articles about teachers and writing research tended to concentrate on summarizing recent findings and encouraging teachers to use them (Haynes, 1978; Vukelich and Golden, 1981). Lee Odell (1976) encourages English teachers to conduct research, although he assumes that the methodology will be experimental, using control groups and comparing teaching strategies. Ann Berthoff (1981) emphasizes the importance of discovering and writing about the theory underlying teaching practices and applauds teachers conducting basic research.

There are other beginnings. Dixie Goswami suggests that classroom teachers conduct case studies of themselves as writers and teachers of writing followed by the study of a student writer. Nancie Atwell (1982) in Boothbay, Maine, is leading a group of teachers who are following the Goswami model. Lucy Calkins, a research associate of Graves's, has served as consultant to a program in Scarsdale, New York, where teachers work in collaborative relationship with college researchers to conduct classroom writing research toward writing a new curriculum.

In England, Nick May of the University of East Anglia is collecting data on the teacher as researcher. He represents a growing interest in teacher research also evidenced by Nixon (1981), whose series of articles defines action research as inquiry by teachers into their teaching practices. Nixon offers many suggestions for conducting such research and for using the findings in curriculum planning.

At least two teacher-researcher reports have been recently published. Mary Ellen Giacobbe, who taught where Graves conducted his two-year study of elementary students' writing, conducted and published a study (1981). The Bay Area Writing Project is encouraging teachers to conduct classroom research and has now published its first teacher-researcher report (Wotring and Tierney, 1982).

I found out about these far-flung efforts at encouraging teacher-researchers because, althought a high school English teacher, I am on leave for two years to work with the Northern Virginia Writing Project at George Mason University. In my new role as a college professor, I am expected to conduct research, and in 1980–1981, I completed a study of the revision processes of high school students and college freshmen. I struggled to write my findings as a combination research report and practical handbook for teachers.

Reflecting on my roles as teacher and researcher, I realized that when I began to think of myself as a researcher, I began to teach differently. I had kept a teaching journal for years: it had become a research log. I had begun asking my students questions and recording their answers to study as data, not to grade. My students were becoming experts on their revision processes and that was helping them become better revisers. The more I thought about this and wrote about it (Mohr, 1980), the more I noticed that "very little is known" about what happens to teachers who conduct writing research in their classrooms.

The first questions led to many others:
What kind of research questions do teachers have?
Will teachers do valuable original research?
Does conducting research cause teachers to have role conflicts?
What is the effect of their research on their students?
Do they change as teachers and if so, in what ways?
What do they need as support systems?
Are they more valued as teacher-researchers by their school systems?
Will they become more interested in the research of others?
Will they continue to investigate new research questions?

Through the NVWP and GMU, I offered a course called "Writing Research: A Teacher-Researcher Seminar." Twenty-one teachers signed up. All but one had taken at least one background course in the teaching of writing. All but five had been in the NVWP Summer Institute. Otherwise, they are a heterogeneous group with a variety of teaching assignments—twelve in high school, three in intermediate school, and six in elementary school.

Some teach the most able students in their schools in newly organized courses for "gifted and talented" students or courses labeled "advanced placement." Others teach in courses variously labeled "basic," "consumer," "Level II," or "academically unsuccessful," all referring to the less able students in the schools' programs. Some teach classes of students at many ability and achievement levels, including students for whom English is a second language.

Some teach in special resource programs—one in reading, one in learning disabilities, and two in Title I. Two are temporarily out of the classroom, one as a general resource teacher for a group of schools and one on maternity leave. (Although irrelevant to the study, it should, I think, be noted that two of the teachers left the course for a couple of weeks to have babies, returning to complete their research.)

The elementary teachers, of course, see writing as a part of all the disciplines they teach, and one did her study on writing to learn math. At the secondary level, one member of the class is a history teacher, one teaches mostly Latin although she did her research in her one English class, and one is writing a follow-up study of research conducted the year before on writing in high school chemistry. (She is co-author of the Bay Area Writing Project research report mentioned earlier.)

The course plan was to meet every two weeks during the school year (a three-credit course lasting two semesters) and to spend the first half of the three hours either discussing a series of research articles or talking with a visiting researcher, and the second half meeting in small groups of four to discuss research in progress. Eventually, Anne Legge, a GMU research intern, and I prepared a bibliography for the class that included additional sources as well as the articles we were all reading together.

The pivot of the course action was the folder of each teacher. At each class meeting they turned in sample of their logs, data, and analysis. I read them and wrote comments on the folder. They developed research questions, gathered data, analyzed data, and wrote up their findings either as an article, an I-search paper (following the Macrorie model, 1980), or a research proposal.

At first I had planned to continue my revision research with my freshman composition students as a way of sharing the experiences of the teachers in the course. By the second class meeting, however, I decided to begin a study of the teachers themselves, assuming the same role with them that they assumed with their students. My early research log entries, like those of the teachers, are almost entirely questions with plenty of self-doubt.

> Oct. 14—First night. Excitement. What changes may happen to these teachers? What do I think will happen? What do I want to happen? What should I look at? What model? What did I assign? Another observation? Should I set goals for each group meeting? What do I want to know? How teachers change?

In addition to my research log, I decided to analyze their research logs, notes and tapes of class discussions, and records of individual conferences. I did not observe in their classrooms, partly for lack of time but also because something held me back, as if doing so would indicate that I did not find their self-reports accurate and trustworthy. I did not wish to undermine my teaching role as one who believed in their capabilities and believed that they could be honest observers of their own teaching. This situation, I was to discover, is a teacher-researcher role tension. When were we teachers, when researchers? We learned to be both and to record our actions carefully.

We all worked hard and were conscious of being in new territory. Many times during the year, we doubted what we were doing and wrote research log entries full of questions. The course is now over and the teachers' articles are the final addition to my data collection. As I finished reading the drafts of the articles, I felt envy that the other teachers in the class were nearing the end of their analysis and I was just beginning. But, I also felt excitement at knowing, already, what a wealth of interesting discoveries were to come.

Like the other teacher-researchers in the class, I have studied and analyzed data that I collected and have some confidence that my hunches will develop into findings. At present they divide into answers to three questions:

1. What happened in their research processes?
2. What happened in their teaching?
3. What are the implications of the findings for research and for teacher education?

What follows are my earliest attempts to answer these questions.

What Happened in Their Research Processes?

1. No longer awed and intimidated, they became intimately involved with research. They grew more confident reading and criticizing the research findings of others as they became more involved in their own. In one class discussion late in the course, the discussion leader said of a well-known writing research article, "93%—humph! Do you know how many students he's talking about? Only 14!" They respected and eagerly read the work of other teacher-researchers. When documentation of the articles was being discussed, a repeated question was how to cite a fellow class member. They began to look at all writing about classroom practices more carefully, asking questions such as, "Is this research or a report or lesson plans?"

2. They developed research questions of their own, repeatedly modifying their questions and their methodologies. Most rejected the conventional hypothesis. One teacher reported on the final evening of class that she had finally come up with her research question. Another stated that he still wasn't exactly sure of his. The evolutionary nature of the process became a class theme, sometimes treated humorously, sometimes with rueful respect. If one source of data didn't give them the information they needed, they tried another. If one piece of data was puzzling to them, they went back to their students and asked more questions. They followed up on their hunches.

3. Considerable role tension resulted as they looked closely at how they taught, questioning, evaluating, and writing as they observed. Typical comments were, "I personally cannot split myself in two" and "As a researcher, I'm changing behavior." Tension arose when they observed behavior of their own or of their students and wished to change the behavior. Frequently, this resulted in a change in teaching method. Several, dissatisfied with answers to their original questions about writing, went back to the students using a different method, thus changing their approach to the students and eliciting the information they were seeking. They were full participant-observers and made full use of themselves as data. They described their interventions openly, sometimes with pride. In their articles, their personalities are revealed. Sometimes they record raw relationships with students, the kind that rarely surface in research reports. They do not spare themselves.

4. Their research studies are fully context dependent. The context is readily apparent, almost tangible. Many of the reports refer to shortened periods and restless students during the series of snowstorms this past winter. Classroom management strategies and student behavior are treated as important variables. One teacher referred to these variables as the "extra murals." Another observed in her log: "When people want to be liked and you tell them you don't like them, you win." She is recording her feelings about managing a class of students and responding to their writing.

5. They were cooperative rather than competitive and eagerly shared the progress of their work with each other, pleased when two of them found something similar. They supported each other with suggestions, encouragement, hard questions, phone calls, and visits. They checked out data with each other, validated their analyses, and did not rush to be first with their findings. They enjoyed pooling data and looking for similarities. One wrote a long analysis of another group member's draft article and mailed it to her during the interim period between classes. Another group held a special meeting at the home of one of the new mothers so that she could have some responses to her analysis. She, in turn, agreed to give some typing help to another. They did not see research as a way of getting ahead in their careers, but as a way of finding the answers to their questions and sharing those answers with other interested teachers.

6. Although referred to as "writing it up," data anlaysis was their hardest task. The process of getting through the data analysis followed a general pattern.

    a. *Deciding what is data and what isn't.* At first teachers were not confident that records of their interventions in the class should be part of their data. They saw data as pure, meaning uncontaminated by teaching. After deciding that everything that happened was data, they began collecting with a thoroughness that in at least one case resulted in "a volcano of data."

b. *Broad theorizing, confidently relating the collected data to their knowledge of writing process and to other research.* The confidence was sometimes undermined by the realization that while everything was in the data, perhaps nothing was in it that was special or that could be "found."

c. *"Confused, unsure, overwhelmed, discouraged" feelings about data analysis.* I wrote this in my research log, recording the repeated words they used to describe their feelings. Some felt that their data was of no value. A typical statement: "I'm seeing it, but I'm not interpreting. I never learned to interpret."

d. *Tentative emergence of patterns and classifications of data.* One teacher writes, "My categories seem to mean maybe something." Although a few later said that they thought of giving up, most are typified by the teacher who persevered, as she put it, undaunted by her ineptitude.

7. Repeated discussion of findings led the teacher-researchers to see comparable concerns in the research of the class as a whole, repeated patterns that crossed grade levels and disciplines. On December 16, I wrote in my log, "Maybe we won't be able to answer questions, but we are going to know what the questions are." Now I would translate the word *question* into *issue.* Issues of importance representing repeated patterns are:

a. Student ownership and control of writing process.

b. A classroom atmosphere that rewards change, risk-taking, and revision.

c. A relationship between self-confidence and writing confidence.

Repeatedly, also, motivation came to be seen as a false issue once certain classroom conditions were achieved.

8. The written reports of their research lack educational jargon for the most part and acknowledge unanswered questions. One English major researcher remarked that the writing was more difficult than what she was used to because she "didn't have *Hamlet* to fall back on." The reports reflect enthusiasm. One teacher uses an exclamation point when her student subject catches on after repeated trials! As they wrote, they asked repeatedly, "Who is our audience?" and came to expect it to be other teachers. They wished to write so as to be true to the classroom, to be recognizable by other teachers.

9. Their research is valuable, solid, and, in some cases, innovative, adding real and useful findings to the field of writing research. Their research questions are the same as those of other researchers.

Where they have looked at questions that have also been studied by other researchers, they have added context. The kinds of findings they produced range on a continuum from case study records of personal journeys ("It had to happen with me first") to a follow-up article on research conducted before the class began. In between are many variations of student and class studies. Their topics reflect a wide range of interests. (See the appendix at the end of the essay for a list of titles.)

10. The research was not completed even after the final articles were written. Both the teacher-researchers and their students had a continuing sense of their projects. Students who had been involved in the study would return to discuss their writing. Some changed their attitudes and behavior, regardless of the fact that the teacher's paper had already been written. Many teachers stated that they intend to continue their research, to ask more questions, and to keep writing in their research log.

What Happened in Their Teaching?

1. Writing honestly about classroom problems, failures as well as successes, in a supportive atmosphere, led to more self-assurance and encouragement to change. The research logs, written under stress as they often were, in minutes between classes or during the times when the students themselves were writing, were honest writings, harsh sometimes, despairing sometimes. These writings and their authors were accepted by the other teachers and many found they shared the same problems. Teachers who avoided difficult questions about their teaching, who tried to avoid sharing their writings, were pulled up short by the other teachers in their response group. They would say to each other, "Maybe something else is going on. Have you thought about . . . ?" Being honest with themselves and with each other seemed to enable them to change. It was a difficult triple whammy—observing, writing, and analyzing what happened in their classes—a strain, as it was repeatedly described. It was also liberating.

2. Their research plans became their lesson plans. At first most felt they were working double, both teaching and conducting research. As the weeks passed, partly out of necessity to save time, but also out of response to their student responses, some changed their plans to make them more in line with what they were discovering. They began to see teaching more as a learning process rather than a daily routine or performance. The teacher who studied the use of writing to learn math began to develop and change her math curriculum as she discovered more and more things that her students

could do. A questionnaire would lead to another followed by an open class discussion that was taped and analyzed. Because they were more in touch with what their students were thinking, they did not plan in the same way that they had done previously. Tight rigid lesson plans began to give. One teacher invented a mid-term exam that reflected her changed teaching ideas, met the requirements of her principal, and became part of her data. Another wove his data and findings back into his curriculum in a series of studies of American literature, at the same time recording the changes he himself was going through. For many their teaching and research became unified. One teacher wrote that she now "takes the lead from her students."

3. They switched from evaluating to documenting. Initially, some expressed disappointment with their data, as if it were a lesson plan gone awry rather than simply what they were going to analyze. The switch to documenting reassured teachers who were accustomed to being disappointed in the work of their students. Irritating classroom behavior, seen as data, became interesting. Error became a sign of growth.

4. They became more tolerant of creative chaos in their thinking (not in classroom behavior) and therefore more understanding of its appearance in their students' thinking and writing. One teacher called herself "a wishy washy Pisces researcher" as she continually refined and developed her research question. They knew from experience what it means to discover your idea gradually as you write and do research. Revision became a commonplace, a fact of life. One teacher reported a sense of "messiness" as part of her teaching, another that she felt she was "fluttering around hither and thither" as she did her research. Although the teachers were not completely comfortable with these feelings, they were acknowledged as part of the research process and therefore as legitimate parts of the learning processes of their students.

5. They changed their focus from teaching students to finding out what their students knew and then trying to help them learn. One teacher wrote, "I'm to the point where I ask them before I ask them." They discovered that their students knew more and could learn more than they had imagined. They reported asking more questions, listening more, and respecting the worries and concerns of the students as legitimate, waiting rather than rushing in with a suggestion. They received the cooperation and interest of their students in their research. In some cases, the students became partners in the project. The students became more aware of their own learning and writing processes. One student chose her own research name. Many of them read the drafts of the reports and made comments to the

teacher-researcher. The teachers and their students became learners together and the students began to see their teachers as learners. The teacher-researcher modeled the learning process for his or her students.

6. The teachers were able to try new ways of teaching because they were very sensitive to the classroom variables. While researching, they were examining the context simultaneously with the teaching. Perhaps what happens with some attempts at teacher change is that even though teachers accept new ideas presented in an interesting, authentic, and enthusiastic manner, if the ideas are not compatible with their classroom context, they will not work as they did at the in-service program. During research, however, the context is an examined integral part of the practice and the teacher is receiving constant response from students concerning the context, so that the idea gets a full trial.

7. As a teacher of teacher-researchers, I found the same changes taking place in myself that I noticed happening to them. We became colleagues learning together. I made honest and direct comments and responses to them about their work. I took more notes on what they said and talked less. On January 20, I noted in my log, "I'm developing a new teaching technique—sending out comments when they're too late to do any good and having them reaffirm what the researchers have already figured out for themselves." This happened accidentally at first because of the many times I returned comments to the teachers later than I had planned. I know that I was helpful to them on some occasions, and they helped me with the material I'm putting together for this essay. I'm not sure how permanent the changes are, but I know that I felt uncomfortable with some of the teaching I was doing in another course for teachers, and I began to modify what I was doing there as well.

One teacher who helped me by giving comments on this essay in process asked, "Are you going to say how hard it was?" It was hard because of the circumstances under which we were working and because we were new at it. One January night after I got home from class, I received a phone call from one of the teachers who said, "It's the first night I haven't been tired since the vacation." We worked hard, but it was a different kind of tired.

Implications for Research and Teacher Education

1. Teacher-researchers need the opportunity to conduct and follow up on their research, to see it as an ongoing professional activity. Most of the teachers in the course have much more data than they can possibly analyze in these first reports.

2. Most teacher research is qualitative and naturalistic, the kind teachers are best qualified to do because of their experience. If, however, many teachers in a school system were involved in classroom research, their findings could be combined and the beginnings of meaningful quantitative studies be made.

3. Researchers outside of the classroom, possibly associated with local school systems and universities, may wish to do their research in a community where teacher-researchers are at work. If so, they will need to accept the teacher-researchers as equals.

4. The creating of a community of teacher-researchers could change the hierarchy of educational prestige. Their position in the educational community as well as in the community at large seems already to be changing toward one of respect. Several of the teachers have been asked to share their findings with the faculties of their schools, although their studies are still in process. They are eager to publish.

5. Teachers will have a changed attitude toward research, but they will insist that if they are to be consumers, research, however complex, must be readable, considered in the context of real classrooms, and related to practice.

6. Teacher-researchers will write up their findings differently and other teachers will read and respect their research. They will need a place to publish. They will give presentations about their findings, showing other teachers how to make use of them in the classroom. One teacher, excited over the group's discussion, said, "We could change the face of the earth!" She was only partly joking.

7. Pre-service and in-service programs should include naturalistic research projects conducted in classrooms as part of the curriculum. Teachers need to be encouraged to come up with their own research questions and retain ownership of the research process.

8. Teacher-researchers need a support system that includes university resources and the backing of their local school system. They need the support of fellow researchers, flexible scheduling, released time to analyze data and write, and, as one teacher put it, "xeroxing without guilt."

9. Teacher-researcher positions, grants, and released time in grades K–12 will become a way of rewarding good teachers that goes to the heart of education—its capacity to effect change. Good teachers will stay in the classroom.

10. Teacher-researchers will influence other teachers. What they find out will have happened in the classroom next door. What they write will be read. They will be especially good mentors for beginning teachers.

Implications for Further Study

1. Teacher-researchers need to be observed in the classroom to further document their changing teaching practices. One way this could be done would be to have them work in pairs, team teaching and observing each other. Their students' comments on their teaching methods should also be a part of this documentation.

2. The idea of the teacher as model, the way that teacher-researchers model learners for their students, needs further study. Students learn to know what their teachers want; in fact, they may learn this better than any other lesson. The model a teacher projects, his or her feelings about learning, may be best developed through the excitement and confidence a teacher receives from conducting research.

3. Teacher-researchers in other disciplines should be studied to discover how the ideas presented here transfer into fields other than writing research.

In the spring, another group of teachers in another northern Virginia county became interested in conducting writing research in their classrooms. Seven of the teacher-researchers in my class were invited to meet with the new teachers and discuss their research with them. These discussions provided additional commentary (while I was not present) on their feelings, attitudes, and thoughts as they began teaching others to do what they were doing. As an experienced teacher-researcher discussed methodologies with the group just beginning, one of them stumbled over his words and asked, "Do you think of yourself as a teachers-reacher?"

As I listened to the tape of that conversation, I thought of another comment made about two-thirds of the way through the course by a teacher who used an *Alice in Wonderland* image to explain how she felt about doing research: "I am grasping a giant window ledge and peeking over a gigantic window sill." Her image was appreciated by all of us, and would, I think, be greeted with a sigh of recognition by most researchers. For me, now, it represents both where we are as teacher-researchers in the larger community of education and, closer to home, where I am in this research. It is an exciting place to be.

References

Atwell, N. (1982, January). Class-based writing research: Teachers can learn from students. *English Journal 71,* 84–87.

Berthoff, A. E. (1981). *The making of meaning* (pp. 30–40). Montclair, NJ: Boynton/Cook.

Giacobbe, M. (1981). Kids *can* write the first week of school. *Learning 10*(2), 130–131.

Graves, D. H. (1981). Research update: A new look at writing research. *Language Arts 58* (2), 197–206.

Haynes, E. F. (1978). Using research in preparing to teach writing. *English Journal 67*(1), 82–88.

Macrorie, K. (1980). *Searching writing.* Rochelle Park, NJ: Hayden.

Mohr, M. (1980). The teacher as researcher. *Virginia English Bulletin 30*(2), 61–64.

Nixon, J. (1981). *A teacher's guide to action research.* London: Grant McIntyre.

Odell, L. (1976). The classroom teacher as researcher. *English Journal 65* (1), 106–111.

Vukelich, C. & Golden, J. (1981). The development of writing in young children: A review of the literature. *Childhood Education 58* (3), 167–170.

Wotring, A., & Tierney, R. (1982). *Two studies of writing in high school science.* Berkeley: University of California: Bay Area Writing Project.

Appendix

The following articles are from *Research in Writing: Reports from a Teacher-Researcher Seminar,* a collection of research reports on the writing processes of students, grades 1–12, prepared by the participants in a teacher-researcher seminar. The seminar, conducted in May 1982, was sponsored by the Northern Virginia Writing Project at George Mason University, Fairfax, Virginia.

Blake, A. B.	The Discoveries of a Teacher of Basics.
Curtis, P.	What Happens When Tenth Graders Use an Adult Editor?
Ernst, E. M.	Students Write and Teachers Write Back—Can it Make a Difference?
Falcone, B. S.	Why Students Won't Write: A Personal Search.
Fant, V.	Conceptualizing the Main Idea Through Writing Process.
Gibney, B.	Four out of Seven: Characteristics of Four Competent Seventh-Grade Writers.
Gibson, M.	Dear Mrs. Gibson.
Glaze, B. M.	Role Writing to Understand the Past.
Graap, P. V.	Open the Door to Inductive Application: Release Anxiety and Math Frustration.
Grossman, N.	What Happens When Mickey Writes? Reading Between the Lines.
Johnson, G. B.	Facing the Blank Page.
MacLean, M. S.	Voices Within: The Audience Speaks.
McDonnell-Culley, P.	After the Writing Project: A Teacher Rights Her Wrongs and a Student Writes Better.

Rothman, G. A.   "Are You Going to Write Another Twenty-Seven
                      Page Story?" Second-Graders Can Help Each Other
                      Write and Revise.
Schulman, M.   The Novice Writer.
Sevcik, A.   What Happened When Research Guided My Grammar
                      Lessons?
Swernofsky, M.   The Ungraded Journal.
Welker, P. E.   Teaching English to Eleventh-Graders.

Buena Vista Writing to Learn

Teachers as Agents for Educational Change

LYNNE B. ALVINE
Parry McCluer High School, Buena Vista, Virginia

In August 1983, I invited several teachers from various grade levels in my school division to join with me to investigate how writing could function as a tool for learning. Believing that an examination of our own learning and composing processes could help us to understand those of our students, I proposed that we meet informally to explore our findings. By finding a new way of looking, I believed that we could become not only participants, but participant-observers in our classrooms, and that our changed perceptions would result in changes in belief and practice. Initially, I expected to provide the direction for our reading and discussion, but I hoped that we would gradually form a cooperative learning community.

Initiating the Buena Vista Writing to Learn Inquiry and Response group was, for me, like starting to roll a snowball down a long incline. I was unsure where it would go or what shape it would find along the way, but the process became a minor miracle. Perhaps my telling of the story of our journey together will help other teachers to see themselves as real agents for change in the educational process.

My work with the Buena Vista Writing to Learn Project has had the support of several cooperative learning communities. I am indebted to Jane Armstrong, Teresa Ellison, Lorene Weing, and Fran Williams for their willingness to find a new way of looking at themselves and their classrooms and for the sharing of their journals and their time, and to Amanda Branscombe for extensive telephone consultation and for her expertise as a visiting consultant in April 1984.

An Invitation

That summer I had studied "Writing, Thinking, and Learning" with Nancy Martin, Peter Medway, and John Dixon at Oxford University as a part of my Bread Loaf MA degree program. As the readings and discussions there began to come together, I looked for ways to apply what I was learning to my own classroom practice and for ways to transmit the energy charge to some of my colleagues.

In early August, I wrote a Bread Loaf research grant proposal for "Buena Vista Writing to Learn." One section was a tentative timetable for our explorations (see the table, "Tentative Schedule"). On August 11, two days after returning from England, I went to my division superintendent and director of instruction with the proposal. They agreed to support the project and approved the granting of three units of continuing education for each teacher who completed the "course." Within the next few days, each of the four building principals had agreed to cooperate and I was ready to begin inviting teachers to join the project.

Knowing that we would be finding our way together, and painfully aware that I had lots more questions than answers, I looked for people with whom I felt I could work comfortably as well as who would probably work well with each other. The previous spring, I had interviewed several teachers on their beliefs about children's writing. I went through the transcripts of those interviews, listing insights to build upon and deeply held convictions to which I had to be sensitive. Those interviews helped me to realize that I was looking for veteran teachers who had not become fossilized, teachers who were confident in their own performance, and who were recognized by their students, the administration, and the community to be very good teachers. I also felt it was crucial that I include only people who had time to meet regularly.

While I wanted teachers from each school, representing a range of grade levels, I felt it was important to keep the group small. I invited eight, hoping to wind up with four or five. I didn't want to see "Writing to Learn" billed as a typical in-service course, yet I also didn't want to exclude anyone who might be genuinely interested. Thus, I gave a brief summary of my summer at Oxford at the division-wide pre-school faculty meeting and asked people interested in hearing more to talk with me later. Then, I went after the people I wanted. By the time school opened on August 22, six teachers had agreed to attend the initial meeting on August 29 to hear a more complete overview of the project.

Opening Night

I had arrived back at my classroom an hour early to get set up.
As I moved to adjust the air conditioner, my copy of Macrorie (1984)
caught my eye. I opened the front and read. "Lynne—Virginia is the
birthplace of Presidents. Remember that. Ken." I drifted back to that
summer day at Bread Loaf in 1981 when I had told Ken how much
being in his class had meant to me. I could hear his voice: "When you
meet someone who is a so-called 'authority' on something, and you
see that he is just another person like you, it gives you the confidence that you too can become an authority." I wasn't an authority;
I wanted to know more.

Six of the eight teachers I had invited showed up that first night.
It was a crucial session. I had one chance to articulate my goals for
the group—and to secure their commitment. I began by asking everyone to answer five questions:
1. What questions do you have about your students' writing?
2. What frustrations do you have about your own writing or
   learning?
3. What can you learn from your students?
4. In your classroom, how do you function as a researcher?
5. On a Monday evening the second week of school—with plans to
   make and perhaps papers to grade—why are you here?

Then I began by explaining how the project related to my graduate
work at Bread Loaf—about what being involved in that program had
done for my personal and professional growth. Most importantly, I
talked about my own classroom investigation on storytelling and
about how my teaching had changed once I began to learn about
reading and writing with my students.

Then I shared how I had come to invite each of them and re-
emphasized that participation was strictly voluntary. I gave each a
proposed schedule. I had built in enough flexibility to allow us to
find our way together, but I did list five rather specific requirements:
1. We would each do case studies of ourselves as writers and
   learners.
2. We would each choose two subjects as case study subjects, save
   copies of everything those two children wrote, and record observations about their learning along the way.
3. Later, we would each focus on some aspect of the writing
   process.
4. In April, we would reflect and write about what we had learned.
5. We would eventually publish our findings so that we might share
   with our colleagues and others.

TENTATIVE SCHEDULE

Dates	Focus	Implementation	Theoretical Base
Aug. 15	Approval by division superintendent for the granting of 3 CEU's.	For application	Britton, 1983. Goswami—importance of teachers' participating in classroom inquiry.
Aug. 19	Selection of participants	Criteria for invitation into a dialogue: 1. Interest in investigation of learning and composing processes. 2. Willingness to follow through the projected activities. 3. Potential for complementing the make-up of a cohesive group.	
Aug. 29	Initiate case studies of ourselves as writers and learners.	Write about own own earliest memories of learning to write and read. Inventory kinds of writing in which we engage for one week. Begin a reflective journal which we will continue to keep through the project. Writing freely—response groups for feedback on writing.	Britton—functions of writing Nancie Atwell—The Boothbay Harbor Writing Project. Macrorie, 1984. Elbow, 1973.
Sept. 12	Selection of two students by each participant—to serve as subjects for case studies.	Discussion of management techniques. Photocopies of papers to be saved. Parental consent waivers.	

Date	Topic	Activity	References
Sept. 19	Exploration of the differences between spoken and written language.	I have tapes (and transcripts) of my own spoken language to compare with written expressions. Do the same with example of student.	Kress, 1982, chap. 2.
Sept. 26	Comparison of interactive and didactic models for learning. Scaffolding, sustaining, and extending learner's topics.	Compare tapes (and transcripts) of examples of interactive and didactic language acquisition.	Wells, 1982. Bruner, 1965
Oct. 3	The importance of talk. Importance of student-sponsored topics.		Medway, 1980a. Brannon and Knoblauch, 1982.
Oct. 17	Sociocultural differences in patterns of language acquisition.	Inventory literacy events in homes of students—students acting as investigators and collaborators of information.	Heath, 1982, 1983. Medway, 1980a.
Oct. 24	Skills and heritage model vs. personal growth model in teaching English.	By this time in the project, I expect that what the teachers are observing in their own classrooms and through their case studies will lead us to our focal points for our inquiry and response sessions. It is very important here not to "teach a class" on the two models.	Martin, 1975.
Oct. 31	Learning to look at achievements and constraints in student writing (e.g., levels of abstraction).	Return to focus on our own writing. Use examples of my students' writing. Then look at other age levels.	Dixon, 1975.

TENTATIVE SCHEDULE (cont.)

Dates	Focus	Implementation	Theoretical Base
Nov. 7–Dec. 12 (weekly)	Diverging inquiries: move participants toward focus on individual explorations of students' writing at their grade levels of interest.	Continue to meet in inquiry and response sessions. In these meetings, various participants will take the lead for the focus of exploration.	All theorists I've been drawing on should be relevant to this.
Dec. 12–Jan. 7	None	Enjoy Christmas.	
Jan. 9	Implications and directions for further inquiry sessions.	Take stock of where we are and what we have learned thus far.	
Jan. 9–Feb. 6	Individual directions.	Sessions will meet biweekly to give participants an opportunity for a response to what they're learning.	
Feb. 6–Mar. 6	Reflection.	Each participant will write up what she has learned through the course of the project.	
	Revision and editing.		
	Dissemination.	Publish pamphlets and share with other staff members, area teachers, and (of course) Bread Loaf mentors.	

I proposed that we keep journals throughout the year, where we would reflect on our early memories of learning to write and our own learning processes, where we would record what was happening in our classrooms, and where we would react to readings and the insights gained through our discussion. Later, I would collect, analyze, and interpret those journals along with the one I was keeping on the project. In addition to continuing the storytelling research project in my own classroom, I was interested in studying the interaction of the group that we were forming.

As a model for our project, I told what I knew of the work of Nancie Atwell and her colleagues at Boothbay (Maine) Region Elementary School and of the discoveries they had made about themselves and the writing processes of children when they began to see themselves as classroom researchers. I challenged those present to help me transform the classrooms of the Buena Vista City Schools into communities of writers and learners. I reminded them again, as I had in the earlier interviews, that I'd had very little contact with children at various grade levels—that they were the real experts in their own classrooms as I considered myself to be in mine. And I proposed that we might all come to a better understanding through our sharing. I made it clear that I would accept the responsibility for leading the group initially, but that we should find our way together and become an interactive learning community before the course had ended.

As a basis for our dialogue, in the second session to be held September 12, I had provided copies of three articles (Atwell, 1982; Berthoff, 1981; and Martin, 1973). Talking about next time meant that we were moving toward the subject of commitment. I suggested "assignments" for anyone who was planning to continue:

1. Read the three articles and make some kind of written response in the spiral notebook.
2. Begin thinking about selecting two students to serve as subjects for case studies.
3. For one week, keep a log of all personal and professional writing activities, including the date, description, purpose, audience, and function.
4. Answer eight questions listed on a separate handout in the journal.

These questions were ones we would be answering every two or three months as a way of monitoring our changes:

1. Describe your English classes (or classes in which you teach English).
2. How much time do you devote to writing?
3. How much time do you devote to talking to writers?

4. What are some priorities in teaching writing at your grade level?
5. How would you describe the comments you make on student papers?
6. How do you grade student writing?
7. Do you write?
8. How do people learn to write?

The "assignments" were perhaps more than enough to ask of volunteers during the first few weeks of the new term, but I wanted to stimulate a rich discussion for our second session, and I wanted to indicate that our sharing would strike a balance between internal and external texts and contexts.

Up to that time I had requested that no one write in the spiral notebooks. Now, however, they could open the journal and write freely for about ten minutes about their reactions to our introductory meeting before they left. And, when they departed, they should either take the materials with them or leave them, depending on their decision. I offered to stay for anyone who wanted to talk after the meeting.

As the room cleared, only one person handed back the materials, explaining that it sounded good, but that it wasn't the year for her to get involved. As I turned off the air conditioner and locked the door, I felt good. We were six. We were the Buena Vista Writing to Learn Project.

What Are We Doing?

When we met again on September 12, the atmosphere was much more relaxed. In that second session, we were to discover our guiding question for the project. We had begun by sharing responses to the question: What are your frustrations about children's writing?

"They don't write in complete sentences."

"They hook everything together with *and*."

"They don't know how to punctuate."

As we went around the circle, reading our responses, the pattern quickly became obvious. We were all saying the same things. It was Jane who asked, "How can we get the skills we work on in English classes to carry over into their writing?"

I said, "Maybe we're asking the wrong question. Maybe we need to ask why we don't get a carryover of the skills lessons to their writing." None of us knew the answer to that either.

Jane went on. "If this complete sentence thing is a problem from grades one through twelve, what are we doing?!"

We had found our beginning. We couldn't answer *how* or *why* until we had begun to describe *what* was happening in our classrooms. Throughout the year, when we were tempted to give simplistic answers to why and how questions, we would return to that single enabling question for the project: *What are we doing?* Asking *what* again and again eventually enabled us to come back around to asking *how* and *why.* As we discussed our responses to other questions that night, we were exploring our assumptions about how people learn to write. And we were checking our perceptions, beliefs, and practice against Nancy Martin's article (1983) about the importance of interactive learning. In our third session two weeks later, we continued our discussion of those initial readings and moved to sharing our journal entries about our earliest memories of writing and the kinds of personal and professional writing we did ourselves.

Discussions, Discoveries, Dilemmas

In the five sessions we held through October and November, we stayed fairly close to my original schedule (see the table, "Tentative Schedule"), but remained flexible enough to respond to the "emergent occasion" as John Donne might have called it. Some of our discoveries, discussions, and dilemmas related to the following:

1. Functions of writing.
2. Similarities and differences between acquisition of speech and acquisition of writing.
3. The role of the teacher in evaluation.
4. Colleagues who use writing as punishment.
5. Invented spellings.
6. Peer response and peer editing.
7. Moving from expressive to poetic modes.
8. Interactive and didactic learning models.
9. Teaching penmanship.
10. Writing to learn in various subjects.
11. The value of real audiences for writing.
12. Management of data collection for case studies.

In our journals, we were recording:
1. Discoveries made about our own learning processes, including reflections on our early memories of learning to write.
2. Observations of what was happening in our classrooms in relation to writing, including changes in teacher and student behaviors.
3. Notes, questions, and insights on articles read and discussed.

Although the specific focus for each evening varied, our agenda usually included time for:

1. Discussion of common or individual readings.
2. Sharing of journal entries about our own learning or our classroom activities.
3. Discussion of insights which had led to new beliefs and/or changes in our practice.
4. Discussion of project "business" such as agendas, scheduling, etc.

After the fourth meeting, Mary, a tenth-grade English teacher, pulled out of the group, explaining that with her teaching and family responsibilities, she was unable to find the necessary time and energy to continue the project. A result of her leaving was that the five of us who remained strengthened our commitment to the project and to each other. We were also gradually to turn our main focus to writing in the elementary school with the focus of my research becoming the interaction of the group itself. At the end of October, instead of a regular group meeting, I met individually with the other four to discuss specific problems each was having. It was at that time that we first began to integrate social interaction as a part of our learning process.

I met informally with Jane and Teresa after school one day in Jane's third-grade classroom. They were having problems with the management of data collection. We decided to use some of our research grant money to order individual hard-covered composition books for each of their students. They would keep the books in the classroom so that their young authors could have access to them during the day.

That same week, Fran and I discovered that we had tickets to the same concert theater series. We combined dinner before the evening of baroque music with a discussion of how she might extend her units in social studies, science, and health with writing activities. The next night when Lori joined me for dessert and coffee at a local restaurant, she explained her concern for a student who always wrote on the same topic because she was afraid to risk using words she didn't know how to spell correctly. We talked about possibilities for helping the girl generate new topics and develop the confidence to risk new words.

Jane and Teresa, who were both members of the Shenandoah Valley Reading Council, suggested that for one session we attend together a dinner meeting of that organization in Harrisonburg, Virginia. After school on November 10, we were off on our first "Writing to Learn" road trip. At our next meeting late in November, Jane and

Teresa offered to share a book about writing they had each bought at an earlier SVRC meeting. Instead of my classroom in the high school, we were sitting around my living room in front of the fireplace sipping coffee and eating brownies. Instead of "taking a course," we were sharing conversation as colleagues and friends.

Coloring Our Own Trees

Maintaining communication with fellow students and faculty members from Bread Loaf throughout the past three winters had been an important source of energy for me. Though we were creating a similar communication network right in our own community, I had continued to rely on telephone consultation with Bread Loaf people as I determined directions for our Writing to Learn group. My most important interaction had been with Amanda Branscombe, a 1983 Bread Loaf graduate, with whom I had spent the past three years talking about writing and learning.

On a Wednesday night in April, Amanda rode the train from Atlanta, Georgia to work for two days as a voluntary consultant to our project. She spent that Thursday morning reading our journals and the afternoon in my classroom. That evening at Teresa's house, she did a remarkable job of helping each of us to see where we made similar discoveries at different times. More importantly, she helped us to understand that the differences in our paths of discovery were to be expected and that each of us, in her own way, had some very exciting things happening in her classroom.

She read to us from Leo Buscaglia (1972). With the anecdote about the teacher who wanted kids (who had seen, climbed, touched, tasted, and smelled real trees) to color trees all the same, Amanda made the point that their writing activities were allowing kids to color their own trees. After Amanda had spent Friday in the others' classrooms and had departed for Atlanta on the Friday night train, I realized that the message was also for us. Everyone in the project needed to move in the direction that was right for her; each had to color her own tree.

Interactive Learning

Knowing that the time before Christmas can be especially hectic for teachers, I had scheduled no meetings during December. (See the table.) When we met again in early January at "The Ranch" restaurant, our focus was to plan for a January 16 guest night to which each of us would invite one colleague. Two aspects of that planning session were to become important factors in the next seven sessions between Christmas and Easter: (1) we were continuing to involve social interaction as part of our learning process, and (2) we were taking the first steps toward sharing the story of our classroom research with an external audience.

Through the winter and early spring, we continued to meet at restaurants and at each other's houses. In April, we took our second road trip, a two-day jaunt to Williamsburg for the Eastern Virginia Writing Conference and a shopping spree at the Williamsburg Pottery Factory.

In retrospect, I believe the increasing social interaction was more important than I realized at the time. As the other members of the group became more involved in when and where we would meet, they contributed more input toward our meeting agenda, our discussion topics, and our readings.

As we became comfortable with each other, we grew willing to risk more as well. On February 20, our session was to involve giving response to each other's writing—other than journal entries. At that same meeting, I first proposed that we submit a proposal to tell our story in a panel presentation at the VATE Conference in Roanoke the following October. And it was that night that Teresa said, "Some of us have been talking among ourselves, and we've decided the project isn't a one-year thing. Would you consider continuing our meetings through next year?" Would I, indeed! I knew then that they would probably continue to monitor their own perceptions and practice and would probably discuss their findings whether I met with them or not. But I had found that the network we had established was giving me new energy for my own teaching and I wanted to continue. As Jane put it, "This has become a way of life."

The Unveiling

At the end of April after a full week's Easter vacation, I met individually with the others to reflect on Amanda's visit and to talk about the focus each had found. Everyone agreed that I should go ahead with the VATE proposal, and that our next step in sharing with external audiences might be to present our story to the two local elementary faculties before the end of school. Talking about what we had done would also give us an opportunity to invite some of our colleagues to join the project for the following year.

At our last evening meeting at Lori's house on May 7, we framed the panel discussion. The following week we were ready to "go public." After school on May 14, I gave a brief introduction to the faculty of Kling School. The following is excerpted from a tape of that presentation. The participants tell the rest of our story.

LYNNE: I kept the initial invitation limited because I wasn't sure where our journey would take us. Now that we know where we've been, we would like to share with you what happens when a group of teachers say, "We're going to meet together to explore new ways of looking at what's happening in our classrooms in relation to how writing can be a more effective tool for children's learning."

So that you can get some sense of what we have discovered and consider whether you will respond to our invitation to join the project next year, I have asked these people to respond to two questions: (1) What have been some of your changes in perception this year? (2) How has your classroom changed as a result of the project?

LORI: When I first started, I'd had very little experience teaching writing, but I'd had a great deal of experience teaching penmanship. They're two entirely different things. I used to give children assignments, have them do them, and turn in the papers. I would mark the errors, give a grade, and hand them back. The children would look at the grade—ignore the rest—then stick them in their book bag or crumple them and throw them away. And they never made much improvement.

This fall I began to determine what should be my function, what should be my goals.

One of the things we've done in the group is to examine our own past—what were we doing with writing at age 3, 5, 8, etc. I tried to remember what helped or hindered my own learning to write.

My conclusion was that I shouldn't be just an evaluator. I began to see that my role was to generate and maintain a flow. I wanted to get the children to enjoy writing, to do it willingly. I wanted to make writing in my classroom a pleasurable activity. I also saw that I could introduce skills as the children developed a need for them in relation to what they wanted to say.

FRAN: When Lynne approached me about becoming involved in the group I told her, "I don't teach English. We group in the fifth grade and Mrs. Cash does the English. I do the social studies. Since you learn the rules in English and that's where composition should take place, I don't think I would have much to offer a group like this."

But Lynne insisted she wanted me to be involved, so I agreed to give it a try.

As we started meeting and reading and talking, I kept trying to find a half hour period where we did just writing. But I didn't have any extra time for composition. One day after school I went by to talk with Lynne. I came away with a whole new idea. I didn't have to do writing separately. I could just incorporate it as part of social studies, science, and health—in all the subjects I taught.

For example, in science, we've used writing as a means of learning and reviewing material. I've had students write down just one thing they remembered from a chapter. We talked about all they had written—as our review. Then I had them write everything they remembered in the chapter, and they got into groups of four or five to talk about what they had written. In looking at test scores compared to previous years— I think this method has been very successful.

I used to think that if the children wrote something, I had to read it; I had to grade it. I had to get my red pen and circle everything that was wrong and give it back and that was it. Now I see that if writing is the means by which kids learn, it doesn't have to be graded because the learning is what it's all about.

TERESA: As a result of the journal entries I've made this year, I've discovered a lot about my students. I would put down a couple of words or phrases while I was working with the students and then go back later to write in more detail what had gone on during the writing session. I kept notes on problems and questions the students were having individually and as a class. By recording those bits, I can identify where they need extra work. I've also discovered that worthwhile writing can be done in ten- or fifteen-minute periods of time—that we don't always have to have long blocks of time for writing.

The journal also gives me a way to see where I've had misperceptions. One time I introduced what I thought was an interesting writing activity, but the students didn't respond. I wrote "Total flop" in my journal. Later, I read that entry and realized that we had needed more discussion before we wrote. We discussed it, and it became one of our best activities of the year. Without the journal, it would never have happened.

My journal writing needs improvement, but it has been invaluable as a way for me to become both a participant and an observer in my classroom. Sometimes when the kids see me jotting things down, they ask, "What are you writing?" I tell them I'm writing about what we are doing in class. Sometimes they ask me to write what they're writing and when I do, I share my writing with them.

LYNNE: So the students are seeing you as a writer also. That's important.

JANE: In the fall, when we began doing interesting things with writing, I didn't say, "You have to write." One of the first times I got excited about seeing a child who didn't like to write show interest happened when we were taping stories we'd written. We were listening for pauses as we played them back to see what the punctuation should be. One little boy who'd said he didn't want to do it came up and started poking at me. I said, "I told you you didn't have to do this; go on."

He said, "But I have to ask you something."

And I said, "I'm sorry but you aren't part of this group. You didn't want to be in it."

He said, "But all I want is a piece of paper. I want to write, too."

We also had sessions where we put one child's paper on the opaque projector and talked about editing—and later revising.

But through all of the fun activities, I was having one serious problem. I wanted to keep the children's papers. At the end of each week, I was running in to make copies of stacks of papers. Teresa was having the same kind of management of data problem. Lynne suggested that we buy individual hardbacked composition books with research grant funds. As it turned out, the children thought they were real authors. They dated each entry, and I did not mark in their books. Instead, I used those sticky yellow note papers.

One child said, "You know, we had better be careful what we put in here because we might keep these and our children might read them someday. We don't want them to think we weren't very good students."

I also want to talk about audience. I found that the children liked to write letters to people we might get to respond to us. We wrote to everyone who came to the room to talk with us: a former student of mine who is in the service, a geologist from the college, the people who performed the play *Dandelion* here. We also responded every week to the "Mini-forum" (Roanoke *Times-World News* children's page). At first the children weren't too sure, but once they began to see their own names and writing in there, they got more excited, and they brought copies in every Tuesday morning.

TERESA: I want to follow up with one thing about those composition books. We're now in the process of publishing a class book. Each student is choosing two selections from his own book to be put together and bound. Each child will get one to keep at the end of the year. The students are helping one another select and edit what goes in. And I have three of the better students who are helping edit in groups. We have increased our interaction all year. The peer response groups for editing have been valuable because the children share with one another, they learn from one another, and they have respect for one another's writing. They've learned to question one another: "Did you need a capital letter here?" and "Don't you need to add something to this?" or "Did you punctuate correctly?" They also suggest topics for each other.

LYNNE: When you have students working in groups, doesn't the noise level get pretty high?

TERESA: They are noisier, but I find that most of them stay on task with what's going on, and I'm always walking around having short conferences with them—one or two minutes each. Sometimes one will tell me, "I think you need to look at so-and-so's book."

FRAN: This is what we've come to call "messy learning." Lots of what I have done in working writing into the various subjects has been done in small groups. The noise level is higher, but they're learning. The structure is there. They know what they're supposed to be doing and they do it.

If there was any doubt in my mind, it disappeared when one of my students I had identified as a slow learner came up to my desk after one of our small group reviews in science and said, "Mrs. Williams, you know it really does make more sense when you write it down and then talk to somebody about it."

We went on sharing other anecdotes and findings. When we finished, the assistant principal made my final point for me. She said, "Lynne, I wrote something a while ago in my notes. Excellent inservice—and we didn't have to go elsewhere to find the experts."

References

Atwell, N. (1982, January). Class-based writing research: Teachers learn from students. *English Journal.*

Berthoff, A. E. (1981). The teacher as REsearcher. In *The making of meaning.* Montclair, NJ: Boynton/Cook.

Brannon, L., & Knoblauch, C. (1982, May). Students' rights to their own texts. *College Composition and Communication.*

Britton, J. (1970). *Language and learning.* Harmondsworth: Penguin.

Britton, J. (1978). The composing process and the functions of writing. In C. Cooper and L. Odell (Eds.), *Research on composing* (pp. 13–22). Urbana, IL: National Council of Teachers of English.

Britton, J. (1983, April). A quiet form of research. *English Journal.*

Bruner, J. (1966). *Toward a theory of instruction.* Cambridge, MA: Harvard University Press.

Buscaglia, L. (1972). *Love.* New York: Fawcett Crest.

Calkins, L. M. (1983). *Lessons from a child: On the teaching and learning of writing.* Exeter, NH: Heinemann.

Dixon, J. (1975). *Growth through English: Report of the Dartmouth seminar, in the perspective of the seventies.* New York: Oxford University Press for NATE.

Elbow, P. (1973). *Writing without teachers.* New York: Oxford University Press.

Heath, S. B. (1982). What no bedtime story means. In *Language in society.* Cambridge, England: Cambridge University Press.

Heath, S. B. (1983). *Ways with words: Language, life, and work in communities and classrooms.* Cambridge, England: Cambridge University Press.

Kress, G. (1982). *Learning to write.* London: Routledge and Kegan Paul.

Macrorie, K. (1984). *Writing to be read* (3rd ed.). Upper Montclair, NJ: Boynton/Cook.

Martin, N. (1975). Subject English. In *The Martin report on the state of English teaching in Western Australia.*

Martin, N. (1983). Genuine communications: The enfranchisement of young writers. In *Mostly about writing.* Upper Montclair, NJ: Boynton/Cook.

Medway, P. (1980). The Bible and the vernacular: The significance of language across the curriculum. *English Education 14*(3).

Medway, P. (1980). *Finding a language: Autonomy and learning in school.* London: Writers and Readers Publishing Cooperative.

Wells, G. (1982). *Language, learning and education.* University of Bristol, Center for the Study of Language and Communication.

PART THREE

Planning
Classroom Research

Interview with Patricia Reed

NANCY MARTIN: Pat, I'd like you to say something about what happens to you and to your class when you do classroom research.

PAT REED: OK. It makes me a lot more alert as to what's really going on. I think I'm always fairly alert, but I think it especially makes me aware of what's not working well in the classroom, and the minute I find out, I sort of drop whatever my research proposal says I'm going to do and I concentrate on trying to do something to change that situation.

MARTIN: So you have a plan, a question or questions that you want to explore?

REED: Yes. I was interested in students' attitudes toward their past writing. How from the present they view what they did last year or the year before that. I had them look at their writings from past years and then from that begin to find some attitudes that were very much hurting the way they were presently writing, and I tried to work on changing them.

MARTIN: Does it have any noticeable effect on your students?

REED: I tell them at the beginning of the year a little bit about what I'm interested in looking at, and then I don't mention it the rest of the year. The effect is indirect in that I do so much more to tune in to what exactly they're thinking about.

MARTIN: Do you want to take it any further in any way?

REED: What I found was that gender difference will affect writing. And that's a very scary topic to me. I think it was scary because I was thinking about it in a psychological, analytical way. Then, in a small group meeting of teacher-researchers at Bread Loaf, someone said to me, "Don't do that. Just describe what you see. Don't comment on it and analyze it; describe what's happening." When I did my brief research report this summer, I tried to do that—describe what I saw—and that works fairly well. I don't feel I'm doing something that I haven't the knowledge to do. If I describe what I see going on without being judgmental, then that seems to work. It's like Michael Armstrong's *Closely Observed Children*—recording observations, and that seems to work really well. It doesn't scare me; I'm not afraid to put what I find down on paper.

This year I got into what my students thought writers were. I just asked them to tell me what a writer is, and I was astounded by the misconceptions they had. I would like to pursue that topic somewhat to see generally what the image in a lot of students' minds is about writers and writing because that affects their reading of literature and their own writing.

MARTIN: At the moment, then, you're holding back. In the end, do you want to be able to either comment or act on what you've found?

REED: Well, in a way I have commented in that I have talked before groups in my own area about what I've been finding. It never crossed my mind that gender would affect students' attitudes towards writing. Especially, I never thought that a girl being a girl would affect how she feels about what she does right and what she does wrong in her writing. I feel I've already had an effect. In my classes here at Bread Loaf, men have come up and said, "Thank you! I never even thought about it."

MARTIN: So you're letting the information make its own mark?

REED: Yes. I can go beyond my classroom without thinking about and treating people like specimens under a microscope. There's a difference between what I thought research was and what I came to know my research was. It's exploring how to help everybody.

Planning Classroom Research

LEE ODELL
Rensselaer Polytechnic Institute

Although classroom research is a natural outgrowth of teaching—should, in fact, be an inseparable element of our business—it seldom figures in undergrad or graduate education courses. Thus, those of us who enter into it most often do so with little formal guidance (or, even worse, persuaded that any inquiry must meet exacting empirical standards). In other words, it remains easy to become lost or overwhelmed—to wonder if and how our study has concluded, and what its actual outcomes are.

Here, Lee Odell, well known for his contributions to research in our field, offers ways to help teachers become researchers. For Odell, "the process of exploration and discovery arises from a sense of dissonance or conflict or uncertainty." While nearly any ventured exploration is better than teaching to unexamined assumptions—ever a source of dissonance—Odell shows us how best to question these assumptions, to structure our research, and to measure its outcomes. The end of classroom research is not data-gathering, despite its requisite formalities; it is, in Odell's words, "continual redefinition and renewal."

The purpose of this essay is to help classroom teachers function as researchers. Consequently, most of it will consist of suggestions for planning research and analyzing data. But these suggestions rest on three assumptions which need to be made explicit at the outset.

The first assumption is that all researchers must be able to (1) formulate and reformulate the questions that will guide their research; and (2) describe carefully the data they have collected. This assumption is particularly important since the process of asking questions and describing data is compatible with the normal demands of teaching. Consequently, the research described will involve teachers in doing what they have to do anyway—paying careful attention to what is going on in their classrooms.

The second assumption is that research is an ongoing process of discovery—a process that continually requires us to rethink not only our understanding of our discipline, but also our sense of the questions we should be asking and of the best procedures to analyze our own and our students' work. Consequently, there is a sense in which research is never finished. As we learn new ways of describing what is going on in our classrooms, we see new questions that need to be answered; as we answer those questions we see other questions that didn't exist until we had answered the previous ones. Exploration leads to still further exploration, discovery to still further discovery.

The final assumption is that most researchers will not function well if they do all their work in isolation. At the very least, a researcher needs someone who can respond sympathetically to both the joys and the frustrations that are part of any research project. More important, researchers need colleagues who can listen critically to the researcher's inspirations and tentative hypotheses, people who can play devil's advocate when a researcher's enthusiasm begins to run rampant or who can see unexpected possibilities in data that leave the researcher confused or disappointed. And there will be times when any researcher needs the counsel of someone more experienced or more knowledgeable (Perl and Wilson, 1986).

Beginning and Directing Our Own Research
Formulating Research Questions

The process of exploration and discovery arises from a sense of dissonance or conflict or uncertainty. Something isn't quite clear to us; something just doesn't add up. A sense of conflict can arise from various sources. For example, it may arise from students' performance. Maybe the reading or writing of one group differs greatly from the reading or writing of another ostensibly similar group of students. Or perhaps the work of a single student (or group of students) varies widely and inexplicably from one occasion to the next. Conflict may also arise when theory or expectations seem inconsistent with our sense of the reality of our own classrooms. Perhaps someone else's notion of what can or should go on in a classroom is incompatible with our knowledge of what actually occurs. Or it may be that our expectations aren't consistent with students' performance. For example, we may find that, after we have invested a great deal of time and effort in planning a series of lessons, students have improved less than we had thought they should. Or it may be that a particular unit of study was far more successful than we had anticipated. And, finally, a sense of conflict may arise because we realize that apparently reasonable theories are inconsistent with each other.

Being aware of conflict, of course, is not enough. To do research, we have to use this dissonance to formulate a research question which will guide our efforts to gather and analyze information. No one can predict exactly when or how we will arrive at the final version of a research question. Sometimes we know from the very outset exactly what question we want to answer. But, at least in my experience, this is fairly unlikely. There is a much greater chance that we will muddle about a good bit, examining and thinking about our data, posing possible questions, discarding or revising them when we realize that they don't quite work. And when we have our question well worked out, we may realize that we have to go back and gather more or new kinds of data. In short, research questions usually arise from a complex reciprocal process in which the collection and analysis of data may lead to a revised question, and that question may lead to more data gathering, which, in turn may require further revision of the question.

At times, this process of formulating a research question will seem totally mysterious and needlessly frustrating. In fact, it is neither. A well-stated research question is essential to our work. It will help us see more clearly what we need to do, and it will enable us to determine when we have done it. In some types of research, we need to have the research question carefully formulated before we begin our study. In other instances, it may be necessary to allow the research question to emerge as we conduct the study. (For further discussion, see pages 132–135.) But, in any event, a carefully constructed, well-defined research question is essential. Moreover, it's important that the question be *ours*; for it is unlikely that we can work effectively or enthusiastically with a question that someone else has formulated.

Although no one can say exactly what to do in order to guarantee the formulation of a good research question, we can take steps to increase our chances of asking a useful one. Since the question-formulating process is so complex and so essential to good research, I want to examine it in some detail, trying to illustrate that process and to suggest things we can do as we try to formulate. The basis for this illustration will be three pieces of student writing, answers to an in-class essay exam. The students, tenth-graders, had been studying parliamentary procedure. As one part of the exam, the teacher had written the claim, "Rule by the majority is not always best," and had asked students to explain why they agreed or disagreed.

> I agree because not always is majority vote best. Look at our 13 colonies that started from minority.
>
> Damon

> The majority is quite often wrong. Because the majority has more than 1/2 the people for them, they rule. Say out of 100 people 51 are for air pollution and 49 are against. So the air is polluted heavily and the 49 who voted against have to suffer because two more people wanted air pollution. This is an exaggeration; but it does prove majority rule is not always best.
>
> Twig

> (a) I think the majoritty should rule but the rights of the mainority should be protected no matter what happens.
> (b) The majortty rules, but the minority should have there say about the motion.
> (c) Also the rule by the majorty is best because that's what more pepol want, but you should protecte the minorty again.
>
> Larry

I showed these answers to teachers at several different grade levels and asked them to raise as many questions as possible. As I read and reread these lists of questions, it occurred to me that they fell into groups; certain motifs or themes recurred:

Questions about instruction:
- How can these students be directed back to their answer so that they might learn how much material (or what kind) is necessary to back up a statement like I agree/disagree?
- How can students be taught to give reasons that support a stated claim? How is that logic developed?
- How can I get Damon to understand that his first sentence doesn't stand as a complete answer, that it simply contains his belief in both clauses?

Questions about students' perceptions of their task:
- What do students think the teacher expects for the answer?
- Do students understand the term *essay*?

- Did the students have an audience in mind? Did they imagine anyone reading this? What characteristics did the students imagine the reader having?

Questions about student performance:
- How do students express agreement/disagreement in other writings? In work for other teachers? In discussion?
- Why are the answers so brief?

Questions about teachers' values:
- Is spelling an important factor in student essays?
- How will teachers grade the answers?

Questions about the context in which the writing was done:
- Why are students being asked this?
- What sort of learning does the teacher want this exercise to stimulate?
- Is Larry's use of a.b.c., a result of his being previously taught to outline answers?
- How much time did students spend thinking? Did students who spent more time thinking write long essays?

These groups of questions help to model some of the general procedures I mentioned a few paragraphs earlier.

We need to begin with the widest possible range of questions and then look for recurring themes. Our interests as teachers may lead us to focus exclusively on questions about instruction. Indeed, in an earlier article (Odell, 1976), I equated classroom research with research on the effects of instruction. It is, of course, entirely reasonable to do this sort of research. But we needn't assume that it is the only kind of research we can or should do. As the groupings indicate, there are several different types of questions we might want to pursue.

We need to examine the assumptions underlying our questions. Consider, for example, those in the question, "How can I get Damon to understand that his first sentence doesn't stand as a complete answer, that it simply contains his belief in both clauses?" This question assumes that we ought to be focusing all our attention on Damon. Moreover, it assumes that our main interest is in getting him to remedy a mistake he has already made. Both of these assumptions are troublesome, especially if we are interested in instructional research. For other types of research (see lists of questions on pp. 143–144, 147, 151, 156), we might want to focus on one student or on a small group. However, instructional research is likely to focus on improving the work of large groups of students. Furthermore, our concern is not with correcting past performance but with influencing what students do in the future.

Another problematic assumption is contained in the question, "How can students be taught to give reasons that support a stated claim?" This avoids the two difficulties of the previous question: it applies to more than one student and it emphasizes future performance rather than past. However, it does make new assumptions: that we understand what types of reasons or persuasive strategies students currently use, as well as the range of strategies that they might learn to use. If this assumption is valid, we can go ahead with planning instruction. But if it isn't, we should probably change our research emphasis. Instead of doing research on instruction, we need to examine the performance of student (and perhaps professional) writers. We need to change our question to one such as: When students attempt to assert agreement or disagreement, how do they go about it? What strategies do they presently use? This will help me illustrate a third step in formulating a research question.

We need to reformulate our research questions until they give us as much guidance as possible. More specifically, we need to try to specify what we will be doing, what students will be doing, and what context the action will take place in. For example, if we want to define the phrase *assert disagreement,* we'll need to think about what people do when they express disagreement. Consider, for instance, the last time you disagreed with another's point of view. How did you try to make your case? Did you offer counter-evidence? look for inconsistencies in the opposing statement? point out its flawed consequences? use still other strategies? As we draw on our own experience to identify some of the strategies people use in expressing disagreement, we get a better sense of what we want students to do.

In addition, we also need to decide exactly what our role as teachers wll be. Will we be the person who makes the statement the students are to disagree with? If so, will we actively challenge the student's comments? And, if so, what strategies will we use? Will we, for example, argue by carrying students' comments to logical absurdity? Will we play devil's advocate? Finally, we need to consider the context in which the argument takes place. Will it be in a class discussion, in response to a statement we make? In a class discussion (or perhaps a formal debate) in response to comments other students make? In a small group which has the task of, say, reaching a consensus on a problematic issue?

This process of making questions operational may be one of the most difficult aspects of our work. Certainly it will require that we formulate and reformulate our ideas. Assume, for example, that we tentatively define "assert disagreement" as "noting inconsistencies in an opponent's statement." As we read student essays, we may realize that students are using other strategies and that we want to expand our definition so that it includes these strategies. However, as we make the question operational, we improve our ability to gather and analyze data. Once we know what we mean by the phrase, "assert disagreement," we know what we need to look for when we analyze student talk or writing. Depending on the final form of our definition, we know that we should look for statements in which, say, students refer to authority or note inconsistencies in an opponent's argument. And, once we determine where the argument will take place and what our role will be, we get a better sense of what data we need to gather and of what we need to do in order to enable students to provide us with this data. (For a detailed explanation of this point, see Odell, 1976.)

Having defined important terms in the question, we need to consider one further issue: *A "No" answer must be as significant as a "Yes" answer.* Perhaps because we are teachers, because we want to believe that schooling has a positive effect, we tend to think that successful research questions must be answered affirmatively. Thus, we sometimes ask questions for which the only good answer is a "Yes." For example, in responding to the essays on rule by the majority, one teacher asked: "How much time did students spend thinking about their essays? Did students who spent more time thinking write longer essays?"

If the answer to the latter part of the question is "yes," the teacher might think he should be pleased; he would have confirmed his original hunch and could begin to define an instructional strategy: have students spend more time thinking about what they write. But if the answer is "no," the teacher is stuck. The hunch is not confirmed and he has allowed himself no subsequent direction. Even if the answer is "yes," there is still a problem. The significance of the amount of time spent thinking is reasonably disputable. As a teacher, I know that it isn't as important as what students do during the time available. Further, as a researcher, I know of no theoretical or empirical basis for assuming that length of time spent thinking is necessarily reflected in the length of writing that is produced. From my perspective as a teacher and researcher, a "yes" answer would produce only the response, "So what?"

To preclude this sort of response, it is necessary to locate any given study in a larger context. Perhaps we can show how the study helps solve a pedagogical problem that other teachers are concerned about. Perhaps it confirms or calls into question the results of other studies. Or perhaps it gives us some new insight into the theory that underlies our teaching or our conception of, say, good writing. In any case, researchers always need to relate their investigations to issues that go well beyond a specific bit of data. For further information about this point, a discussion of theoretical perspectives that might inform an analysis of various facets of writing is given by Myers (1985). Also, see the theoretical perspectives discussed by Cooper (1985).

To illustrate this point, let's consider the original question about the relation between time spent thinking and length of writing. In the other questions posed by this teacher, there were two recurring themes: an interest in student performance and an interest in the relation between writing and thinking. Since we have already identified some of the problematic assumptions underlying the original question, we can go on to try to reformulate, making it focus on the relationship between writing and thinking. To explore this relationship, we could reformulate his questions thus: What kinds of thinking are reflected in students' papers? Do some groups of papers (we could consider longer vs. shorter, but we also could consider better vs. poorer) reflect thinking that is different from other groups? More operationally, does one group use strategies (e.g., setting up hypothetical sequences, elaborating the consequences of a particular statement) that differ from the other group? If we find that there are no differences between the thinking in the better and poorer papers, we may have to go back and examine the assumptions that underlay our evaluation of the papers. If the answer is "yes," we may improve our understanding of what we need to teach students who wrote the poorer papers. In either case, we have an answer to the question, "So what?" In the first case, the results lead us to reconsider some of our basic assumptions about writing; in this case, our assumptions about "good" writing. In the latter case, we have learned something that will help us improve our teaching.

Choosing an Appropriate Research Methodology

Near the beginning of this essay, I mentioned that most researchers will occasionally need to consult with more knowledgeable, experienced colleagues. This is particularly important when one is trying to choose a research methodology. It is possible to find descriptions of experimental designs (Campbell and Stanley, 1966), survey research (Anderson, 1985), or ethnographic research (Doheny-Farina and Odell, 1985). But there is a good chance that simply reading about various research methodologies won't be enough. Such readings will probably have to be supplemented by frequent conversations with someone who understands both research methodology and the goals of a specific research study.

In preparation for these conversations, it might be useful to be familiar with some distinctions mentioned by Miles Myers (1985). Myers identifies three types of research: *rationalist, positivist,* and *contextualist.* Myers' terms are not as widely used as, say, *qualitative research* and *quantitative research*; yet his terms suggest distinctions that are important for the purposes of this chapter.

For many people, elements of the positivist design are considered to be synonymous with *research,* the assumption being that research must entail a comparison of the performance of experimental and control groups and that the results must be subjected to a statistical analysis to determine whether or not they are reliable and significant. In both rationalist and contextualist research designs, a researcher's claims are not based on a statistical analysis of the performance of control groups and experimental groups. Rather, as Myers points out, researchers using these designs examine "contrasting pieces of data and [use] the logic of reason and the insight of intuition to make claims about the significance, reliability, and validity of a hypothesis" (p. 15). The contextualist design is further distinguished from the positivist in that the former doesn't rely on specially designed experimental tasks, but rather examines behavior (reading, writing, discussion) in the contexts where it routinely occurs. In addition, Myers explains, contextualist research differs from rationalist research in that the latter is particularly well suited to the examination of completed products, whereas the contextualist approach is particularly well suited for examining the dynamics of a process which is repeated over time. Finally, to add to Myers' explanation, contextual research is concerned with interrelations between behavior and the context(s) in which it occurs. For example, a contextual study of classroom discussion would seek to determine how that discussion shapes and is shaped by the attitudes and practices that characterize the classroom in which the discussion takes place.

In the discussion of research on composition (see pages 145–151), I'll suggest a procedure (the use of pre- and post-tests) that is usually identified with positivist research design. More typically, however, I've tried to emphasize research questions that are compatible with the rationalist or the contextualist approach.

Areas for Research

The remainder of this essay identifies three likely areas for research. For each, I'll suggest some research questions and also demonstrate or give references to procedures for analyzing data. Most of these discussions of research questions and procedures will examine the talk or the writing of students. However, the close examination of classroom talk and writing isn't enough. Ultimately, we must recognize that we are part of a professional community, and our research will reflect our awareness of that community.

This awareness of a professional community doesn't mean that we should feel obliged to go public with our research. It can, of course, be rewarding to write articles, make talks at professional meetings, or conduct in-service meetings for colleagues. Indeed, in at least one school district, a large part of the district's in-service program consists of workshops in which teacher-researchers describe specific teaching procedures and present their assessment of them. However, it can be equally rewarding to do research simply because it satisfies our own curiosity about what is happening in our classrooms or it lets us to a better job of working with a particular group of students. But, in either case, we have to remember that it's very likely that others have thought about some of the same issues we are concerned with. Whether or not we accept them, these ideas can provide useful reference points as we try to understand what is going on in our own classrooms. Thus, I'll frequently refer to current work in our profession—pedagogy, theory, and research—which can and should inform the expectations we bring to bear on our individual classes.

In identifying possible areas for research and in suggesting research questions and procedures, I mean to be illustrative rather than definitive. (Because it's impossible to discuss all possible areas of research, I have left out such important topics as teacher-student conferencing. For an excellent introduction, see Freedman and Katz (in press). For other possible research topics, consult the semiannual bibliography in *Research in the Teaching of English*.) Ultimately, the best research question is one that arises from an area in which we are interested and with which we have experience; the best analytic procedures are those that we modify or invent to answer our own questions. I hope that the following sections may provide some useful starting points for classroom research.

Reading/Literary Study

For all practical purposes, we tend to treat reading and the study of literature as two entirely separate disciplines. Those who are trained in one area may know relatively little about the other. And the content of a course in reading is likely to be quite different from that of a course in literature. Although some of these differences will (and maybe should) continue to exist, recent work in reading and in literary criticism identifies at least one important assumption both disciplines can share, an assumption that can enable classroom teachers to investigate students' ability to read any sort of text, literary or otherwise. The assumption is this: reading is not simply a process in which a reader derives meaning from a text by decoding the text or observing its formal properties (e.g., rhyme, metaphor, plot). Rather it is an active process in which readers bring to bear their values, prior experiences, and expectations in creating the meaning of the text. Some theorists go so far as to pay almost no attention to the text itself, arguing that what is important are the associations a reader brings to the text (see Petrosky, 1982; Bleich, 1978). Other scholars see reading, to use Louise Rosenblatt's term (1978, 1985), as a *transaction,* a process in which one's values, knowledge, etc., influence the reader's attention to specific parts of a text, and the text, in turn, has some influence on the reader's knowledge and values.

If we see reading as an active attempt to create meaning rather than a realtively passive attempt to discover meaning that exists within a text, we can make one further assumption that will help us as teachers and researchers: The process of reading, that is, of creating meaning, isn't limited to those times when readers are actually decoding a printed text. Rather the act of reading goes on each time readers try to articulate their reactions to, perceptions of, or understanding of a text. Thus, if we want to learn something about our students' reading, we can examine what students say or write about the materials they have read. In the next several pages I'll illustrate one procedure for analyzing students' comments about what they have read. (For other analytic procedures, see Cooper, 1985; Purves, 1973; Odell and Cooper, 1977.) Put simply, the procedure requires that we examine students' spoken or written comments with this question in mind: "What questions are answered in the students' comments?"

To illustrate this procedure, I want to consider seven short pieces of writing done by eighth-graders. Each is a journal entry prompted solely by the instruction that the students were to spend four 20-minute periods each week writing about whatever they were reading. To make comparisons easier, I'll examine journal entries written by seven students who were reading the novel *Roll of Thunder Hear My Cry.*

The first three entries are in some ways quite similar; all discuss plot and character, making no attempt to talk about the theme of the book or about the way the book affected the reader's thoughts or feelings.

[Student 1]

This Book has started to tell the story of a Mississippi family and their problems and how they struggle to keep their land every year from the state and taxes.

In the first part of this book it talked about the problems the Logan children had in school and on their way to school. It also tells about some miner characters and some of the problems they face. One thing the author describes pretty thoroughly in the chapter is How the father gets laid off then goes to St. Louis to find work to save the land so they could save the land so they so they wouldn't have to sharecrop.

Some of the characters are Cassie Logan who is telling the story only Logan daughter, she is in the 4th grade.

Little Man Cassie's youngest brother he is just starting school tries to keep neat and clean all the time, when he finds out what the white people call him and that they are giving the books only

[Student 2]

Roll of thunder her my cry. Im going to write what happens at the end of the book. T. J. came over to get Stacey to help him get home because the Averys bet him up. Stacey had to no why so T. J. told him it was because he was going to tell him they were beating up on some people. So Stacey took him home and on his way back he saw headlights so he ducked in the bushes. A bunch of pople pulled up to the Averys and started beating on them Cassie ran home and told her parents his father and Mr Morrison left Then Cassie went out side and saw a fire so Mary and Big Ma ran to fight it. When they were finished Stacey told Cassie that every one was there. And that David might have started it.

[Student 3]

As I read on most of my questions have been answered. I just got done with Chapter 6 and I want to know how are the Logans going to pay for waveing back. I wonder if they are going to get burned or the house will be burned? This weekend is gonna be alazy one I know it. I will probably draw, read, watch T.V. But mostly draw its a way that I can settle down and relax. I love art and I think I may take an art course in college. I'm defenatly gonna in high school.

Despite their similarities, these three statements reflect different concerns; each student seems to be asking somewhat different questions. The first appears to have asked: What is this book about? What important problems do the characters encounter? Who are some of the principal characters and what are their distinguishing characteristics? The second student focuses her concerns much more narrowly ("I'm going to write about what happened at the end of the book") and answers these questions: What happened in this episode? Who did what? Why did the characters act as they did? More specifically: What does the text say about why the characters acted as they did? Student 3 is also concerned with the text's narrative, but her comment seems somewhat more assertive than does the second student's. Instead of passively following the text, she asks whether, at a particular point in the narrative, the novel has left questions unanswered.

Student 4's response is quite different from the first three:

[Student 4]

One of the main points this book seems to point out is the Black segregation still in this area of mississippi even after the the civil war was over and slaves—black people were free. It seems some of the people like the Wallaces didn't like it when the north won and to try to prove their anger took it out on black people and their families.

Besides the Wallaces through Harlan Granger another white per son in the country seemed to have distaste for the war after it was over and seemed to irrelivate his anger by trying to live in the past and trying to do what his ancestors had done in controlling the town and having people take their problems to them and have them solve them. But Harlan Granger's problem is he still wants the Logan land that used to be Granger land even if he has to have people burned or murdered to get it.

More segregation comes from the economy. The Wallaces, the sharecropperss landowners make them pay 50 or 60 percent of what they make so there is just enough left to pay the store bill and they can't put a down payment on land and move away. The last weapon of segrgation would probably be trying to poison the minds of the black children with alcohol, drugs and "candy" so they will be in the palms of their hands and do anything they want them to do.

This student has considered not just characters' actions but also their feelings, values, and motives. Moreover, he has answered this question: How can I classify characters' actions? Do the same kinds of things happen again and again? What prompts people's behavior? Do these recurring actions and motivations add up to some central point? In short, this student is not just summarizing the book; he is interpreting it, trying to decide upon its meaning. Student 5 takes a much more personal approach:

[Student 5]

I'm on chapter 9 now and I think the book is getting better.
T. J. gets me so mad. I can't believe he talked Stacey into giving him Stacey's coat. Sometimes I wish Stacey would beat him
up. I like Little Man but sometimes I feel sorry for him. I don't
under stand why Cassie is treating Lillian Jean like that. If I
where her I would just ignore her.

In this brief journal entry, the student talks about her personal
reactions to the book (it "is getting better") and to the characters
T. J. and Little Man. At one point she mentions a character's action
that underlies her reaction. Finally, she at least raises a question
about motivation ("why Cassie is treating Lillian Jean like that") and
concludes by saying how she would react if she were in a character's
position.

As did Student 5, Student 6 gives her personal reactions to aspects of the novel but goes well beyond that:

[Student 6]

Since I said in a previous journal entry that I was going to develop the characters, I might as well. Cassie, is the "teller" of
the story. She is a member of the Logan family, and they are
black. Cassie, is the only female child in the family. She is in
the fourth grade at school. Cassie is a "stubborn" type of person, as you will find out. If there is one thing that Cassie can't
stand, it's being discriminated against because she's black. As I
said before, I don't blame her. Who really cares what color ones
skin is anyways, back to the book. Cassie had three brothers.
Stacey is the oldest Logan child. He is around thirteen, and in
the seventh grade. He has his "mama" for his teacher. Stacey
is a responsible child, and although he doesn't like being discriminated against, he can better handle it than Cassie. He is
also honest, unlike his best friend T. J. Avery he doesn't cheat.
More than once, Stacey has been punished instead of T. J. Because while trying to straighten T. J. out, he was caught with
the "cheat notes". Needless to say T. J. Avery is an irresponsi-
ble child. Back to the Logan family. There are now two Logan
children left, Little Man and Christopher-John. First, Little-
Man. Little-Mans real name is Clayton Chester. He hates that
name, and he is rarely called it. Only occasionally when he is
in trouble. Little Man is the youngest child, he is in first grade.
He is a very clean person. He is to young yet, to clearly understand why the whites treat him as they do. Christopher-John
is basically a cheery person. He gets out of his "bad moods"

easily. He's either in second or third grade. Now, to mama, also known as "Miz Logan." She is the seventh grade teacher at the black school. She is a woman who stands up for what she believes in. She is kind gentle, kind, yet firm. She must be, because at this point in the story, her husband David is away at his job, working on building a railroad.

This student is the only one who gives herself directions and follows them. She had concluded the previous journal entry with this statement: "I will develop the characters more in my next journal" (the entry printed above). In "developing" the characters, this student identifies the character traits that make each character stand out: Cassie is "stubborn" and bitterly resents discrimination; Stacey is gentle, and he is better able to handle discrimination than is Cassie; Christopher-John is "basically a cheery person"; and so on. Further, she mentions the characters' attitudes: like Cassie, Stacey resents discrimination; Little Man "hates" his real name. And the student suggests the circumstances that seem to prompt a character's trait; Miz Logan is "gentle, kind, yet firm" because, at the point in the story, she has sole responsibility for raising the children.

Like Student 6, the next student occasionally gives himself directions. However, those directions produce results that are quite different from and in some ways more interesting than what we find in the other students' journal entries.

[Student 7]

Roll of Thunder, Hear my Cry is an awsomely boring book. It is so boring and dumb that it is a shame to waste lead and paper writing about it. No. Seriously, it is pretty boring but it's ok, but you see I am used to the books that teachers give us being exceptionally good, and this deffinately isn't exceptional in any way. Of course you know what the book is about and I hope you don't think that I would lie to you about reading it so, I don't think I'll write any summaries of parts of the book. Really their isn't much else I can write about it for four journals so what the hell, I guess I will write summaries. First lets start with T. J. I think well I don't know, theres something wrong with him. First of all I would think that it would be degrading for white people to go around with black people at that time, when T. J. was hanging around with the Simmes. And I thought that the only people T. J. could be friends with are the ones that he could tease. But I guess he could be friends with the Simmes because they gave him everything he wanted, and I don't see why they would do that anyway. And I would think that they would have other friends they're own color and their

142

own age. Cassie though I don't know why she was the one whom the author told the story from. She didn't do anything of importance. And she seemed to be everywhere that the action was except for a couple of times. I think that the book should had been written from Stacey's point of view.

On the face of it, this would seem to be some of the worst writing in our sample of seven journal entries. There are frequent mistakes in spelling, syntax, and punctuation. And the student frequently changes his mind and ignores the directions he gives himself; he never does carry out his plan simply to "write summaries." But to be fair to the student, we have to remember that this is a journal entry, not a formal essay. Although the teacher was not eager for students to make so many mechanical errors, she had told the students that for this type of writing, she wasn't concerned with editing. And she had emphasized that students were to use the journals to explore their ideas, reactions, and responses. Given this instruction, the student does some very interesting things. He identifies aspects of the book that bother him ("there's something wrong with [T.J.] ") and tries to identify what causes him to feel bothered. He makes assertions ("I thought the only people T. J. could be friends with are the ones he could tease") and then in the next sentence acknowledges an exception to his assertion. And he questions the author's decision to tell the story from Cassie's point of view.

As the last student makes clear, these journal entries are not intended to be finished pieces of formal expository writing. Yet these brief analyses of journal entries indicate some of the very diverse questions students appear to have considered:

- What is this book about?
- What major problems do the characters encounter?
- What does the text say about the reason characters act as they do?
- At a given point in the narrative, what questions are left in my mind?
- Are there any recurring patterns in the book?
- How can I categorize events or characters' feelings?
- Do these recurring patterns add up to a central point?
- What is my reaction to these characters?
- How might I have reacted if I were in a character's situation?
- What personality traits distinguish the characters from each other?
- How does a particular character feel about other characters or events?
- What bothers me or confuses me about the text?

• Are there any exceptions to the assertions I have made about the novel?

This list of questions doesn't describe every intellectual activity students engaged in while they were thinking about the book. Indeed, we might want to supplement this analysis by interviewing students about the works they are reading. But the questions identified above do have a heuristic value. They could help a reader begin thinking about the book and, insofar as they prompt further insight, they could help the student make meaning out of a novel. Assuming that we understand some of the questions these students have considered, we are ready to go on to consider various possibilities for research on the topic of reading/literary study.

One important area for research would be *student performance.* We might begin our research with such questions as those discussed below. In posing them I have relied in part on intuition and in part on my familiarity with recent work that suggests questions that can help writers with the process of discovery. (For discussions of this work, see Larson, 1968, or Odell, 1968). My assumption is that questions which guide this process for writers might also be useful for researchers. However, I reiterate my earlier caution that questions raised by someone else can, at best, serve only as a starting point for your own attempt to formulate a research question.

1. How do these students differ with respect to the questions they answer? How do they differ from other students in their own class or in other ostensibly comparable classes? How do these students' questions differ from what we value? For example, are they considering the type of questions we are trying to teacher them to consider?

2. Do these students ever vary the questions they consider? When they come to the end of a novel, do their journal entries contain answers to the same kinds of questions found in entries written while they were reading the early chapters? Do we find that during the course of a school year students begin to consider new kinds of questions?

3. Do we find that all students answer (or fail to answer) the same types of questions? Do students at one grade level consider issues that students at another grade level rarely or never consider?

4. How do these questions relate to the intellectual and social life of the classroom? How do the actions of teacher and students create an atmosphere that is (or isn't) conducive to the consideration of certain questions? How do patterns of classroom interaction stimulate (or inhibit) students' willingness to consider certain kinds of questions?

To answer these questions about students' performance we would need to (1) require students to keep folders of everything they write about the text they read, (2) employ a set of categories that will let us describe students' work fairly, and (3) record (perhaps in a journal) our own observations of how students interact with us and with each other. (For an introduction to procedures for recording observations, see Doheny-Farina and Odell, 1985, pp. 520–522.) For the sake of our sanity we'll also need to place some limits on our investigation, perhaps examining the works of a few students in great detail or studying only two or three aspects of an entire class's work.

These questions about student performance lead naturally to a research question about *instruction*: Does my class seem to have any effect on the way my students respond to a literary text? More specifically, we might ask: When students write in their journals, do we find that they are considering questions in more detail? Are they considering more kinds of questions? Are those questions the same ones I have emphasized in my teaching? To answer these questions, we proceed just as before. We'll need to collect a sample of students' journal entries, some from early in the year, and some from late in the year, and we will need to describe them carefully.

Assume, however, that we want to study students' perceptions of the work we have assigned. This may be an especially good idea when students are doing what may be an unfamiliar task, such as writing a journal entry. In this case, there are several procedures we might follow. For example, we might assign this:

> Assume that a new student has joined our class and has never done a journal entry before. Assume that this student doesn't understand exactly what he/she is supposed to do and asks you for help. Explain to this student exactly what he/she should do.

Or we might give the student several sample journal entries, each representing various levels of sophistication. As before, we might ask students to explain to a newcomer why one of these samples was better than others.

Composition

The past ten or fifteen years have seen an extraordinary amount of work in composition theory, pedagogy, and research. As a result, there are several assumptions which, if not universally accepted, are at least widely discussed and are good beginning points for research:

1. *Rhetorical context is important.* In order to write well, writers must have some understanding of the audience they are addressing, the purpose they wish to accomplish, and the voice or per-

sona they wish to project. Furthermore, this context may influence the way writers spend their time during the process of composing (Matsuhashi, 1981), and it may also—especially as writers mature—influence syntax, dictation, and even the type of arguments writers advance in support of their point of view (Rubin and Piche, 1979).

2. *Good writing in one context may be different from good writing in another.* We may argue that all writing will have certain very general qualities: it will not be unnecessarily difficult to read; it will be appropriate for its intended audience and purpose. But, of course, the specific qualities of language, syntax, evidence, and reasoning that are appropriate for one rhetorical context may be less appropriate for some other rhetorical context (see Lloyd-Jones, 1977).

3. *Errors may reflect a certain logic* that makes them understandable, if not acceptable in formal discourse. Some errors, of course, occur because of a momentary lapse of a proofreader's attention. But, as Mina Shaughnessy (1977) has pointed out, errors sometimes fall into patterns that can be the result of a writer's attempting to follow a rule that he or she doesn't quite understand or that is simply not appropriate.

4. *The writing is, to some extent, knowable and teachable.* No one would responsibly claim that we can understand all the intellectual activity that goes on when one writes. Nor should anyone assume that the composing process can be reduced to a neat set of rules which, if followed carefully, will inevitably produce effective writing. However, we do have ways to glimpse that process. And those glimpses tell us several things. First, the process can be one of formulating ideas, of creating meaning rather than simply transcribing ideas which already exist in one's mind. Further, this process may be recursive. Instead of following a neat progression from asserting a thesis to developing it and then revising and editing, writers may find that the process of looking for examples leads them to rethink their thesis; they may find that the process of revising and editing began well before they have a completed draft. Although it is complex and, in part, mysterious, important parts of the process are teachable. We can give students help with the process of discovery, either by teaching them a relatively unstructured discovery procedure such as "free writing" or a relatively structured procedure that entails using specific observational activities (cf. Hillocks, 1979) or asking certain questions (cf. Rabianski, 1979). We can also teach students specific strategies to revise their writing (Rawe, 1981).

If one attends enough professional meetings, and reads enough journal articles, many of the preceding statements sound like truisms.

Yet any of these can serve as the basis for research. Consider the following questions, which we might ask about any of the preceding assertions:

1. Is this assertion always valid? Under what circumstances and for what writers is this valid? When and for whom is it not valid? More specifically, is the principle justified by the actual practice of writers, especially writers whom we believe to be particularly skillful? If successful writers avoid following one of these principles, how are they able to do so?

2. How do writers (student or professional) perceive some of the principles referred to above? If, for example, we think rhetorical context is important, to what extent are our students aware of context? What do they understand context to be? Can they relate that context to their choices of language, syntax, organization, or content?

3. How are these principles manifested in the intellectual and social life of a particular classroom? For example, if a teacher is using peer response groups to help students with the composing process, we might ask such questions as: How do students perceive the function, goals, and value of these groups? How do students' perceptions relate to the way they behave in these groups? How do student writers assess the comments made by other members of their peer response groups?

4. If we accept these principles, is our teaching and evaluation consistent with them? If we don't, what assumptions are implicit (or explicit) in our teaching and evaluation? What basis do we have for those assumptions?

5. How can we use these principles to improve student writing? If we design teaching procedures based on these principles, how can we determine whether our efforts are paying off?

This last question is the one that lends itself most readily to a conventional research procedure—the use of pre- and post-tests and the use of an experimental group and a comparison group. The use of comparison groups entails problems that lie somewhat outside the province of many classroom teachers. Consequently I will be solely concerned with pre- and post-tests.

For purposes of illustration, let us assume we want to answer this question: How can I improve students' sensitivity to rhetorical context? To devise an appropriate pre- and post-test, we'll have to follow some of the procedures mentioned earlier.

For one thing, we'll have to make the question operational. That is, what do we hope students will do? What will we do? For example, consider some of the things students could do to show us they are sensitive to rhetorical context. They could:

- Describe their audience in some detail, noting relevant characteristics of the audience's values, interests and knowledge.
- Describe the purpose for their writing; explain how they want their reader to think/feel/act after reading their work. Or explain how the reader intends to use the text the student has written.
- Vary features of the text (word choice, sentence structure, arguments) according to the stipulated audience and purpose.
- Refer to a description of audience and purpose in justifying choices (of syntax, etc.) found in a text.

We must also decide exactly what to do to improve students' sensitivity to rhetorical context. For example, we might:

- Provide model essays in which a writer has effectively considered audience and purpose; we might analyze those models for students or we might teach them a procedure that would let them analyze those models.
- Provide models of ineffective writing and teach students how to recognize deficiencies and how to remedy them.
- Teach students how to work in peer editing groups, responding to each other as to how appropriate a given piece of writing is for its audience and purpose.

Our decisions here become the basis upon which we plan our teaching.

Once we have decided what we want students to do and how to plan the teaching, we must devise a pre- and post-test that are appropriate for the questions we ask and the teaching we do. For example, let's assume we are teaching students to vary word choice, syntax, and arguments to suit a particular audience. If we are to find out whether students can make those variations, both the pre-test and the post-test will have to include at least two writing tasks, each specifying a different audience. Insofar as possible, these tasks should be comparable in every respect except the one (in this case, the audience) we are concerned with. That is, it would be inadvisable to create some tasks that required students to draw upon their personal experience and others that required students to analyze a written passage. Further, it would be unfair to base some tasks on topics about which students have strong feelings and to base other tasks on topics about which students are neutral.

There is no way to guarantee that the tasks will be perfectly identical. But there are some precautions we can take: first, we can test the assignments by having them done by students who are not directly involved in our research. Do these students seem to do especially well on one assignment and less well on others? Second, we can analyze the assignments and perhaps do them ourselves, asking: Did one task require me to do something that the other task did not?

Once we have tested the writing assignments, we can take one further precaution. Assume that we have four tasks—A, B, C, and D. We would divide our students into two groups. Group 1 would do tasks A and B for the pre-test and C and D for the post-test. Group 2 would do tasks C and D for the pre-test and A and B for the post-test. This procedure would let us determine whether one task was especially easy or difficult.

Once we have collected all pre- and post-tests, we must have the papers assessed. For a very informal study of, say, the students in our class, we may do the assessment ourselves. However, if we are dealing with large numbers of student papers and if we plan to do any statistical analysis, we must train other readers to make reliable judgments about the quality of the papers (see Cooper, 1977). In any case, no matter who is doing the reading, we must be sure that judges use the appropriate criteria. That is, if we are interested in students' ability to vary their writing according to their audience, our evaluation must focus specifically on this issue (see Odell, 1981).

Although a pre-/post-test design is widely used, it does have some problems. It is a very limited sample of a student's work. Since anyone can have an especially good or bad day, the pre-/post-test design won't let us assess the individual performance. It will only let us talk about the average performance of groups of students. Furthermore, to the extent that pre- and post-test essays are written under test situations, they may be something of an anomaly, especially if we encourage students to take several days to produce a piece of writing—drafting, getting peer response, and revising (see Sanders and Littlefield, 1975). And finally, a pre-/post-test study may make demands which are inconsistent with our practices as teachers. As Reising and Milner point out (1982), such a study may require us to commit ourselves to a very specific, well-defined set of teaching procedures and objectives. However, it may be that our understanding of students' needs may change as we go through the year. Consequently, we may want to modify or discard some teaching procedures and acquire others. This course of action is reasonable, but it may be incompatible with the demands of a well-defined, pre-/post-test study.

As either an alternative or a complement to pre- and post-test studies, we might also do descriptive studies that are based on a comprehensive sample of students' work in a given area. We would gather this sample not by assigning a pre- and post-test, but by asking students to keep a writing folder in which they place everything they write during the course of a semester or school year. With these folders, we could either do a very detailed analysis of a few students' work or we could focus on only a few aspects of the work of a large number of students. As Reising and Milner point out (1982), descriptive studies are not without their shortcomings. But these studies do allow us to base our research on materials that are produced under circumstances that are as favorable as possible. Furthermore, our profession has come to the point where we have available a wide range of procedures for describing written products and the writing process. All of these procedures are relatively new; all have some limitations. But, if we are conscious of these limitations, and if we realize that we may have to alter a given procedure to suit our own needs, we can use these procedures.

One of the most popular methods of examining the composing process is to ask writers to compose aloud, not only speaking the words they set down on the page but also verbalizing the thoughts, questions, reactions that occur while they are in the act of writing. The great advantage of this method is that it captures some of what goes on while the writer is in the act of writing (see Flower and Hayes, 1983; Atlas, 1979). The disadvantages are that (1) not all writers are comfortable composing aloud, and (2) the act of writing is so complex and demanding that a writer may be able to verbalize only a small part of the knowledge and strategies he or she brings to a writing task (see Odell, Goswami, and Herrington, 1983).

Other procedures entail observing writers while they are writing (see Graves, 1983) and, immediately after the writer finishes writing, interviewing him or her about times when there were pauses or apparent troubles with a particular passage (see Matsuhashi, 1981; Rose, 1984). For another approach to interviewing, see Odell, Goswami, and Herrington (1983). For a critique of retrospective interviews, see Atlas (1979).

In addition to directly observing the act of writing we may look at written products to make some inferences about a writer's thinking. As I explained in the Reading/Literature Section we can examine a piece of writing, trying to identify the questions a writer appears to have answered. Or, using procedures described by Bridwell (1980) or Faigley and Witte (1981), we can try to categorize the kinds of revisions students make.

Finally, we can examine written products, not for insight into the composing process, but for insight into students' ability to produce a finished piece of discourse. We can examine sentence structure (see Hunt, 1977), cohesion and coherence (see Cooper, et al., 1983), and errors (Shaughnessy, 1977).

From just this cursory review of descriptive procedures, it is obvious that it would be impossible to illustrate all or even most of them with any thoroughness. Fortunately, detailed illustrations are available in the sources cited just above. What I want to do now is to suggest some of the kinds of questions we might try to answer by describing what we find in students' writing folders.

Let us assume for a moment that we want to focus on the work of a few students who are for some reasons especially interesting to us—perhaps their work is some of the best we have seen, or perhaps we suspect that their work reflects problems that may be typical of our weaker students. Also, for purposes of our illustration, let's assume that we're concerned about students' sensitivity to rhetorical context. Here are some of the questions we might ask:

1. If we ask students to describe the audience and purpose for their writing, do we find that those descriptions become more detailed, more comprehensive, more useful? Do we find that students are increasingly able to specify audience characteristics that could help them decide, for example, what kinds of arguments might be most persuasive?

2. Do we find that the writing becomes more appropriate for the intended audience and purpose? Do we find a decrease in the number of places where the student uses language, sentence structure, organizational patterns, and arguments that are inappropriate for the intended audience and purpose? Do we find an increase in the number of instances in which a student's language, etc., seems especially appropriate?

3. Do we find that a student's sense of rhetorical context begins to enter into the composing process? If, for example, we examine a student's revisions on a series of papers, do we find that those revisions make the writing more appropriate for the specific audience for whom the writing is intended?

4. Do we find that students increase their references to rhetorical context when they refer to decisions about their writing? If, for example, we asked students to explain why they made a certain revision in their writing, would we find that students increasingly justified their revisions by referring to their audience and purpose?

5 How are students' perceptions of rhetorical context influenced by classroom interactions? Do their comments about rhetorical context suggest that they are beginning to internalize comments made in peer response groups or class-wide discussions?

Listening/Discussing

Many of us are openly proud that we do not lecture but, rather, conduct our classes by means of discussion. Yet this is an area to which we may have given little rigorous thought. We teach students how to read, write, and analyze literature. And we evaluate them on their achievement in these areas. But, in my experience, at least, we rarely set out to teach students how to function well in a discussion. And we rarely grade students on their discussion skills, unless we base part of their grade on "class participation." This seems unfortunate since—as both James Moffett and James Britton have argued—talk is the matrix from which both reading and writing arise. In order to read or write well, one may need to talk (and listen) to others— before, during, or after the process of reading and writing.

It's difficult to teach or to study discussion skills. Talk is evanescent; unlike written material, it doesn't hold still for scrutiny. Unless we record it, talk vanishes. And if we rely solely on our ability to listen to a group discussion and take notes, we will inevitably miss some (or much) of what goes on. Furthermore, it can be difficult to say exactly what we are looking for when we try to analyze a discussion. We know we want the discussion to be stimulating, lively, and productive. But it can be difficult to identify those elements of a discussion that help make it successful. And finally, many of us are not trained to teach or analyze small or large group processes.

Fortunately, there are several texts which help overcome the problems I've just identified (see, for example, Stanford and Stanford, 1969; Stanford and Roark, 1974). All of these texts describe classroom activities that can work with students of almost any age level. Furthermore, all the exercises are based on substantial theory about what helps or hinders communication.

An important part of this theory has to do with the fact that participants in discussions may take recognizable roles: some will play, in effect, a devil's advocate role, consistently challenging what others say; some will take the role of conciliator, trying to reduce friction, defuse anger, look for compromise or consensus; others will digress, raising extraneous issues or making jokes; still others will try to keep the group on task, reminding others of the subject at hand or suggesting procedures that will help resolve a problem or move the group toward its goal.

Another important part of this theory has to do with listening. Different texts provide different activities to help people learn to listen to each other. But all of these texts share some assumptions about basic listening skills. The most rudimentary skill is passive; it is simply a matter of being quiet while others are talking, of not interrupting until others have had their say. A somewhat more active and more difficult skill is paraphrasing or summarizing what someone else has said. This entails restating others' ideas or feelings in such a clear, accurate way that they can say, "Yes, that's exactly what I was getting at." The third skill is still more demanding. It involves certain basic mental processes that are as important to reading and writing as to engaging in a discussion. One text refers to this skill as "looking for areas of agreement" (Stanford and Stanford, 1969), another calls it "discovering the region of validity" of another person's point of view (Young, Becker, and Pike, 1970), still another refers to it as playing the "believing game," as opposed to playing the "doubting game" (Elbow, 1975). All of these texts make the same assumptions: (1) that there is a perspective from which almost any statement makes a certain amount of sense; (2) that part of our job as listeners is to try and identify that perspective, to look for ways another's point of view might seem plausible; (3) that after we have played the believing game, we may also play the doubting game, raising questions, looking for inconsistencies in someone else's statement, trying to think of facts that refute or modify someone else's assertions

To illustrate this theory, consider the following transcription of a discussion in two different tenth-grade classes. Both groups have been shown a small statue and are trying to determine what civilization it came from. (These transcripts are taken from Massialas and Zevin, 1967.)

Group 1

(Statuette is passed around among the students, who take about fifteen minutes to examine it.)

TEACHER: What do you think this is?

GARY: A Buddha.

IVAN: A girl who lost her hair!

KEN: It's not a girl, but a man. Have a closer look.

GARY: A Buddhist monk.

IVAN: Is it Chinese? Aztec? Mayan?

MICHAEL: The Rolling Stones!

CYNTHIA: His ears don't match.

MARY ANN: And his head is lopsided.

CARLA: One eye is lower than the other.

IVAN: It's a Chinese god.

MICHAEL: It's an Egyptian god.

GARY: Some guy struck his father and they cut his hands off.

MARY ANN: It's some kind of priest.

NELL: Does it say anything on the bottom?

BILL: Made in Japan!

MICHAEL: It looks like a god.

BILL: It's a slave from Egypt.

GARY: It looks like a monk.

PAULETTE: It's a surgeon who got his hands cut off.

CAROL: But his hands look like they were broken off.

IVAN: Is it Chinese? Tibetan? Laos?

NELL: It's from a museum. Someone reproduced it in a museum. The hands were destroyed some time ago.

Even in this fragmented discussion, there is at least some listening going on. At two points, students do listen enough to contradict the previous speaker (Ivan: "It's a girl"; Ken: "It's not a girl but a man"; Gary: "It's a surgeon who got his hands cut off"; Paulette: "But his hands look like they were broken off"). At another point, Cynthia notes that "his ears don't match," and Mary Ann and Carla immediately note other physical details of the statue. However, the listening skills of the first group are much less sophisticated than those of this next one.

Group 2

(Teacher passes the object around the room. As the artifact circulates, the discussion resumes.)

SUSAN: It looks like a voodoo doll to me.

LARRY: I think it looks like Mrs. Doe in a nightgown.

(General laughter)

MARC: I definitely think it is not a Mrs.

(More laughter)

DAVE: It's a statue.

JOHN: That sounds safe.

(More laughter)

MARC: It's of African origin.

MIKE: No, it's a statue of an Egyptian priest.

EDWARD: I think it's a priest, but I'm not sure it's Egyptian.

PAM: It looks Middle Eastern to me.

MARC: Maybe it's Aztec or something like that?

LOIS: Yes, I think it's American Indian because of the dress— the dress looks like it's made of feathers.

EDWARD: Maybe he's a ruler?

EUGENE: I wonder why he is bald. That must be some kind of sign of some one special.

NANCY: Perhaps it's an idol of some sort.

JIM: It looks strange—maybe it's a Chinese lord.

*   *   *

BARBARA: I think we could try to eliminate some of the suggestions.

JOHN: Mrs. Doe for instance.

RONNA: I think we should try to establish where it's from.

EUGENE: Yes, I think we can definitely say that it's not African, or a Voodoo doll, or anything like that.

TEACHER: Why? Do you have a reason for saying that?

EUGENE: From the sculpture, we can see that this person would be of the Caucasian race. His features are definitely not Negroid.

BERNIE: Then we can rule out that he is an Asiatic on the same grounds. He is not slanty-eyed or particularly Oriental-looking.

BARBARA: That narrows down our choice. Now we only have to find out what society this statue is from. I think this figure represents a person of the Caucasian race.

EDWARD: Maybe so, but it's still a strange-looking statue— nothing like an American or European.

PAM: It's not anything from any society I'm familiar with. It must be an ancient object.

DAVE: Yes, yes. I agree too.

As did Group 1, Group 2 begins with a couple of humorous assertions, and there are instances in which students seem not to be listening to each other. No one responds to Pam's comments that the statue looks "Middle Eastern"; no one picks up on Edward's comment, "Maybe he's a ruler." Also there is at least one instance where a group member uses one of the rudimentary listening strategies found in Group 1: when Marc asserts that the statue is "of African origin," Mike immediately cuts him off: "No, it's a statue of an Egyptian priest." However, in the very next student comment there is a more sophisticated form of disagreement than we have seen thus far. Edward disagrees with Mike's claim that the statue is an Egyptian priest. But Edward begins his response to Mike not by asserting a disagreement, but by identifying an area in which he and Mike agree: "I think it's a priest, but . . ." Although we can't read too much into a single example, Edward has done something that theorists would argue is valuable: he began his response by playing, however briefly, the believing game rather than the doubting game; he looked for an area of agreement before asserting disagreement.

Other students in this group play the believing game in different ways. When Marc asserts that the statue is "Aztec or something like that," Lois provides support for Marc's claim: "Yes, I think it's American Indian because of the dress. The dress looks like it's made of feathers." Somewhat later, we find Bernie playing a different form of this game: when Eugene argues that the statue is Caucasian, Bernie accepts this claim and uses it as the basis for a further conclusion: "Then we can rule out . . ." And finally, the excerpts from

Group 2 show one student emerging in a very clear role; on two occasions, Barbara tries to establish procedures for the group: "I think we should eliminate some of the suggestions" and "Now we only have to find out . . ."

This brief analysis suggests how we might go about describing students' discussion. We might begin with categories developed by communication theorists and attempt to find students acting in ways that represent those categories. And as we attempt to use these categories, we might find statements that help us redefine the categories (as did Lois's and Bernie's remarks, noted above), or we might find ourselves rejecting certain categories and replacing them with categories—perhaps of our own invention—that seem more truly descriptive of what our students are doing.

It's unlikely that a look at two brief passages of student talk will give us as firm a basis as we need for research. But for the sake of illustration, let's assume that we want to do research on some of the discussion skills I identified a couple of paragraphs earlier. A number of researchable questions readily come to mind:

1. Does Barbara *always* take the initiative and suggest procedures for the group to follow? Does anyone else in the group take such a role? How do members of the group respond to Barbara or to others who take this role? Do other members of the group consistently take other roles?

2. How often do students in the group play the believing game? What form does this take? For example: Do their comments suggest that they are empathizing with the person they are listening to? Do they try to justify what a classmate has said? Do they accept a classmate's assertion and begin to speculate on the implications of that assertion?

3. Under what circumstances do students play the believing game? Are there certain topics or speakers that seem to prompt students to play the doubting game? Do students increase in their ability to play the believing game at least enough to see possible merits of something they would have otherwise unthinkingly rejected?

Any of these questions could help us understand better our students' discussion abilities. In trying to arrive at this understanding, we would need to observe students over a long period of time, perhaps tape-recording discussions, perhaps taking careful notes about what people do and say. In any given discussion we will, inevitably, miss a good bit of what goes on. But, as we continue to observe students, patterns will begin to emerge, and we can test and refine our understanding of those patterns if, as we observe each new discussion, we ask such questions as these: What is going on in *this* discussion? Is there anything that contradicts the generalizations I am beginning to form? Do I need to modify these generalizations? Do I need yet another category to account for as much data as possible?

So What?

Early in this essay, I mentioned that there are some research questions that particularly invite the response, "So what?" In fact, researchers must always be prepared to answer such questions as these: What is the significance of what we have learned? Is it really worth all the time and effort we put into our work? Does it matter that we have found an answer to the question we started out to answer?

Now that we have considered a number of possible research questions, it seems appropriate to think about why those questions are worth trying to answer. If we have been trying to assess the effects of instruction, we will have relatively little difficulty. If we find out whether students' reading/writing/discussion skills have improved and if we have a rational basis (in theory or research) for thinking those improvements are desirable, then we, in effect, preempt the question, "So what?" But if we are not trying to assess the effects of instruction, *then* what do we say?

One response is implicit in the kinds of questions raised throughout this essay. Frequently, the issues I have touched upon lead us to see connections among the various elements of the English curriculum. The section on reading/literary study emphasized the analysis of students' writing. And the discussion of discussion skills emphasized at least one intellectual activity (playing the "believing game") that is not just limited to discussion. As Peter Elbow has argued (1982), the ability to empathize is essential to our full understanding of a literary text. And it seems clear that if a writer is to understand and argue well against someone else's point of view, it can be useful to try to see the region of validity for that point of view. The attempt may help a writer rethink his or her own convictions or it may simply help the writer understand more clearly the limitations of another person's point of view. In other words, many of the questions we have been considering will help us understand relationships among apparently diverse activities in the English classroom. As we understand those relationships, we should be able to make our teaching more unified and more effective.

One further answer to the question, "So what?" is that a close analysis of our own students' work can let us test and perhaps modify assertions from current theory and research. Although small-scale studies don't let us refute or confirm beyond all shadow of doubt, they can let us say, "Theory *X* or Research finding *Y* doesn't quite fit what I find going on in one specific situation." Such assertions help the rest of our profession rethink some of the claims we are beginning to accept. A good theory, for example, must account for a wide variety of sets of data. If we produce data that seem inconsistent with a particular theory, then it may become necessary to reexamine, perhaps modify that theory. In other words, our small-scale investigations can let us contribute to our basic understanding of our profession.

One final answer to the question, "So what?" is concerned only indirectly with benefits to our students or our profession. It is concerned, rather, with benefits to us. As we continue to do research, we continue to grow. We continue to learn. Our work cannot become stale, because we are continually redefining it. And this process of continual redefinition and renewal helps us retain the enthusiasm and commitment that brought us into this profession in the first place.

References

Anderson, P. (1985). Survey research. In L. Odell & D. Goswami (Eds.), *Writing in non-academic settings.* New York: Guilford.

Atlas, M. A. (1979). *Assessing an audience* (Tech. Rep. No. 3; NIE Contract No. 400-78-0043). Pittsburgh: Carnegie Mellon University, Document Design Project.

Bleich, D. (1978). *Subjective criticism.* Baltimore: Johns Hopkins University Press.

Bridwell, L. S. (1984). Revising strategies in twelfth grade students' transactional writing. *Research in the Teaching of English 14*(3), 197–222.

Campbell, D., & Stanley, J. (1966). *Experimental and quasi experimental designs for research.* Boston: Houghton Mifflin.

Cooper, C. R. (1977). Holistic evaluation of writing. In. C. R. Cooper & L. Odell (Eds.), *Evaluating writing.* Urbana, IL: National Council of Teachers of English.

Cooper, C. R. (Ed.). (1985). *Researching response to literature and the teaching of literature.* Norwood, NJ: Ablex.

Cooper, C. R., et al. (1983). Procedures for describing written texts. In P. Mosenthal, L. Tamor, & S. Walmsley (Eds.), *Writing research: Methods and procedures.* New York: Longman.

Doheny-Farina, S., & Odell, L. (1985). Ethnographic research. In L. Odell & D. Goswami (Eds.), *Writing in non-academic settings.* New York: Guilford.

Elbow, P. (1975). *Writing without teachers.* New York: Oxford University Press.

Elbow, P. (1982). *Systematic doubt and systematic belief.* Stony Brook, NY: State University of New York.

Faigley, L., & Witte, S. (1981, December). Analyzing revision. *College Composition and Communication 32*(4), 400–414.

Flower, L. & Hayes, J. R. (1983). Uncovering cognitive processes in writing: An introduction to protocol analysis. In P. Mosenthal, L. Tamor, & S. Walmsley (Eds.), *Writing research: Methods and procedures.* New York: Longman.

Freedman, S. W., & Katz. A. (in press). Pedagogical interaction during the composing process: The writing conference. In A. Matsuhashi (Ed.), *Writing in real time: Modelling production processes.* New York: Academic.

Graves, D. H. (1983). *Writing: Teachers and children at work* (chap. V). Exeter, NH: Heinemann.

Hillocks, G. (1979). The effects of observational activities on student writing. *Research in the Teaching of English 13*(1), 23–25.

Hunt, K. W. (1977). Early blooming and late blooming syntactic structures. In C. R. Cooper & L. Odell (Eds.), *Evaluating writing.* Urbana, IL: National Council of Teachers of English.

Larson, R. L. (1968, November). Discovery through questioning: A plan for teaching rhetorical invention. *College English 30,* 126–134.

Lloyd-Jones, R. (1977). Primary trait scoring. In C. R. Cooper & L. Odell (Eds.), *Evaluating writing.* Urbana, IL: National Council of Teachers of English.

Massialas, B. G., & Zevin, J. (1967). *Creative encounters in the classroom.* New York: Wiley.

Matsuhashi, A. (1981). Pausing and planning: The tempo of written discourse. *Research in the Teaching of English 15,* 113–134.

Myers, M. (1985). *The teacher-researcher: How to study writing in the classroom.* Urbana, IL: National Council of Teachers of English.

Odell, L. (1976, January). The classroom teacher as researcher. *English Journal 65*(1), 106–111.

Odell, L. (1976, Summer-Autumn). Question-asking and the teaching of writing. *The English Record 27,* 78–86.

Odell, L. (1981). Defining and assessing competence in writing. In C. R. Cooper (Ed.), *Competence in English.* Urbana, IL: National Council of Teachers of English.

Odell, L., Goswami, D., & Herrington, A. (1983). The discourse-based interview. In P. Mosenthal, L. Tamor, and S. Walmsley (Eds.), *Writing research methods and procedures.* New York: Longman.

Perl, S., & Wilson, N. (1986). *Through teachers' eyes.* Portsmouth, NH: Heinemann.

Petrosky, A. R. (1982, February). From story to essay: Reading and writing. *College Composition and Communication,* 19–36.

Purves, A. C. (1973). *Literature education in ten countries.* New York: Wiley.

Rabianski, N. M. (1979). *An exploratory study of individual differences in the use of freewriting and the tagmemic heuristic procedure: Two modes of invention in the composing process.* Unpublished doctoral thesis, State University of New York at Buffalo.

Rawe, F. (1981). *A study of seventh grade writers who are introduced to invention/revision strategies as part of their composing process.* Unpublished doctoral dissertation, State University of New York at Albany.

Reising, R. W., & Milner, J. (1982, December). Classroom experimentation and good teaching: Are they compatible? *English Journal 7.*

Rose, M. (1984). *The cognitive dimension of writer's block.* Carbondale, IL: Southern Illinois University Press.

Rosenblatt, L. (1978). *The reader, the text, the poem: The transactional theory of the literary work.* Carbondale, IL: Southern Illinois University Press.

Rosenblatt, L. (1985). The transactional theory of the literary work: Implications for research. In C. R. Cooper (Ed.), *Researching response to literature and the teaching of literature* (pp. 33–53). Norwood, NJ: Ablex.

Rubin, D. L., & Piche, G. L. (1979, December). Development in syntactic and strategic aspects of audience adaptation skills in written persuasive communication. *Research in the Teaching of English 13,* 293–316.

Sanders, S., & Littlefield, J. (1975). Perhaps text essays can reflect significant improvement in freshman composition. *Research in the Teaching of English 9,* 145–153.

Shaughnessy, M. P. (1977). *Errors & expectations.* New York: Oxford University Press.

Stanford, G. (1977). *Developing effective classroom groups.* New York: Hearst.

Stanford, G., & Roark, A. E. (1974). *Human interaction in education.* Boston: Allyn & Bacon.

Stanford, G., & Stanford, B. D. (1969). *Learning discussion skills through games.* New York: Citation.

Young, R. E., Becker, A. L., & Pike, K. L. (1970). *Rhetoric: Discovery and change.* New York: Harcourt Brace Jovanovich.

PART FOUR

Research Close-ups
Bread Loaf's Teacher-Researchers

Interview with Betty Bailey

DIXIE GOSWAMI: Betty, how long have you been interested in class-room research and inquiry?

BETTY BAILEY: Six or seven years.

GOSWAMI: At Thayer Academy, do you get rewarded in any way if you continue to ask questions and to do classroom research year in and year out?

BAILEY: No, nothing direct. There have been many rewards, but nothing in my salary that I could point to.

GOSWAMI: Well, why do it? It's a lot of work. Why?

BAILEY: I don't think I can remember why I did it the first time. That might have been just to see what it was about. I think I know why I do it now, and I do very directly plan to do it. I plan one or two studies a year to do in my ninth-grade classroom. There's such a great contrast between my role in my classroom when I'm conduct-ing an inquiry and when I'm not. The biggest difference, which I noticed in my earliest studies, is that when I'm trying to study some-thing, I work with my students in a very different way. Instead of dominating the class, which I tend to do—I need a protection against myself—instead of dominating the class, I really have to step back and let *them* do some things. In a way, I have to step back so that they can produce "data" for me to look at. I can't be running the show because I can't be looking when I'm running the show.

It's also a lot more pleasant and efficient when they're helping me with my study. Besides producing what I'm looking at or doing what I'm looking at, they enjoy and learn from and are eager to take part in collecting, logging, finding categories. We do that a lot as a group. For example, if we are passing in writing folders and making a table of contents, that table will be an annotated table of contents. As a group we'll make up categories and labels they can use to cate-gorize the various pieces of writing in their writing folders. We get to hear all kinds of different things that writers consider important about their writing. From the wide range of things they hear, they select some categories they think are important that apply to their own writing. I learn so much from that, plus I get categories chosen, and when they're using the categories, they can use them so much better if they make them up than if I make them up.

It's much less drudgery. I have much less the feeling that I'm slogging through a pile of material on my own—even if it's for their benefit. It's much less lonely when they're participating. I used to take batches of papers home every night to my apartment, sit, cor-rect them, hand them back to the kids, take a new batch home, sit, smoke cigarettes, drink coffee, correct. But now we talk about papers in class, or groups of us talk about them, or I have conferences with students about them. And they help me talk about what we're going to talk about. Instead of trying to figure out on my own, "What do these kids need me to say to help them get better?" I ask them, "What do you need help on? What's going on here?" There are a lot of things that might seem somewhat burdensome about doing class-room research, but overall it makes day-in-day-out teaching much less burdensome, less lonely.

Since 1982, a number of teachers who have come to Bread Loaf to study the teaching of writing have planned and carried out inquiries about language and learning. These Bread Loaf teachers don't aspire to become miniresearchers producing minidissertations; nor have they attempted quantitative, evaluative studies. Instead, they have become listeners and observers of a new kind, working with students and colleagues to develop cultural and linguistic understandings at the classroom level. Such efforts continue to provide important information about teaching and learning in rural schools, about which we know relatively little, although these kinds of inquiry can and should happen anywhere. The following six essays describe inquiries conducted by Bread Loaf teacher-researchers.

From A Letter to Bread Loaf

GAIL MARTIN
St. Stephens Indian School, St. Stephens, Wyoming

. . . My research project was hard to contain and continues to grow. It's nowhere near completion at this point, and I will continue working on it long distance from New Mexico this year. I've scheduled a meeting with the teachers at St. Stephens during my Christmas break to review what we've done and continue our discussions.

Revising School Writing

Many of the assumptions behind my project turned out to be wrong. I assumed that one reason our Arapaho students had such a difficult time writing was that they believed that their grades would be affected by their poor writing skills. Yet, they all told me that it wasn't the grading of their work that worried them. They simply didn't feel comfortable putting thoughts into writing, partly because they weren't competent writers but for other, more significant reasons as well.

After talking with our school elder, Pius Moss, and my Arapaho teacher's aide, Margaret Littleshield, I realized that part of their fear of writing came from over a hundred years' distrust of written words. Until the white men came with their written treaties, the Arapaho had not been exposed to any form of writing. The treaties proved to be dangerous lies.

Until four years ago, there was no written form of the Arapaho language. Because Pius Moss was worried that the spoken language was being lost, he began a project to transform the spoken language into written form to preserve it. The plan met with much resistance at the beginning. Many of the old native-speaking tribal members saw the writing down of the Arapaho language as one more "white man manipulation" and said that if a man spoke words, those words were the truth. What was spoken could not be changed later by anyone who chose to. The thought comes from the heart when it is spoken. It took Pius Moss, a well-respected member of the tribe, some time to convince other tribal leaders that if the language was not written down, it might soon be lost for good because fewer and fewer of the young people were using it.

After becoming aware of the community's mistrust of writing, I began to wonder if this mistrust might not somehow be related to my students' unwillingness to revise beyond correcting spelling words. I talked with each student every other week about a piece of his or her writing. I asked Valinda Swallow how she felt about a story she'd written. She replied that she didn't think it was very good for several reasons. When I suggested that she rework the story to accommodate her new ideas and understandings, she said no, she didn't think she could. Even though her story was not as successful as she'd have liked it to be, it was already down on paper and had been there for a week already. To change it in any way would be wrong. She preferred writing a completely new story.

I observed that when my students used the word processor, they did not hesitate to add or delete sections of their writing as long as it was still on the screen. But as soon as their writing came through the printer and they had a copy in their hands, they stopped revising. The school allows my students computer time only rarely, so I didn't have time to explore this line of inquiry further. I've requested that in the future my writing classes have the use of the computer on a regular basis.

Writing Stories

St. Stephens' teachers met every other month to discuss our students as writers. One of our major concerns was that many of the stories children wrote didn't seem to "go anywhere." The stories just ambled along with no definite start or finish, no climaxes or conclusions. I decided to ask Pius Moss about these stories, since he is a master Arapaho storyteller himself. I learned about a distinctive difference between Arapaho stories and stories I was accustomed to hearing, reading, and telling. Pius Moss explained that Arapaho stories are not written down, they're told in what we might call serial form, continued night after night. A "good" story is one that lasts seven nights. On the seventh night, the story should end. Arapaho stories seldom tell what happens to main characters before or after particular segments of the stories.

When I asked Pius Moss why Arapaho stories never seem to have an "ending," he answered that there is no ending to life, and stories are about Arapaho life, so there is no need for a conclusion. My colleagues and I talked about what Pius had said, and we decided that we would encourage our students to choose whichever type of story they wished to write: we would try to listen and read in appropriate ways.

Writing Outside of School

Another of my mistaken assumptions was that our students used writing in and out of school in more ways than they realized. Three times during the year I asked my class to complete a five-day home writing survey (drawing on Shirley Heath's work). They noted any writing done by any member of their families. We discussed the kinds of things that might appear in their surveys: homework, notes, lists, letters, and so on. After the first survey was due, only seven students returned their papers. The rest said that no writing had taken place at home that week. The seven who turned in their papers indicated that they'd done two kinds of writing: homework and the filling out of government forms. On later surveys, students reported that their parents had written letters to the editor of the local newspaper concerning the controversial upcoming tribal election. I called the editor and she told me that since 1981 the government had received about 80 percent more letters from tribal members than in the preceding ten years. She also said that many of the letters needed so much editing before being printed that she feared her editing might have competely changed the letter-writers' meanings and intentions. She agreed to let me have some of these letters so that I could search for clues that would improve my chances of helping my students become writers.

After studying many of these letters, I had a new and deeper understanding of the difficulties my students and their parents share when it comes to writing in English. I took comfort, however, in the evidence I had that Arapaho adults were using written English to express their views and to accomplish social and political goals.

With this understanding behind me, I looked for ways of giving my students reasons for writing outside of school. I wanted them to find pleasure and satisfaction from writing, and I hit upon a rather obvious, simple solution to my problem. I gave each student several stamped envelopes and wrote a note to their parents asking them to help their children write letters to friends or relatives living outside our county. I asked the students to ask for answers to their letters by return mail. Several students wrote to brothers and sisters away at boarding schools and to friends out of state—parents sent me a note each time their child wrote a letter. For each verified letter, children earned points towards a fishing field trip or a picnic. If a student received an answer, they could share these with the class, if they chose, and each reply was worth ten bonus points. By the end of the year, my students reported that they were beginning to feel like good letter-writers; some had received as many as ten replies. Several parents were adding a few lines to their children's letters to relatives. I'd like to know if these children continue to write letters, if they have an expanded notion of how written English might function for them.

Becoming a Community of Writers

All year my students and I exchanged notes and letters that we kept in a private writing file. The file served as a source of ideas for writing and talking for all of us. In March, students reviewed their writing folders and chose several pieces to submit for publication in a collection. Later, the class voted to invite all students in the school to submit pieces for publication. My class helped a committee of teachers, community writers, and high school students select the best writings. We distributed copies of the booklet to every student in the school.

Studying Language and Learning

I believe that even though I have a long way to go, my inquiry has helped me develop as a teacher of Arapaho children. I've taken the first step by learning to ask questions and to listen, not only to the children but to their parents and other members of our community. Here are some things that I've noticed happening at St. Stephens since I began my classroom research project:
- We are making conscious efforts to understand and value our students' culture.
- We are beginning to view our own classroom and school as a community with its own social realities and their consequences.
- We are working cooperatively with students.

168

- We grade very little writing.
- We have doubled the amount of time we are spending on writing in class. This year we had thirty-minute writing classes every day.
- My students voted their free-writing time as their favorite class.

I have many questions I'd like to try to answer, with the help of my students and my colleagues, if I were able to continue the inquiry I've only just begun at St. Stephens.

An Analysis of Peer Group Dialogue Journals for Classroom Use

DALE LUMLEY
Butler Senior High School, Butler, Pennsylvania

Most writing teachers agree that students need to write every day as part of the learning process, and that, along with the traditional writing required by schools for grading by teachers, students also need to write to audiences other than the teacher and for purposes beside grades. The problem which faces us as writing teachers, especially those who must concurrently teach composition and literature, is how we can provide daily writing opportunities and real, responding audiences for our students. I believe a valuable writing opportunity for students can be provided through peer group dialogue journals. I offer my dialogue journal concept as a workable approach for secondary teachers who must deal with large numbers of students on a restricting period-by-period schedule. My use of dialogue journals and my belief in their value require some detailed background.

During the last three years, I have randomly paired average level high school juniors, from different sections of my American literature and Composition classes, as journal partners. For example, a student from period two might write to students from my period four and seven sections taking the same course. Each student then has one or two journal partners for the length of the journal exchange.

During the last ten minutes of class, students write in composition or spiral notebooks which I provide and which never leave my classroom. I collect the journals at the end of the period, again, for example, period two, and redistribute them during the last ten minutes of the later sections. These later students respond to their partners, who must wait until the end of the period, the following day, to read and again respond. The cycle forms an ongoing written conversation, a direct link between students. I become only an occasional participant, reading and responding to each journal group intermittently as time allows.

While the dialogue journals are not graded or scored in any way, I do place several demands on writers. I ask that they use ink, date each entry, write a minimum of ten lines each day, and that they somehow relate each entry to class. At the outset, some students complain that relating entries to class is too restricting. I explain that the term "relate" actually gives them freedom. They can ask questions, offer anecdotes, share personal experiences, give insights and reactions to an assignment, class discussion, or lesson. I further explain that I hope students will not adopt a routine of class summary. I advise students to focus on "I" in the journal rather than "we," but refuse to direct writing beyond these comments and earlier restrictions. I am primarily interested in the dialogues they create within this framework, with what they make of the journals.

To see just what they make, I taken an active role in the journal process. I respond to each journal to gain a broad sense of students' views and the impact of the journals themselves. I also keep a daily log of reactions and insights to journal comments and processes. To gain a more detailed perspective, I focus observations on specific journals, two or three per term, to trace their developments throughout the exchange.

What came to light during the first year of journal exchange and study is that each journal team creates a unique dialogue based on the terms and ideas which partners choose as meaningful to them. Still there were recurrent patterns of language function apparent in almost all journals. With the help of Dixie Goswami at the Bread Loaf School of English in Vermont, I was able to identify and label the functions of language in the dialogue journals in two principal ways. The journals provide, first of all, a context for *social interaction* about the class in general. Social interaction includes addresses, concerns about quizzes and tests, remarks about homework and reading progress, comments on personal matters and closings. These general comments lead to another level of language which specifically explores class reading and discussions. I refer to these specific comments generated by the class content as *topic exploration.* As an example of these levels of language, I offer a brief excerpt from the beginning of Matt and Darrin's journal, written during our study of *The Adventures of Huckleberry Finn.* The statements of topic exploration are italicized.

Matt: January 14

.   What's up? My name is Matt B. and I guess were stuck being partners. *Well, what do you think about Huck and Jim when they escape from the King and duke? What about when they run back into them on the river? Pretty crazy, eh? Well, I think huck is a great person and I would like to do some of the things he does.* Later.

Darrin:

   What's up with you not much here. *I didn't get that far yet but from what we talked about [in class], it is.* My name is Darrin N. *I agree with you about doing some of that stuff.* I hope the test on this stuff won't be hard. See ya around.

The most significant conclusion I drew from that initial study was that the combination of social interaction and topic exploration in the dialogue journals indicate that students, if given the chance, can converse and interpret while writing about the reading they are doing in school. Using the context of class, students were able to sustain their own conversation on terms of their own choosing while considering and exploring their reading and class discussions.

Using these insights, I decided to directly join the use of dialogue journals with the *Huck Finn* unit the following year. My explanations and procedures were essentially the same. My study concentrated on the subjects which students initiated in the journals and specifically what relevance these subjects had to the novel. I had students do their own topic analysis of their journals, listing the topics most mentioned and tracing a topic's recurrence and development over several days of the exchange. Students also wrote evaluations of the journal exchange and attempted to summarize individual roles within the journal process.

While it is difficult to summarize their comments, we did discover that the social interaction about homework, class procedures, and personal matters made the journals most enjoyable for the students and was vital to the ongoing dialogue. The ability to interact on a personal level in the journals made the writing real communication for them rather than a writing task. The importance of the social interaction as a way to establish personal relationships and to provide opportunities through which students can explore the novel became even more apparent to me.

With the help of John Dixon in Oxford, I began to see the link between the comments students made to interact socially and the levels they reached in responding to the novel through topic exploration. From the student summaries and evaluations, we found that most journal partners agreed that it was important for each person in the journal group to initiate new topics by asking questions. Most specifically, we discovered that questions became the springboard through which most topic exploration occurred, and that of the levels of questions in the journals—factual speculations about future events, and opinions about character and plot—those which solicited opinions gave the students the most valuable way to respond to the novel and to build ideas.

In the third year of the study, I again joined the dialogue journals with the *Huck Finn* unit. I explained my past discoveries to the classes and also said I hoped to connect the writing of the dialogue journals with writing done outside the journals. I wanted to see if the dialogue journals could be used to spark topics for expository essays. In the midst of the journal exchange, however, it became evident to me that a closer look at the topic exploration was needed to better understand the potential of dialogue journals as a device for reading and responding to literature. Through my observations, I became interested in the strategies students used to build their topic explorations. While we had determined that questions were a valuable way to explore the novel, I sensed that other strategies were also at work in the journals, and I wanted to identify and label some of these strategies, if possible.

To limit my observations, I focused on a section of one journal written by three girls over a three-day period, interrupted by a snow day and an Act 80 half-day. In the excerpts which follow, I present only those questions and statements which are topic explorations. While I realize a true sense of the discourse is missing without the social interactions, I hope the close analysis of the topic exploration will lead to a clearer understanding of the strategies these three writers created in exploring the novel.

The girls—Connie, Carol, and Evon—have already been writing in the journal for several days when we join the conversation. I think it is relevant to mention that I had not responded to their journal in any way prior to these excerpts. I will present and comment upon each completed round. Ellipses are used where social interaction existed in the midst of topic exploration.

Connie: January 24

Alot of things Huck has been doing, I've done. For instance, when he sneeks out of the house to go with Tom. When I was his age my sister and I used to sneek out and go moonlight riding on our horses. We always had a good time. Although, going through the woods scarred me. I always thought some escaped convict was going to capture us and never let us go. Well, enough about me sneaking out. I want to read some of your experiences like Huck's.

Carol:

Huck is a lot like me, but I think Tom is more like me. I like to tell stories, sometimes I really get into it. I used to go around having fun all the time too. I'm glad I've grown up some.

Evon: January 28

I really can't relate to Huck and Tom like you both say you can, but I do like the story. . . . Huck Finn and Tom are about the same age as my little brother, so I can just imagine him doing the things they do. The way Jim talks in the novel is funny. It's sort of hard to understand the vernacular in this novel—for me anyway.

Connie clearly establishes the framework upon which these entries are built. She draws a parallel between her life and Huck's fictional existence. She cites a specific connection, sneaking out, and gives a brief but complete narrative. Her last sentence makes a direct demand which shapes her partners' thoughts and responses.

Before I proceed, I think Connie's mention of being scared in the woods and captured by an escaped convict also deserves comment. Why does she mention that? Tom and Huck, you remember, sneak out at night into the woods and form a band of highwaymen. They talk of kidnapping and ransom, even though they don't know what "ransom" means. I think Connie, along with making the connection between Huck's late night adventure and her own moonlight ride, is responding to the romance and mystery of the novel, the excitement and fear called to mind while reading.

Interestingly, before Carol follows the pattern established by Connie, she explains a closer tie to Tom than Huck. Like Connie she also offers an example of the similarities—telling stories. But what interests me is what follows the example: "I used to go around having fun all the time too. I'm glad I've grown up some." Rather than extend her comparison by telling a story, she pulls herself back. She feels she is more mature than Tom. She used to have all that childish fun but not so much anymore because she has grown up some. Why doesn't Carol offer an instance of having all that fun, one time past, the way Connie does? Carol's comments are far more general because she doesn't enter the personal narrative. That doesn't mean Carol's response is any less important or effective; instead, it shows she is responding to the novel in a slightly different way. Her comments show she is evaluating Tom and, in a very subtle way, herself. She sees Tom's immaturity, remembers when she was the same, and probably recognizes the foolishness as well as the fun of those experiences.

Evon also constructs her comments according to Connie's request, and, even more so than Carol, draws back from the projection of self into these imaginary characters. She can't relate to either Tom or Huck and so substitutes her little brother into their roles. She seems to be making the same statement as Carol and supporting her; yes, I enjoy these characters but I am older now, more mature, and can't cast myself into their parts. Additionally, she initiates a new topic, Jim's dialect, and judges that the vernacular makes the novel difficult to comprehend. (We discussed use of the vernacular in an earlier unit, and students had even written tall tales using local idioms.)

All three girls, then, offer some sort of parallel between their lives and those of the characters in the novel. While building from that foundation, there is also a movement away from Connie's personal narrative to Evon's problems with the vernacular, the comment of a reader outside the plot. There is a distancing by Carol as she reflects upon and evaluates the past. There is an implicit connection as Evon moves even further away from personal narrative to the process of reading and understanding the novel. Evon manages to respond on several levels: to the characters, to the comments of each journal partner, and to the reading process. Her remarks about Jim give impetus to the next entries.

Connie: January 29

I also, like the way Jim talks, but I have to read real slow so I can understand what he's sayin. In a way I feel sorry for Jim, cause he has to take the wrap for killin Huck. But maybe Huck will come to his scences and go back to town and tell the truth for once.

Carol:

Huck is some guy. I wouldn't mind having some of the fun he does.

Evon:

I about died when I read that chapter about Huck dressin up like a girl. I just picture my little brother doing that! What a roll!

Connie directly supports Evon's enjoyment and difficulty in reading Jim's dialect, which Evon, by adding at the end of her earlier entry, "for me anyway," seemed to be soliciting. Connie also says she reads "real slow," possibly suggesting Evon do the same, and sympathizing with her problem. Connie also extends the new topic of Jim, empathizing with his plight of being accused of Huck's murder. She even anticipates a possible solution—Huck's return to clear Jim's name. Connie seems to be passing judgment on Huck, in the similar, subtle way Carol had done earlier to Tom, when she says "maybe Huck will come to his scences . . . and tell the truth for once." In this brief topic exploration, Connie responds to Evon's comments, continues to project herself into character (this time Jim), and to evaluate Huck.

Carol's response seems a bit out of touch with her partners. She doesn't comment on Jim. Instead, she vaguely generalizes about Huck; he is "some guy." The theme of having all that fun continues, but nothing else is added. Part of Carol's social interaction provides a clue to this entry. She explained that she was behind in the reading, and, so I take it, hadn't yet encountered the problems of reading long passages of Jim's talk. Still she remains part of the exploration by commenting on earlier themes.

Evon's response again proves interesting. She writes of a new episode—Huck's disguise as a girl. She connects the episode to her little brother, continuing to imagine him in Huck's ploys. She enjoys the episode—"about died"—and enjoys making the connection— notice the exclamation marks. Why does that personal connection remain for Evon when Connie and Carol have seemed to alter that angle? Possibly Evon had anticipated from yesterday's entries that the connection of personal experience would continue, and perhaps this affected how she responded to the novel as she read it, working in the tie to her brother as a link to her journal partners. Yet, something more can be seen in Evon's brief response.

There seems to be a greater sense for Evon to respond to the novel as a piece of literature. While Carol doesn't give her much to build upon, Evon could have repeated Connie's feelings of sorrow for Jim or predicted another solution. Instead, she brings in a new episode, responding with delight as a reader to the text. Her link with experience, however (in this case her brother), remains intact. Thus, she again responds to all three levels in the journal: partners, character, and novel. Evon's freedom to respond to an episode again guides the next day's entries.

Connie: January 31

How about the snake episode? Do snakes really wrap around their dead mate. If they do I think it's gross. If I were Huck Finn's friend I don't think I would want to sleep out in the woods with him. He's too mischievious for me to handle.

Carol:

> How would you like to run away like Huck? That would be fun. I don't think I could think of all them things to do, like cutting up a pig. . . . I wish my life could be filled with all that fun.

Evon:

> Did you read the part where Huck and Jim are trying to figure out where the stars came from? Jim says he things the moon laid them like eggs. I thought that was pretty good.

All three girls use similar strategies in these entries. Each offers something of a rhetorical question (notice that none gets a reply) along with a personal opinion or insight. Connie asks about the snake episode and specifically if snakes wrap around their dead mate as Huck claims in the novel. Here is a question she really would like answered. She concludes that "it's gross" and eventually evaluates Huck, "he's too mischievious for me," by again imaginatively projecting herself into the fictional world.

Carol's response follows the pattern, but she continues to travel on more general ground. She questions about an earlier episode, Huck's escape, and reiterates that running away could be fun. She also recognizes Huck's superior intelligence in the elaborate plan he concocts. Carol is still behind in the reading, yet she remains involved in the discussion by drawing on the knowledge she holds.

Evon's episode of interest deals with Huck and Jim's conversation about the stars. Unlike Connie or Carol, she does not place herself into the story; she does not see herself running away or sleeping out in the woods with him. She only says, "I thought that was good." What does she mean by the pronoun *that*? Does Evon mean she thinks the episode is good? The discussion interesting? Probably. But more, I think, she is again responding as a reader to the text. Connie sees herself in the plot: "If I were Huck Finn's friend." Carol, slightly removed, wishes she could have the excitement of running away. Evon, however, seems to comment upon the innocent charm a reader senses when Jim concludes that perhaps "the moon laid them [all those stars] like eggs." The pattern, which we've seen throughout, shows movement from a personal response, closely involved in the plot, to a response of a reader to the language of the novel, from the inside to the outside looking in.

Overall, what can we say of these brief transcripts; what conclusions can we make? I think it is evident that this written discussion closely resembles talk. The dialogue shows an implicit understanding where all three participants exchange points of interest and build a meaning based on what each member perceives and feels. A friend pointed out that this conversation, especially the later entries about episodes, sounds similar to the way movie goers discuss a film, each person mentioning a special scene and adding notes of interest and opinion. In my classroom, I've heard pieces of such discussions about literature as well as movies without giving them much weight. But, here in the journals, a close look reveals a natural construction of ideas, a strong potential for learning. The conversational tone allows freedom and provides openings for each girl to explore and contribute.

It is important, I think, not to begin evaluating the comments of Connie, Carol, and Evon in a hierarchical way. While I feel Evon responds more by interpreting the novel, it doesn't mean her entries are more significant than the others. Certainly her responses are valuable, but so are those of Connie and Carol; truly, the girls construct their ideas together. What is significant is to see that each girl has the chance to reach into her own experience, her own level of response, and take part in making meaning. Each brings to the discussion, to borrow Walt Whitman's phrase, "What belongs to him or her and to none else." The fact that the journals leave the way to learning and expression open is the key.

What is also telling is how a close look at this journal reveals a richness, diversity, and complexity of discussion which might have originally seemed insignificant. The girls build and shape by questioning and thinking about *Huck Finn*. The sharing and exploring gives the dialogue journal meaning within the classroom.

Now to those original questions: What are the strategies which Connie, Carol, and Evon use to respond to the novel and how might we label them? I think several kinds of responses are evident. They respond to the novel by relating personal experiences and traits to the events, characters, and personalities of the novel. They empathize with characters and even project themselves into the plot. They evaluate and judge characters, the plot, and the novel itself—remember Evon's comments about the use of the vernacular. They anticipate future events—maybe Huck will come back to town and tell the truth for once. I think we can also see that the girls respond to the language and themes which permeate the novel.

In commenting upon these excerpts, I tried to show the strategy patterns the girls developed and how their responses marked their levels of response. Most clearly, we saw the use of personal narrative, the movement toward a spectator of the plot, and toward a critical reader responding to the process of reading the text.

In many ways, I believe, we as teachers disregard all of these responses and strategies by students as fragmented and off the point Rarely do we solicit such spontaneous and personal responses, at least in secondary school. In fact, I feel we rarely give students the chance to explore and respond to literature with such freedom and value. If we are really interested in what happens as students read and respond to literature, we need to listen closely and take a closer look at both what they say and how they say it. We need to open up lines of communication which allow the freedom to explore the content of the class; we need to allow students to make their own points. We also need to provide opportunities for students and teachers to use their freedom to build with one another and to make meanings together. The use of peer group dialogue journals seems to be a step in that direction.

Everyone Sits at a Big Desk

Discovering Topics for Writing

NANCIE ATWELL
Boothbay (Maine) Region Elementary School

For longer than I care to remember, students in my junior high English classes wrote a composition a week on the good, creative topics their good, creative teacher assigned. Every Monday I orchestrated a pre-writing activity, and every Friday I collected final drafts to read and grade, evaluating, I know now, based on how well each writer had guessed the scenario in my head. Students wrote narratives, poetry, persuasion, essays, journals, and all manner of dramatic writing. And from my perspective of the big desk at the front of the classroom, it looked as if real writing were going on out there. In fact, although some of the tasks were engaging, most were, plain and simple, exercises—what James Britton calls "dummy runs." Underneath the veneer of my assignment lurked some unexamined—and pretty faulty—assumptions.

I assigned topics because I believed most of my students wouldn't write without them. I assigned topics because I believed my structures and strictures were necessary for kids to write well. I assigned topics, when it came right down to it, because I believed my ideas to be more valuable than any my students might possibly entertain. So decreeing topics wasn't just a philosophical issue; it was political, too. Writing well became a matter of writing appropriately and convincingly about my ideas, and I chalked up ineffective or perfunctory responses to low ability or effort.

Lucy Calkins has written about the "underground curriculum" teachers often fail to acknowledge and tap. Sitting there at my big desk, crafting new assignments and evaluating their results, I remained oblivious to the grade-eight underground curriculum—my students' ideas, experiences, and expertise. I remained in charge.

When Students Discover Their Own Topics

Four years ago, a language arts curriculum committee on which I served decided to investigate how children acquire language. It was our good fortune that Susan Sowers was one of the consultants we looked to for answers.

Sowers, Donald Graves, and Lucy Calkins were then nearing the end of their second year as researchers-in-residence at Atkinson Academy, a public elementary school in rural New Hampshire. Under a grant from the National Institute of Education, they spent these two years following sixteen first- and third-grade writers and their teachers, observing students *in the process* of composing to discover how children develop as writers. Susan brought to our curriculum committee meeting copies of reports from their study. She also brought her authority as a teacher and researcher, a wealth of knowledge—and patience. What she had to say was not what I wanted to hear.

Children in the Graves team's study learned to write by exercising all the options available to real-world authors, including daily time for writing, conferences with teachers and peers, and opportunities to draft, revise, and publish their writing; most significantly, they took responsibility for deciding what and why and for whom they would write.

Because the topics were their own, these young writers made an investment in their writing. They cared about content and correctness. They wrote on a range of topics and in a variety of modes wider than their teachers had dreamed of assigning. The writers and their writing flourished as teachers came out from behind their big desks to observe, listen to, and learn from their students.

I kept Susan at our school much later that day than she intended to stay, explaining the reasons her findings couldn't possibly apply to me and my students. All that week I continued to explain, to anyone who would listen, how Sowers had advocated topic anarchy. But on my free periods and in the evening, I read and reread the manuscripts she'd shared. And I saw through my defenses to the truth: I didn't know how to share responsibility with my students, and I wasn't too sure I wanted to. I liked the vantage of my big desk; I liked setting topic and pace and establishing criteria. I liked being in charge. If responsibility for thinking and planning shifted to my students, what would *I* do?

What I did, finally, was to put the question to my students: "Children in an elementary school in New Hampshire are choosing their own topics for writing. Could you do this? Would you like to?" Resoundingly, they said yes, and the underground curriculum surfaced.

Eighth-graders began writing to satisfy genuine, individual needs, discovering that in-school writing can do something for them. They recreate happy times, work through sad times, discover what they know about a subject and learn more, convey and request information, apply for jobs, parody, petition, play, argue, apologize, advise, and, through contests and professional publication, make money.

My students do have ideas for writing. Over the past four years, I've seen the critical role self-selected topics play in their involvement and growth as writers. These writers take chances, trying new subjects, techniques, and formats. They're more apt to revise, so their writing will do what they intend it to, and more careful in editing and proofreading so readers will attend to their meanings, not their mistakes. They seldom lose pieces of writing; they talk about their writing with parents and friends; they spend much of their own time writing and thinking about their writing; they identify themselves as authors; and "literature" becomes a term that embraces students' writing, too. Most importantly, open topic choice allows young writers to tap their own, rich, personal and academic resources. As Pam, one of my students, explained it:

> I get to find out what's important for me, what *I* think and have to say. It might just be some little thing, but it's a thing a teacher wouldn't know about me that I think is important. It's boring when thirty students all write the same thing. It makes me not care about it and not want to do it. . . . I want to tell people things in my writing. I can't do that when teachers tell me what to write about.

Pam describes the sense of authority that comes when she's truly an author, sitting at her own big desk. True authorship begins with a thought that eventually becomes words on the page; with an individual's own interests and concerns. This is the step I'd denied with my assignments—that struggle to discover and clarify what one thinks. In denying that step, I'd usurped my students' authority.

The methods Susan Sowers described to our committee had struck me as permissive, as a sure road to undisciplined and purposeless writing. This has proved not to be the case: open topic choice does not undercut structure. Instead, it hold students accountable for developing and refining their own structures, and allows me to offer individual guidance within the context of each writer's intentions. I know now that one of my roles as writing teacher is, in conferences, to help my students discover and act on their options.

Making and defending writing choices is part of what Tom Newkirk calls "the democratic gamble." I'm not advocating topic anarchy either; I am arguing for a redistribution of the power of ideas and a new kind of classroom seating plan. When each student initiates the writing process by taking responsibility for finding out what he or she has to say, everyone sits at a big desk.

A Writer's Environment

Students in the primary grades have little trouble finding subjects for writing. At this stage, Graves writes, "their voices boom through the print." Young children are playful in their orientation toward language and artwork; they write and draw primarily for themselves and tend not to be self-critical. Older students, inexperienced in writing about their own ideas, have two strikes against them: self-consciousness and a sense of audience that come naturally with age, leaving many kids wanting correctness and acceptance; and too many years on the receiving end of teachers' ideas and assignments, victims of what Graves terms "the teaching cycle that places young people on writer's welfare."

Faced with decisions about topics, secondary students may balk or complain. They may try to figure the teacher's new angle—what we're really after but won't say. Or they may freeze, suffering what one of my students called "a bad case of writer's blues." Given time and a conducive environment, these writers can rediscover their voices and ideas.

During last spring's evaluation conferences—quarterly interviews between each of my students and me about their growth and efforts as writers—I conducted some simple research. Students responded to two questions: "What is your best piece of writing of this quarter? Where did your idea for this piece come from?" Their answers describe a writer's environment—the circumstances, arrangements, and provisions that enable students to discover and explore their own ideas for writing.

Time

Frequent time for writing—in their case, every day—is crucial to my students' topic selection.

Because they write regularly, they anticipate and plan for writing time. Mindy's comment is typical. "'Attic Prize' is my best piece. It's about a personal experience that was really funny, and it sounds just like what happened—the piece is funny, too. Right after it happened I thought, 'This is going to make a great piece.' And I went to bed that night thinking 'Tomorrow, I've *got* to write that.'"

Mindy naturally spent her off-duty time planning her writing because she knew the next day's class would bring her an occasion to write. In situations where students can't write every day, three writing days each week are enough for developing the habit of gathering and considering ideas for writing. And I think the three days should be regular and consecutive—for example, every Monday, Tuesday, and Wednesday—providing the sense of continuity and routine writers need.

Talk

Talking with others—parents, friends, and me—also serves as a springboard for pieces of writing. My students identified three kinds of discussion that elicited ideas: informal conversations, interviews, and writing conferences.

Mike's best piece, "Busch Gardens," came about because of a conversation with his mother: "Mom and I were talking about Maryland and Busch Gardens, 'cause she'd gone with my class on a field trip there. I said, 'Hold on, Mom!' And I wrote it down on a piece of paper to remember it." Amanda's letter to the editor of a local newspaper also started with a conversation at home. Amanda said, "My mother pointed out the paper's mistake in printing the tournament scores and said, 'Is this something to write about?' And I said, 'It sure is.'"

Parents become part of a cadre of interviewers helping students discover their ideas. Bert conducted and wrote a series of interviews with area artists after his father had interviewed him. "Dad said I should do something that interested me; something I really care about. We talked about my interests. Since art is my field, I decided to focus on local artists, to see what I could learn." Mike, Amanda and Bert were sitting at big desks at home, too, where their writing provided a new context for talking about their ideas.

Other interviews that resulted in writing ideas were conducted in school, by me or other students. Blocked writers know one of their options is to ask for a topic conference, where the interviewer asks open-ended questions about the writer's ideas and experiences. For example, an interviewer might ask, "Tell me about your: weekend, family, friends, neighborhood, likes and dislikes, jobs around the house, earliest memories, hobbies, skills, fears, problems that need solving, birthday, Christmas, favorite books, movies, poems, sports, subjects, etc." At first I made copies of questions available, but these sheets saw less and less use as, through writing and conferences, students and I came to know about each others' lives and concerns. Lance wrote "Happy Valentine's Day," about a job that had required him to miss school on a day he'd really wanted to be there, because he and I talked about his situation one day after school: "I was thinking of writing it before—because it was really on my mind—but your interest got me more interested in it as something important to think and write about."

Writing conferences, where students read their pieces aloud, seeking help in the form of questions and comments, are another source of ideas for writing. In conferences, my students hear the topics other writers are choosing. This is how Sandy explained the origins of her essay on the nature of friendship: "Other people were writing about friends. When Mindy read me her story of what we'd be like when we were older, she gave me the idea."

Reading

Students' success in taking responsibility for their writing eventually led me to give over similar responsibility for reading, a separate course which also meets daily. I read to them, and we read stories, plays and poems as a group, but the heart of the reading course is students' self-selected texts. They read, on average, thirty books each year, with two-thirds of each week's class time devoted to independent reading. The impact of others' writing on their own happens naturally as they discover what they like to read and try out themes and techniques of authors who impress them. By example, I think two of my eighth-graders' most significant writing teachers are S. E. Hinton and Robert Frost.

Six students identified elements in their best pieces as being inspired by Hinton's novel *The Outsiders*—from topic (Damon's short story about a boy caught in a gang war) to technique (Tara "made a point" in her narrative "Beautiful Mountains" because she was so impressed by the themes she identified in *The Outsiders*).

Frost's poetry has a similar influence. "Nothing Gold Can Stay" served as a model for almost a dozen student poems, including these by Billy and Dede.

Beyond the Light

The sunset is so lovely,
        with its warm colors and bright glow.
I could sit and stare for hours
        at the elegant sight.
Then I shiver
        as a cold breeze blows—

to warn me of the darkness
and to warn me of the night.
Dede Reed

Dawn

The lake sparkled
in the light of the moon.
Dawn was near—
it would be soon.
The clouds gave off a goldish light
and broke the silence of the night.

Now the dawn has come to be noon,
just like grown-up life—all too soon.
Bill Snow

Others students' published writing—and opportunities for students to publish their writing—are another way reading informs writing. My students have produced dozens of classroom magazines. These are anthologies written by kids who choose to submit something in response to calls-for-manuscripts on various themes. David wrote "The Ski Flip" after the announcement of a forthcoming sports story collection. Vicky's first piece of fiction was inspired by Justine's "A Night in the Life," which appeared in a class fiction volume. Mindy's poem about ice-skating, published in one of our poetry anthologies, gave Phil the idea for his poem about feelings, entitled "What Are They?" It was Mindy's technique that caught Phil's interest: "I liked her poem a lot—the way it wasn't clear until the end what she was talking about. But she really gave it away, and I decided not to—to give clues but not too many."

Wide reading of both student and professionally published writing allows young writers to learn from others' subjects, styles, and formats. In turn, opportunities to *be* read evoke the desire to write and share one's writing. A student left this note on my desk the day after the publication of his class's first magazine:

10/1/82

Dear Ms. Atwell,

I enjoyed *What Are Friends For?* It was great reading stories written by *young adults* of my own age. I especially liked David's and Bert's pieces, David's because he told his feelings and bravery along with helpful details, and Bert's because of his wording and the techniques he used.

I hope more books like this are written. If so, would you please inform me?

Your friend,
Willie

Willie submitted an essay to the next class magazine.

Materials

Several kinds of classroom resources see regular use as sources of ideas for writing. The most important are my students' permanent writing folders. We save all of each eighth-grader's writing, keeping it on file and accessible in the classroom. Sometimes previous pieces of writing suggest new ideas. Daniel's "A Trip Nowhere," his best piece, "captured the way my friend Tyler and I are together. I got the idea from the first piece about Tyler, Gary and me that I wrote. I just thought of other things we'd done. It helps to look back at my writing folder."

Another helpful material resource are sheets headed "My Ideas for Writing," where students can capture potential topics, jotting down ideas as they come. Students carry these lists in their daily or working folders. I've also taught writers how to brainstorm—how to generate, uncensored, as many ideas as possible, and then see what's emerged as a topic possibility. Writers who have a range of ideas to choose from usually have strong feelings about those topics they ultimately select.

My students can also look to writers' sourcebooks, for example, *Writer's Market*; to a "Places to Publish" folder where we've gathered lists of writing contests and magazines that feature student writing; to the address file I set up and they maintain; and to guides such as NCTE's *All About Letters,* where Luanne, Carol, and Leslie found inspiration and models for the resumés and cover letters they wrote in pursuit of summer jobs.

Finally, a variety of materials for writing can aid students in generating ideas: different weights, sizes, and colors of lined and un-lined paper, blank booklets, ditto masters, poster paper, stencils, stationery and envelopes, stamps, a typewriter, and all kinds and colors of pens, pencils and markers. These materials suggest formats beyond the white-lined-paper composition—correspondence, individual collections of poetry, notices and announcements, etc.

Getting Started

After four years of unassigned topics, I'm still slightly panicked the first day of school—afraid that every student in each class will draw a "writer's blues" blank. It never happens. This tells me a lot about the ingenious topics I'd crafted for so long at my big desk. It tells me more, though, about my ingenious students. I've started off our year together in one of two ways; they've proven equally successful.

The first is to ask students, in pairs, to take turns interviewing each other, using the list of open-ended interview questions I referred to earlier. Interviewers take notes on interviewees' "My Ideas for Writing" lists. I model an interview with one student, then he or she interviews me, before the pairs go to work. They have twenty minutes to storm each others' brains.

A second approach is one I learned from Mary Ellen Giacobbe. I describe the topics I considered the night before, lying awake anticipating the day's writing. I purposefully propose, then reject, topics too broad or subjects about which I know nothing, settling on a topic I know and care about and genuinely want to write about. I ask students to sit silently for three minutes, thinking as I thought the night before. Then they describe to a friend the ideas that came to mind. After three minutes, students change roles. (This tight timing focuses writers on the one task before them.) Finally, I bring the group together and ask six or eight volunteers to quickly describe the topics they discovered.

Whichever approach starts the class, the rest of the period is writing time. This is the crucial part of getting started—an expectation that everyone will write and the tacit acknowledgment that everyone has something to say. I transfer authority from the desk at the front of the classroom so my students can assume it; they do, taking their rightful places as true authors.

And I'm writing, too—out from behind my big desk, listening to young writers' voices and finding my own.

Selected Bibliography

Calkins, L. M. (1983). *Lessons from a child.* Exeter, NH: Heinemann.

Day, R., & Weaver, G. C. (1978). *Creative writing in the classroom: An annotated bibliography of selected resources* (104.7). Information about magazines that publish student work and writing contests.

Graves, D. H. (1982). *Writing: Teachers and children at work.* Exeter, NH: Heinemann.

Graves, D. H. (1983). Break the welfare cycle: Let writers choose their own topics. In P. Stock (Ed.), *Fforum* (pp. 98–101). Montclair, NJ: Boynton/Cook.

Murray, D. (1980, May). Questions to produce writing topics. *English Journal, 69.*

Murray, D. (1984). *Write to learn.* New York: Holt, Rinehart and Winston.

National Council of Teachers of English and the US Postal Service. (!979). *All about letters.* Urbana, IL: Author.

Simmons, J. (1982). The writer's chart to discovery. In T. Newkirk and N. Atwell (Eds.), *Understanding writing: Ways of observing, learning and teaching* (pp. 57–62). Chelmsford, MA: New England Regional Exchange.

We Watched Ourselves Write

Report on a Classroom Research Project

VICTORIA L. HOLMSTEN
with the SENIOR HONORS ENGLISH CLASS OF 1983–1984
Laguna-Acoma High School, New Laguna, New Mexico

Background: What I Wanted to Know and Why It's Worth Knowing

I was skeptical. I admit it. I wasn't interested in computers *or* classroom research. It was Bread Loaf that got me into this. I went to the Bread Loaf School of English, Middlebury College's summer graduate English school, last year armed with my writing teacher's notebook full of observations from the '82–'83 school year. I showed the book to Dixie Goswami, director of Bread Loaf's Program in Writing. She informed me that these were the beginnings of class-room research. It seemed that I was already involved in the process. We talked a few times, I attended the research seminars and meetings, and things started to cook. After listening to writing consultant Lee Odell talk about question-forming and listening to the previous year's teacher-researchers discuss their projects, I began to think that maybe I could do this, too.

My original thoughts were aimed in several directions. Dixie encouraged me to write a letter to her trying to pull some of them together. "Yes," she said after that letter, "you've got something going about computers here. Let's follow through on that."

One of the things I had recalled in that letter was the arrival of ten Apple computers at Laguna-Acoma two months earlier. I couldn't help but notice that none of the teachers seemed to know what to do with them, and the only students who got near the machines were the gifted program students who went into the computer room to

The Laguna-Acoma Senior Honors English class of 1983–1984 included Karen Aragone, Sandra Cheromiah, Anthony Concho, Grace Dempsey, Melissa DeVore, Grace Kayate, Michelle Mooney, Kenny Nunez, LaDonna Ortiz, Darrell Phillips, Mary Reed, Natalie Reed, Aaron Romero, Lorie Salvador, and Mel Sarracino.

play games. I considered this a waste. Even in my early machino-
phobia, I sensed that there was something in that computer room
that I might be able to use.

A week or two later, during the '83 Bread Loaf session, I attended writing program assistant Bill Wright's meeting for "teachers
interested in using microcomputers in teaching writing." I walked
into a room filled with foreign language that evening: *word processing, programs, software, hardware, modem, functions, capabilities,
80-column card, 64K, interface, compatability, user-friendly.* It was
just as shocking as my first day in Spanish 1 when the teacher didn't
speak any English for that whole excruciating hour.

Then my fellow student Karen Wessel of Homer, Alaska, made
a useful comment:

"These machines are coming—in fact are here!—whether we
want them or not. The potential for abuse is heavy. It's up to us, as
humane teachers of literature and humanities and the arts, to get in
there and make sure that abuse doesn't take place."

I thought back to the game-playing in the computer room back
home and I was sold. My career in computers was launched.

Through several letter drafts and discussions with Dixie Goswami, I had worked out my research question. I wanted to know
what would happen if I used word processing in a writing class. I
was most specifically interested in the question of revision, because
in five and a half years of teaching, I had never been successful in
getting students to revise their work. Would the students become
better editors? Would the revising process become less painful? All
leading to the ultimate question: Would our writing improve?

"My goal in proposing this project is to complete a piece of
research with my students in order that we might learn something
about our writing processes," I wrote in my original grant proposal.

I received the letter of acceptance for the grant from Paul
Cubeta, Director of the Bread Loaf School, in early September. I
went into my Senior Honors English class and said, "Let's do it."
Most of them seemed excited, chomping at the bit, in fact. They
couldn't wait for the *Bank Street Writer,* our selected word processing program, to arrive.

They reflected on the beginnings of the experience later in their
final reports.

> I wanted to know everything about computers. How to work
> them correctly. I really wanted to see what they were capable of
> of doing. This class has taught me a lot about computers and
> I'm thankful for that. I think it's really good to know about
> computers because in the future that's all we'll be using world-
> wide.

> —Kenny Nunez

The day came when our teacher proposed to our class a computer writer's workshop and really confused us all. We heard a lot about computers and in time, computers were to become one of our daily friends. I wanted to know how the computer worked, how it thought, functioned, and cooperated with my thoughts.

—Melissa DeVore

I got started in the computer program through my English class. I guess you can say I didn't have a choice.

—LaDonna Ortiz

We all got involved in the word processing program when our English teacher told us about it. We were all interested in it cause it had something to do with computers. It also was another way to write without having to throw away papers for mistakes. This processing program was designed to help us write more correctly, to change errors, proofread and revise what we had. To add more on to writings and so on. We wanted to know about that so we could try to improve in writing so that others would understand what point we were trying to get across.

—Mary Reed

My reason for wanting to know about computers and about this writing program is because it might help me to understand a lot about what might be in the future.

—Lorie Salvador

Our teacher had this crazy idea that if we worked with computers that we would learn how to revise better. She brought us into the computer room and told us what she expected from us. At first I thought the hell with this idea. I told myself that I was just going to mess around in the room.

She gave us a few pointers on how the computer worked and I was amazed with all the functions it had. I realized this was a neat thing to learn. I thought it might come in handy in the future because a lot of businesses are starting to use the computer more often.

—Darrell Phillips

Well it started when Ms. H., as I like to call her, came up with this wicked idea of using a computer to process words. To be honest, I really didn't know what she was trying to pull, but after she began to explain herself and make her idea a bit clearer, I thought sure, why not give it a try.

—Aaron Romero

The way we started off on this computer stuff was through Ms.
Holmsten writing to this place called Bread Loaf and getting
the money for the things we needed. We are to do class research
on writing. Most of us didn't know how to use the computer,
and I guess we asked Ms. Holmsten a lot of questions about
how to use them. The main thing I wanted to know was how
to use the computer. I certainly think it's worth knowing since
most everything now in this modern time is done with computers and it seems that in order to survive you need computer
skills.

—Sandra Cheromiah

And so we were started, with all sixteen different sets of expectations and interests.

Procedures: What I Did to Find Out

We used the *Bank Street Writer* word processing program from
Scholastic developed by Bank Street College in New York. It arrived
in mid-October. I gave myself a week or two to get used to it; then
we began the project on October 30, 1983.

I made an effort from the beginning of this project to involve
my students as research collaborators. I believe that this was a very
important part of the procedure and had a dramatic effect on the
results. There were ten computers in the computer room, and the
class totaled fifteen students. On the first day in the computer
room, the students received a copy of my research proposal and
we discussed the question we were to research. I worked out a group
schedule for computer time, with the idea that those five students
not on a computer on a given day would meet together in a writing
group. We discussed this scheduling the first day and I also gave them
my idea of project requirements. I developed the requirements with
two goals in mind: first, to involve students in the research process
and make sure they were observing and writing about what they
saw; and second, to give me something concrete on a regular basis
to satisfy the grading requirement we have to live with in school.

Writing Groups and Project Requirements
October–November 1983

Group 1: Karen Aragon, Grace Dempsey, Michelle Mooney, Darrell
Phillips, Mel Sarracino.
Group 2: Sandra Cheromiah, Melissa DeVore, Kenny Nunez, Mary
Reed, LaDonna Ortiz.
Group 3: Anthony Concho, Grace Kayate, Lorie Salvador, Natalie
Reed, Aaron Romero.

Project Requirements:
> One completed piece of writing per week, your choice of
> subject/format.
> Participation in group work
> One file on your disk labeled "Research," where you store
> observations, questions, notes, etc., on project research.
> One final "Think Piece," reflecting on your experiences, eval-
> uating project.
> Collaboration on final paper, reporting results of project.

I didn't make any assignment of writing topics. The project
was based on a writer' workshop format of classroom procedure,
after Donald Graves' work, that the students had been involved in,
without computers, during the first three weeks of the school year.
Student perceptions of procedure follow:

> At first we had to get acquainted with the computer and learn
> how to use it. Miss Holmsten divided us into groups so we could
> all get a computer. Next she gave us a *Bank Street Writer* to get
> used to the tutorial and how to correct our mistakes with what
> we learned. We learned how to write with the computer printing
> on the screen and us re-reading. I just played around with it until
> I figured out what I was doing and how I was doing it. I tried to
> remember how each part worked and what it was used for. I got
> the hang of the procedure and used it daily in correcting.
> —Mary Reed

> I did everything from asking the computer questions to physi-
> cally abusing the computer. (And it all worked.) I also had a lot
> of help from the other people in the room. Especially the teacher.
> Some of the machinery on the computer drove me crazy.
> —Kenny Nunez

> We built our own computer ability at our own speeds. Some of
> us had a full, completed writing at the end of class while others
> sat dazed by the computer. We evaluated our writings, one turned
> in per week. All of our disks contained what we wanted to write
> and what we liked to write about without being pressured into
> anything. The computer workshop was built with a lot of
> thoughts and personal experiences. We put into it and we re-
> ccived a lesson in return.
> —Melissa DeVore

> We all learned how to use the *Bank Street Writer* and we just
> played around with the computer to find out what it would do,
> just to experiment with what would happen if you pushed a

different button. What would change? Would you destroy all your writing, or what? This went on for a couple of days. . . .

—LaDonna Ortiz

What we first did to find out about computers was to understand how to work the computer. We had to learn how to load the computer and a lot of "do's" and "don'ts." We had to be careful, we had to put things into the computer. We had to find out where to correct our mistakes and how to replace them, We asked questions like, "How do you do this?" and "How do you run this and put things into it?" It took a lot of things just to make it understandable. It was really interesting how to work the computer. So we really did quite a bit of finding out.

—Lorie Salvador

The following is from my research file. These are my interpretations of our procedure.

Week 1: October 31 to November 4. This week we're getting acquainted with the machines and the *Bank Street Writer* program. The interest in the mechanical process is high. There is a certain amount of playing with things on the screen, but also a bit of serious writing beginning to happen in isolated pockets around the room. We're taking turns using the flip side of the *Bank Street Writer* to get into the tutorial program, and also using the teacher and other more computer-wise students to help when problems crop up.

On Friday, we had a brief class meeting before I got yanked out of the room for an English teachers' meeting. Before I left, I asked the students to give me the file name of the writing they were presenting as their week's work, and to fill in the following open-ended sentences:

I learned_____	I was surprised_____
I observed_____	I suggest_____
I liked_____	Next week I will_____
I didn't like_____	

Week 2: November 7 to November 11. The assignment for the week was again to hand in a file name, or printed-out file if the student had learned the printer this week, and the responses to another set of open-ended sentences. I also asked students to begin their research files with last week's responses to open-ended sentences. At the end of all this, we can print out our research files, pool our resources, see what we've learned, then get the whole thing written up into one large research paper. Next week, we'll emphasize the writing more.

Evaluation sentences for this week were:

I observed _____ My writing is _____
My editing/proofreading/revising is _____

November 17. Class meeting at the beginning of the week to discuss what will happen when I am in Denver for the NCTE convention. The kids listened, they talked a little bit, and we came up with some topic ideas, some ways to use our noncomputer time. I re-emphasized the research bit. Since I'll be out of class for four days, I'm anxious that they assume the role of the researcher and continue on here in some sort of serious mode. I'm not impressed with the threat as a means of making a point, but I did remind them that any undue goofing off next week will result in their immediate return to the classroom.

Suggestions for noncomputer time: (1) Talk about your writing with another writer. (2) Brainstorm ideas for topics. (3) Read over printouts, make notes, corrections. (4) Take notes on your observations about yourself, the class, the revising process. (5) Begin and use an *idea* file on your disk for those moments when you really are stuck and do need a topic.

There are four things that I want from students while I am gone next week. I announced these, and posted them on the board for their future reference: (1) One good written evaluation of week's work. (2) Add on to your research file. (3) Print out and hand in one original writing. (4) Share at least one piece of writing with a small group.

I'll leave the following open-ended sentences for the week's evaluation:

I have learned_____ My writing_____
I have observed changes in myself _____
the class _____
my writing process _____
my revising process _____
My plan for the final week of computer writing workshop is

_____

November 30. I reviewed the project requirements and laid out the following end-of-project assignments designed, in my mind at least, to lead to a wrap-up. First, to print out and hand in the entire research file. Second, to write the final report/think piece, using the following guidelines (from William West of the University of South Florida):
1. Background: What I wanted to know and why it's worth knowing.
2. Procedures: What I did to find out.

3. Results: What I found out, including what I observed.
4. Conclusions, interpretations: What I think this information means.
5. Recommendations: What I would recommend as a result of this information.

This, then, is a basic outline of how the classroom functioned during the project, worked out by me with student input. This is what we did to try to answer our question.

Results: What I Found Out

Armed with a procedure, we went into the computer room. We began to watch ourselves learn how to use the machines and use them for writing. This section details what we saw.

> It was amazing, I would get so into the writing that it was hard for me to stop. My mind would just keep on rolling out ideas. There were days that I did not feel like writing or working on anything because it was becoming too much of a routine just like coming to school day after day. There was this small part of the computer that I didn't like. It was the editing process that you had to go through just to delete a small word. So when I felt like it, I would write on paper all my thoughts before I wrote them down on the computer. Since I'm lazy, I usually just wrote all my thoughts on the computer. . . . The writing on the word processing disk is okay for me. It made me aware of all the mistakes I'd make when I was writing. I never knew I made that many mistakes because I never used to proofread. It made me correct more than I used to because I would get to erase whenever I wanted to.
>
> —Darrell Phillips

I liked writing and then seeing it on the catalog, also the computer makes you think faster. . . . I observed that when I write or have an idea it keeps flowing. It makes me want to write more. My writing is getting better as I become familiar with the computer, I make less mistakes. My editing, revising, proofreading are improving. . . . I have observed changes in myself because I was into typing my writing, not just sitting around scribbling on paper. I have observed changes in the class because I guess we're not too good at commenting on each other's writings. On the computer screen, someone would say, "Wow! That's bad!" or something of that sort. . . . I think that the whole class really enjoyed the workshop, even though some days it was hard to get our minds on the assignment. The reason I think everybody likes to type on the computer is they like to see their own writing on the screen.

—Grace Kayate

I was surprised at the open opinions my classmates voiced. I wish we could have more open discussions. . . . The results of learning to word process are that it is very easy to control and it is much faster than writing out an idea on paper first. Why? Because observing your ideas on the monitor helps a person read their ideas. If the person wants to change the idea it only takes a few keys to change the ideas. Other than changing ideas, using the keys saves a lot of finger cramps.

—Grace Dempsey

I like writing on paper still, then putting it in the computer afterwards, correcting as I go along. It makes it easier to write what I think about. . . . It makes you stop and read what you have written down because it is on the screen, whereas on paper I wouldn't have even bothered. . . . I have learned how to correct my mistakes and proofread what I have written which I never did before. It has also helped me to add things on to my writing and to continue with it. . . . I can write better than I did before and more freely. . . . I can write about things, get comments on them and continue on with it, adding more to improve the story or get across what I am saying.

—Mary Reed

I didn't like when you make a mistake, it's difficult to find it and everything gets all messed up. . . . My writing makes more sense while I'm writing on the computer because I can read it and make corrections where needed or add onto it to make it sound better. . . . I realize that English class can be more than just writing nouns and verbs. . . . We all seem to be happier to be writing something on the computer than when we were just writing on paper in our class. And I think we are all learning more about how to use a computer. . . . My writing process has been made easier, because of the advantages I have at correcting my mistakes and seeing exactly where they are and fixing them. . . . Kenny and I started out by having a conversation on computers. Then I started using some of my previous writings, correcting mistakes when I found some. Then I started writing some more stuff just on the computer right away instead of a separate rough draft because I could see if I made any mistakes and I could correct them more easily. I think it's a little more easy to compose on a computer rather than on paper, especially while writing my poems. . . . I have found that I would rather compose on the screen than take the time to write it out on a piece of paper and later put it on the computer. Maybe that proves I'm lazy at times, but I feel strongly that word processing is much easier and much better. But composing on the computer is a lot better for some people only. Some people might rather want to compose on a piece of paper because they find it hard to do on computers, as some people in here have said.

—Sandra Cheromiah

My revising is better because I can understand better what kind of mistakes I make. I can point out my mistakes as soon as I read what I have on the monitor. . . . The class seems to be excited about the whole idea of computers because no one dreads coming to seventh period like before. Everyone is learning what can be done and learned in computers. . . . The computer helps me to understand what I want to know and what I need to understand. I found out that it can really help me put my thoughts into good writing because I can actually read what I'm writing. I seem to have improved my spelling and some other departments in English.

—Lorie Salvador

I used the computer for a rough draft, corrected and revised it, on the other hand I had paper to write and erase. Each way, I revised and corrected until my writing was ready to turn in. I learned to look over my work and take my writing seriously at times. . . . To some it was a new thing which excited us and maybe even made us eager to write. The computers were good, but I think writing regularly is better, it's up to the person. This is only from my point of view. . . . I liked when the class all worked together and when we had open discussions about some subjects! I was surprised that I enjoyed doing my work and liked what I was writing. Every now and then I was surprised everyone was actually enjoying themselves.

—Melissa DeVore

I miss doing English the old way. All you had to do was read from the book, do your work and turn it in. . . . I prefer writing on paper first, then putting it on the computer, because if I write on paper first I can catch my mistakes before I put it on the computer. . . . I learned how to proofread and punctuate. I also learned you can write as much on the computer as you can, I think it is more fun to put writings on the computer than finishing them on paper, it sure beats the pen. . . . The main thing I learned was how to watch for mistakes.

—LaDonna Ortiz

I liked the typing out on the computer because you can type anything without saving it, and it is better than writing on paper. . . . My writing is coming along better than before because now when I put my writing on the computer I can or I will proofread it. But if it is on paper, I don't bother to proofread it. . . . The class seems to be a lot more interested and they are willing to learn and try to do some work. . . . My writing process has improved because I can find all of the mistakes I make.

—Michelle Mooney

I learned how to operate a computer differently than in computer class. . . . I was surprised that everyone caught on so well. . . . My writing is improving. Since we've been working with the computer I have a better outlook on writing. I used to hate to write something, but now I'm anxious to work with the computer so I try to have something to type into the computer when it comes my turn to work on it. . . . My revising and proofreading have become much better now that I'm able to see my mistakes and correct them right away. If I were to write a long story on paper and make one mistake, I would just throw away that paper and start all over. But now that we're using the computer, I can put the cursor at the beginning and at the end of what needs to be erased, then just push a few buttons and it will be erased. . . . I found out that at first this word processing was fun to do, but then as time went by it got boring. I think it was like that for most of us, because we all started slacking off on our writing. In the beginning everyone usually had someting to write just so they could work with the computer and the printing machine, later on no one really cared. Just about everyone dreaded coming to this class because we just did the same things everyday. Sometimes we would just play with the computer or the computer games. As time went by it became harder to come up with things to write. I still prefer to write on paper first, and then rewrite it on the screen of a computer. . . . I think this means that some people like to write on paper and some on a computer. If you prefer to write on a computer, I think that you have to be ahead of your thoughts. . . . If you're the type of person that likes to write on paper, it takes a long time, but at least you can sit there and put together your thoughts.

—Karen Aragon

I learned to use the Apple II correctly without breaking it. I found out you could also make good friends with the computers. It's a good way to break the ice when you're trying to score on a quiet girl. You can talk to another person without getting embarrassed. It can be interesting and exciting. Composing is a lot easier with the Apple II.

—Kenny Nunez

I have observed in myself that writing comes easier when I'm just sitting in front of the computer, it makes me more imaginative. . . . I have observed in the class that they seem to be a little busier in here than in the classroom. My writing process has improved, gotten a little faster on the keyboard and in my head (does that make sense?). . . . Working at a computer is a lot more mind-opening than sitting at a desk writing with a pen. For one thing, your mind begins to notice the futuristic appeal that a computer has for a person, which made me more imaginative. Having the words on a screen in front of you is much easier to proofread and find your mistakes and correct them rather than going back and reading your own writing, which at times can be a strain on one's eyes. I found that words flowed easier onto the keyboard since this is still new to us and we're still interested in it.

—Natalie Reed

I observed how to go about editing a piece of writing. This is the part I also did not like to do. To edit I had to go through too many steps just to edit one or two words and letters. The part I like the most is just to write on the computer screen. I was surprised how the computer kept everything that I wanted to save. I was amazed at how fast I learned to work with the computer. . . . My editing is coming along all right. I am more careful to watch how I spell because it takes too long to go through the whole editing process. I like to revise on the computer because there is no messy ink to erase and it's better to revise on the computer.

—Darrell Phillips

Before I began working on the computer, writing was quite tiring. I would get really bored and my thoughts just wouldn't flow. After a few days on the computer, ideas began to come. Not only was I surprised at the ease of typing words on a screen,

I was surprised by the arousal of my interest. The class really enjoyed using the computers. Many of the students who before-hand could not enjoy writing soon began to create good pieces of writing. After a couple of weeks everyone was willing to do some writing. Just getting a chance to work on a computer was half the excitement. Since the computers captivated the students' interest, the writing process was more productive. . . . Revising with the computer is a great idea. When words can be changed or sentences reworded just by retyping them, a writer does not get so tired. Revising with a computer isn't as time-consuming and therefore there is more time for writing.

—Mel Sarracino

I kept a research file on my desk, too. Here are some of my observations.

Week 1: October 31 to November 4. Several students are work-ing on collaborative writings. They're sitting together at one terminal and writing messages back and forth to each other on the screen. Kenny and Sandra did this on Wednesday and saved that test. Today on Thursday, Lorie and Sandra are working together on another message writing session while Sandra shows Lorie how to use the program.

As noted before, there is a certain amount of text being entered and saved on students' individual disks. Is anything being revised? Yes and no, I think. I've seen people catch errors as they play with mov-ing the cursor around and then go through the mechanical learning necessary to revise their errors. Again, the interest right now is in the mechanical side of the process.

"It would be easier to erase on paper; the screen confuses me; it's hard to see my mistakes," said Karen.

"I didn't like it (the revising). You have to push all kinds of buttons. If you don't push the right one, the computer yells at you and you get all mixed up," Michelle said when I asked how her writ-ing was going.

Because we have only one printer, I had to ask students to give me file names instead of printing out their work. This was an inter-esting experience for me: paper-grading in this computer age. I came in here after class to read student writing from their disks instead of sitting down with the usual stack of papers.

Not very many people managed to hand in file names and fewer managed to get the evaluation done. I blame that on the last-minute meeting that called me out of class. When I came back in to check on things, my students had pulled out the games and were going full steam on those.

Overall, excitement and enthusiasm are high. A real turnaround in classroom interest. I've heard many comments about how surprised kids are to hear the bell ring "already," and I believe word is out and about in school that something is going on in here.

An interesting side note: this project has also sparked a certain amount of interest among faculty members. One has been in here during spare time to learn how to use the *Bank Street Writer.*

Week 2: November 7 to 11. On Tuesday, Karen was sitting at a desk and writing in a notebook. I asked her about her composing process.

"I prefer writing on paper and then typing it into the machine later," she said.

Kenny and Aaron were settling into some heavy work at typing things into their disk files. They both were recording rock lyrics, however, and not original work. Why?

"I just want to check it out and see how it's done," Kenny said. So I'm assuming that the fascination with the mechanical process is still taking precedence over the writing. On this note, Michelle made an interesting comment at the end of last week. "I like this. It's better than writing." There appears to be a distinction here between writing and using the word processor. If you're working on a computer, you can't be writing, for writing is something you do at a school desk with notebook paper and pen at the whim of your English teacher.

Yesterday, Darrell was busily involved with revising his piece of writing on football camp, discovering how to move things around and erase and replace and retype.

Today, only six people are here because of the football game at Tularosa tomorrow and heaven knows what else. Quiet day. The people are investigating the printing process on our one and only printer, so some of the writings handed in this week will be printed. I plan to come in this weekend and print one for everyone so that next week the writing groups have some writing to work on and discuss. There has been no writing discussion in groups away from the computer so far, partly because we haven't had the stuff printed up and partly because those students unassigned to the computer for a day tend to drift and work with other people who are on the computers.

Next week I'd like to emphasize the writing itself. Perhaps the mechanical fascination will begin to wear off. Margaret Jaeger, our local computer teacher, reports that this has happened with her regular computer class. It is possible, I suppose, that a four-week project won't be enough to see this happen. I do know that it won't be easy to get these guys back into the classroom after this. I plan to continue to use this word processing as the year goes on for later composition assignments.

Week 3: November 14 to 18. Teacher feeling like we've reached an impasse. Maybe I'm just grouchy, but it doesn't look to me like a whole lot is going on in here right now.

November 15. I tried to get Grace D. and Sandra to work together today on their printed-out writings while everyone else was on the computers. No go. This is a problem here: the few people not scheduled for a computer on a particular day don't work in writing groups. They either hang out with someone who is on a computer or they sit and draw their graphics on the paper. A few people write at desks, but there seems to be little concentration here. I have the feeling that all this so far is nothing but a computer workshop to these kids, that they have not made the connection that this is supposed to be about writing.

All those rosy evaluations from the kids, are they too idealistic? Certainly they are entertained, but I'm not convinced right now that much serious writing is happening here.

My role so far has been roving helper with mechanical questions, sometime editor, and moral supporter for people attempting new mechanical operations.

November 17. Yesterday was a total bummer. Playing around and not much real work. I was ready to give it all up. Today we had a class meeting at the beginning of the period during which time I expressed these feelings.

"I'm discouraged," I said. "Why all this playing? What is going on here?"

I judge the meeting that then took place to have been a success. Everyone stopped messing around and took part in a serious discussion about what was happening in the classroom. We talked about what could and should happen to improve classroom behavior and we did some important talking about the course of the research. I sense that we're back on course now.

November 29. They were good while I was not here. All substitute reports confirm this. There is not paperwork to show evidence that they were writing, however, so I've asked them today to print out one piece of writing and their evaluations. Walking around the room, I notice that some people have added many new files, notably Sandra and Natalie, so I do know that writing is happening.

What hits me most today is that I am unnecessary here. The work goes on, for the most part, and there is no reason for me to be here. This is indeed a revolution. I'm not quite sure how I feel about it at this moment; it certainly is different than anything I've experienced in a classroom before. I must admit that I feel a little left out, but at the same time I think that what's going on in here is pretty exciting.

At the class meeting tomorrow, I want to hear from them what happened while I was gone and I want to discuss the wrap-up plan for this project. The original plan calls for finishing up and getting the paper going by the end of this week. I think we can stick to that, but that is where I will have to step in as teacher/project director once again and switch the gears on the classroom dynamics.

December 2. I was thinking that I would write in my own paper that the biggest failure here was in the workshop process. I couldn't persuade students to work together in writing groups when they didn't have computer time, and so I felt that no sharing of writing was going on. I'm beginning to suspect that there is indeed sharing happening, but it isn't happening in the traditional small group methods I had planned for.

There seems to be instead a greater sharing during the composing process itself, and a brandnew interest in collaborating, in writing things together on these new mechanical toys. I see one comment by Grace K. that she noticed people looking at the writer's screen and making comments on the writing. In a curious way, writing on this screen has made the writing instantly more public than writing on paper ever could be.

And so, perhaps, the sharing process has taken on a whole new dimension. These people do know what other people are working on in other parts of the room, and they are interested in working together on one piece of writing.

I am beginning to speculate on what may be happening to the composing process with this screen and its instant, painless eraser. I am taken back to Ann Berthoff's ideas about an "all-at-onceness" to the writing process, that to artificially separate composing and revising is wrong because the brain can comprehend the entire process all in one motion, and in fact does compose and revise and edit to a certain extent all at one time.

Maybe Berthoff is right and maybe this word processing experience is reinforcing that, or even proving it, because it sure looks to me right now that this is exactly what happens when a writer composes on a word processor. I see not only fast writing, but also backing up and instant correcting of both typos and word choice, up to sentence level problems.

While I'm engaged in all this heady thought, I notice that my kids are wreaking havoc in the room around me. Aaron is throwing Natalie against the wall, people from here are wandering out into the hall, people from elsewhere are wandering into the room and looking interested, and someone has broken into the file of game disks and has begun to make obnoxious noises on a nearby computer.

And so goes Friday afternoon and any possible intellectual life on the part of this lowly public high school teacher, struggling to stay alive, stay out of the rain, and drink less caffeine.

Conclusions and Interpretations: What This Information Means

Our little research project produced an enormous amount of information in the end. We began to look at revising and, as the project progressed, I began to see that many other things were happening and being recorded in our classroom. As I finally sat down with all the papers put together in one notebook and talked to the students about what had happened, I say that five areas were affected. So I'll now attempt to group the final information accordingly: (1) the revising process on a word processor; (2) computer knowledge; (3) the composing process on a word processor; (4) teaching with the word processor; and (5) the research collaboration process.

1. The revising process on a word processor. As I expected at the outset of the project, revising did seem to come more easily with the use of the machines. After a bit of initial frustration with learning the machine's commands to change the writing, I think most students felt that the word processor offered them a simple route to changing errors in their writing. They were more willing to revise papers they wouldn't have bothered with if it were not for the ease of using the machine to revise the work. Perhaps that is the key point here: writers who would not otherwise bother to revise at all will work at it on the word processor.

I should like to emphasize here that, as they noted in their comments, not everyone was taken in by the ease of the word processor, and they didn't all feel that this was the answer to their writing problems.

2. Computer knowledge. In the beginning of the project, the fascination with the mechanical process was very intense. It was so distracting that I began to think that no one would ever bother to concentrate on what they were writing and observing. This finally did begin to wear off a bit.

For many of the students, I believe the chance to get acquainted with the computer was the main benefit of this project and their major purpose in continuing the work. I suppose this may be the result of the beginning of the computer age in our schools and is inevitable with the introduction of the new devices. In spite of the fact that this seemed to detract from the main objective of the research, I believe this was a very positive movement. I've seen too many dead faces in classrooms to not get excited about this classroom's enthusiasm running very high during our stretch in the computer room. In other words, good things were going on even if they weren't what I initially was looking for in the research question.

3. The composing process on a word processor. Some students preferred to use the computer to compose, others preferred to write on paper and then transfer their work to the computer for further revising and editing. The split between the two groups was about even in this class. Most students advised in their final papers that a writer should give both a chance before making a final decision as to where she prefers to compose.

Collaborative writings occurred spontaneously in this project, and this was quite interesting to me because it was something I didn't expect to happen. I did nothing to encourage students to try this. I believe it was a combination of lack of enough computer space for everyone, and the spirit of helping other people learn to use the machines. In any case, many of the early writings were "conversations" between two people at one machine. This continued on throughout the four weeks of the project, although it was most in evidence during the first week or two.

I also believe that the computers made the writing more public, in that the screens are more visible than writing on paper at a desk. Even though I was at first disappointed that students were not meeting in groups to share their writing, I realized by the end of the last week they were all quite aware of what other people in the room were writing, thanks to those screens and their freedom to wander around the room. They were interacting and talking about writing with other poeple. My students in this school have always been somewhat reluctant to share writings in groups, and so in a curious way, our trips to the computer room caused even more sharing of writing to take place.

As I noted in my journal entries during the project, I believe there is room here to consider Berthoff's "at-onceness" theories about the writing process. Perhaps it is a mistake to separate writing and revising into different steps of the process, because on a word processor, it seems quite apparent that these things are happening together in the writer's mind.

4. Teaching with the word processor. I found that I was less reluctant to suggest major revision in a student paper when I knew it could be easily changed on the computer. There is a fine line between being too picky and thereby discouraging, and being exacting enough to let a student know what good writing ought to look like. When I see a handwritten paper that I know has already been copied over several times, I am not very quick to ask for another revision. A word-processed paper freed me from that problem.

I also found a printed-out draft of a piece of writing to be a wonderful opportunity for conferencing with a writer. We talked about the writing, and with pencils in hand, the writer and I could mark, circle, and draw faces on the paper without fear of the rewriting pain and agony we might be causing. From the teacher viewpoint, I found word processing in the writing classroom to be nothing but a positive addition.

5. The research collaboration process. We learned a lot about computers and revising and learning and teaching. I think the most important thing that happened as a result of this research project is what happened when I walked into the classroom and informed my students that we were going to collaborate on this project and that they were responsible for producing information about themselves and what was happening to all of us.

These students were involved from the beginning and they acted as if this were important to them. They were enthusiastic about what happened with the project. They were motivated to produce the information requested, and they were interested in putting it together and seeing some results.

I, as a teacher, learned to do more disappearing, and I think the students learned to take more responsibility for their learning. It seems to me this is what school is supposed to be about anyway and so I have to say the collaboration was the most exciting part of this research for me.

Recommendations: What I Would Recommend as a Result of this Information

First, I believe that the use of the word processor in an English classroom is appropriate and helpful to the teacher and learner of the writing process. I can't make any sweeping statements about why or exactly how, but it did work quite well in my classroom and I think it could work well in many others. I also firmly believe that we, as high school teachers, need to start producing our own information and reports on our own classrooms. That I may have added a small bit of information to the larger knowledge on writing with microcomputers is very satisfying. If many of us did the same thing in many different classrooms, we would truly have something major to add.

And perhaps most importantly, we need to involve our students in the process of observation because it is a good learning opportunity. I saw something different happening in that classroom when we watched ourselves write. I sense that it was combination of the new—the machines—and the research collaborator status assigned to the students. I put a lot of responsibility on them. I was not in absolute charge of that classroom; we worked together. They made suggestions, watched themselves, and made intelligent observations. I do believe that this collaboration worked and kept working for that group, even after we were officially finished with the research project.

I Gave My Classroom Away

AMANDA BRANSCOMBE
Auburn High School, Auburn, Alabama

When I lost interest in teaching a few years ago, I became a learner and a seeker. At that point in my career, I changed my definition of teacher from a person who imparts knowledge and skills about content to people who are called on to help others (mostly children) learn skills and knowledge, as well as tell their personal stories which will help them make some sense of their lives. Because I believe this to be my mission in teaching, I faced many intellectual conflicts when I entered a classroom with my training in writing exegeses of passages from Shakespeare or T. S. Eliot. I found that my training had very little to do with teaching a child to love literature, to like writing, to tell stories, or even to read.

To resolve this conflict, I used detailed lesson plans, sponsored a newspaper and several yearbooks, coached a tennis team, and took special graduate courses which specialized in teaching writing. Struggling with the impossible task of putting my definition of teaching into a real classroom and never being satisfied with my product, I often felt like Atlas when he wanted to shrug; but I continued to shift to new teaching approaches.

Finally, I realized that there is no formula for teaching the way I wanted to teach. Rather than make my stay in the classroom short-lived, I shifted my teaching to a learning pilgrimage or search with my students. Discovering, as Studs Terkel said, that "growth is forever" and nothing is static or final, I focused on process rather than product, on relationships in a community of learners rather than entangling teacher-student battles, and on learning rather than worksheets. I used research in my classroom as a tool to help me with my new approach to teaching. Ann Berthoff, in "Teacher as REsearcher," best describes what I hoped research would offer in my classroom.

It helps to pronounce "research" the way Southerners do: REsearch. REsearch, like REcognition, is a REflexive act. It means looking—and looking again. This new kind of REsearch would not mean going out after new "data" but REconsidering what is at hand. REsearch would come to mean looking and looking again at what happens in the English classroom. . . . We need to interpret what goes on when students respond to one kind of assignment and others do not.

(Berthoff, 1979)

Dixie Goswami, my instructor at Bread Loaf School of English's Program in Writing developed my skills to do research and directed me as I designed the beginnings of my first project. Through her teaching, I saw research as a way of improving my teaching practices by observing, recording, and analyzing what was happening in the classroom. She showed me that research in a classroom could do just what Berthoff had written.

After spending the summer of 1982 thinking about the kind of research I wanted to do as a classroom teacher, I invited a researcher, Shirley Brice Heath, an anthropologist from Stanford University's School of Education, to work with me. She had taught in both elementary and secondary education and her study of language use in the communities of the Piedmont Carolinas, *Ways With Words: Life Stories Made in Communities and Classrooms,* seemed to be compatible with my ideas and my areas of the South. For that year, she and I joined my ninth grade Basic English students in a research project.

Our project's first phase was a letter exchange between the ninth-graders and my advanced Expository Writing students who were eleventh- and twelfth-graders. I had successfully done such an activity the year before and wanted to repeat it. Why the note exchange?

Note-writing offers people a means of communication within a formal, institutional setting. People love those notes—not formal letters, but those neat little notes one finds in a faculty mailbox, or those that the teacher scribbles on a student paper, or those that a friend writes when he should be listening in a math class. Those notes act as a secret bond—an intimate code between two people. They communicate feeling and information. They even move into adult life in the form of notes on memo pads, notes left on a husband's pillow, or notes given to children when saying "I love you" is too scary.

Students from all levels of academic ability pass and receive notes throughout the school day. When some teachers spot this activity in their classrooms, they usually punish the students by reading the note aloud or correcting it and grading it before returning it to its owner. Instead of doing this, I decided to make the notes a writing activity in my classroom.

My high school provided the perfect setting for such a note exchange because of the school environment. In 1981–82, it had over 1,000 students in grades 9–12 with a 35% black, 65% white ratio. The city school is in a university town, and its university population (18,000+) creates a split in the school's population. Most students are either children of university personnel or children of poor, working-class laborers. The university parents' children are at the top of the academic spectrum, and the others are at the bottom, with a very small group for the middle. Because of this demographic make-up, a student division occurs which can be seen in participation in ourside activities, school dropouts, academic achievement, college attendance, and general student attitudes about school and learning. In a sense, the high school's buildings house two different schools.

Within those two schools, the "school" learning did not function for the students at the lower end of the spectrum. The students simply did not find school to be a place where literacy functioned for them. This kind of detachment was reflected in my school's weaker students by many of their repeated disciplinary problems, low self-esteem, lack of academic success, lower test scores, and lack of participation in extracurricular activities with the exception of football and basketball. Writing in school did not function for them either. Indeed, writing was used as punishment. Students faced writing 500 sentences which started, "I will behave . . . ," or writing an essay about behaving in . . . , and faced sure failure which came with papers with red marks and F's. Thus, most of those students did not write.

Often the college-bound students also saw writing as a form of punishment and failure. They too had to write sentences and received C's on their book reports, but they knew that writing was an entrance into their society. They saw it as practice for college writing, as information gathering, as moving up in their society, as jobs in the community and even as possible articles after graduate school (like those they saw their college professor parents writing).

While both of those groups seemingly had one use of writing in common (sentences for punishment) in the school setting, they shared another common use for it. Both groups wrote notes to their friends every day. Those notes were honest, lively, and showed some degree of skill.

Because of those observations about notes and the school's environment, I decided to use the notes between the older and younger students. I recognized that the notes might just contain gossip, lunch escapades, and "who did what"; but I also hoped that they might contain information about the students' goals, successes, problems, and failures. My goal for the exchange was not to have the students become friends outside the context of the notes, but rather to communicate as equals through writing.

The semester note-writing activity offered the older students an experience with a real audience, practice writing in a mode besides the essay, learning to help another person, and learning to extend their ideas beyond a generalization. It offered the ninth-graders a ten-point bonus for writing a note, a chance to write without teacher comments or grades, and an opportunity to volunteer to do a writing project. For both groups, the exchange was voluntary and at any point the student could stop writing his pal and do a regular writing assignment. (No one did!)

At the beginning of the project I also hoped that the older students could serve as a language model for the younger students. Those students might be able to help the younger students with problems of adjusting to a new school. Since the young students frequently experienced difficulties with learning, the school administrations, and the school social setting, as well as problems with the police and with raising young children of their own, I hoped that the older students could also help the ninth-graders with adjusting to being teenagers. The eleventh- and twelfth-graders had problems of their own, but they were at least functioning in the school's social and academic setting. If their caring and note-writing could help the ninth-grader move into the school's mainstream, then the project would be a success.

It soon became apparent that the advisor/advisee roles assumed by the groups dissolved as both students explored their mutual interests. I realized that the ninth-grader who was being abused by family members often helped the eleventh-grader more than the eleventh-grader helped the ninth-grader. That turn of events was totally unexpected and I recorded the following observation in my field journal after several weeks of seeing such events.

I have noted that at this point the child who has problems with acquiring language at an early age really needs the language model more than the one who does not. The knowledge of who has problems and who doesn't can't be seen in a classroom by an untrained teacher. The early language problem may be as simple as someone not listening when the child wanted to tell him a story or as complex as no one to model for his language. So the *real* model doesn't necessarily stand as the eleventh- and twelfth-grader. In some situations, the ninth-grader is the language model because of work with the communication process.

To me, the child's ability to go through the steps of complaint, conflict, love, anger, etc. [depends on] this early language success. . . . I believe that language and emotional problems go hand in hand. If a child can't express himself because he can't deal with his emotions, then he reacts as Andre did when he fought the white boy and then cursed the coaches.

Each pair of letter writers created their own unique story. The method I used for setting up those pairs was simple. With the first exchange, I told the students to write a page describing their hobbies, themselves, and their jobs (if they had one). After both groups did this exercise, I matched the students based on the interests they mentioned. Using the local Project Uplift Big Brother/Big Sister training manual as a springboard for some of my pairing ideas, I tried to avoid pairing a boy and a girl by adding a third member to such groups. I also made mistakes in the pairings that turned into successes. One such mistake regarded horseback riding. The following is an excerpt from the exchange between the two girls after I told the advanced student about the ninth-grader's love for riding.

CHARLENE (ninth-grader):   . . . and on class i like is math and i think that I'm going to like english. I like to go riding on Sunday. Maybe you would like to go. . . .
LINDA (eleventh-grader):   . . . I used to ride horses a lot before I had hip surgery, but now I can not sit on them. Thanks for inviting me to go riding with you. Where do you go riding? . . .
CHARLENE: I mostly go out riding anywhere. no i do not go on horses. I ride in a car. How else would I be going?

After they cleared up that mistake, they continued the correspondence even when the ninth-grader dropped out of school in November.

When I completed the pairings, I asked the students to write their first notes. The older students wrote first, using a list of suggested topics which I wrote on the board. Some of those included their goals, successes, problems, positive experiences, and stories (about their grandparents, pets, and friends). Students were also encouraged to pick their own topics for the notes. After that introduction to note-writing for both classes, I wrote ideas on the board, talked to individual students about specific notes, asked that they date their notes for research purposes, but did no other formal instruction about those notes or their content.

Both groups stayed interested in the letter exchange. One eleventh-grader asked, "Will he understand what I mean from what I wrote? What if I tell him the wrong thing to do? This is more important than an essay!"

If the pal did not live up to the page length limit for the note, the other pal was angry. They wanted *real* notes which were (to them) a page or more.

The groups also respected my desire to have an hour between the two classes so that the students would not encounter each other and so that I could photocopy the letters. The eleventh-grade class met at the fourth hour, so I collected those notes, copied them, skimmed them (*but never censored or commented in writing*), and then gave them to the ninth-graders at the beginning of their sixth-hour class. Then the ninth-graders read their notes and wrote their pal. This activity took about 20 minutes at first, but as the semester progressed, the students took most of the hour for their notes. Those who did not need the entire hour had other activities to do when they finished the notes. Those activities were always fun so that they never felt that they were being punished for finishing early.

When the students did the note-writing, I observed them and recorded those observations in a fieldnote journal. Typical entries read:

Oct. 5, 1981, 6th hour, 9th English

ERIC: His spelling don't matter to me. What he say does.

TIM: What's he mad with me for? I'm asking how to join a club, not what clubs to join.

TEACHER: Well, tell him that.

TIM: I am.

CASSANDRA: They want to know my business.

BEN: Come here and read Mark's letter. I can't read his writing.

BIG RED: I don't want them to know about me. I just don't feel good. (He puts his head on his desk with his face resting on the note.)

TIM C.: (Summarizes his pal's note as I walk by. He stops me and directs a statement to me.) She says I don't have no run-on sentences in this note. I know about run-on sentences but I get in a hurry and forget to put in periods.

TIM A.: I don't want to write no letter today. I ain't got no knowledge today.

BIG RED: (Raises his head, shakes it and mumbles) I don't. (Check the note from Greg and Eric to see what questions they asked that would upset him this much.)

EUGENE: How do I write this where it makes sense? How do you say it?

TEACHER: Well, how would you say it?

(Eugene tells me what he wants to say and then I suggest that he write what he has said and he does.)

(Thoughts after the class)
. . . I have to modify two things. One, the kids have shot my twenty minutes to hell. They need more time for their notes and take it. They work slowly and take pride in what they do with their letters. My second surprise deals with the topics. Today I really saw this. . . . They are aware of the number of questions in the letters, but they don't know how or don't choose to shift the topics in the letters to something beyond surface chatter. Some of the students are moving into stories but most are just frustrated with the surface chatter and endless questions that they see as prying. . . .

As the weeks passed, the notes varied in length and topicality. Each pair reached a point of crisis in their relationship, however. After that crisis, the students shifted control of the relationship from the eleventh- and twelfth-graders being the leaders to the ninth-graders having an equal amount of power in the relationship. The following excerpts show such a shift.

MARK (eleventh-grader): Man, when you gonna' join a club! I have given you all the suggestion I can. I don't know what else to say to you about this club situation. If you are not going to join a club quit writing to me and asking about them.

TIM (ninth-grader): I'm going to buy you a pair of glasses so you can read. I have not been asking what club to join. I've been asking how to join, and if you were really reading you would have noticed I've been writing about other things too but you insist on telling me about all the clubs because you can't read. I will have you a pair of glasses very soon so you can tell me how to join the anchor club like I told you.

MARK: I have got some bad news for you. I do not need glasses. I already have some contact lenses to correct my vision. It is now 20/20.

I also have some more bad news about anchor club. Anchor club is only for girls to join. Besides, I think its to late to join any clubs.

The notes also shifted from random sentences that had very little relation to one another to flowing prose that had transition and unity. The following shows such a shift as the evelenth-grader shared this experience with his ninth-grade writing pal.

When I got home yesterday I found out that one of my good friends was in the hospital. He broke his leg really bad playing soccer. Another kid kicked him. He thought he was going to have an operation, but the doctor changed his mind. But he does have to stay in the hospital until Wednesday. I went with some other people to go visit him last night. He was kind of depressed. I hope we cheered him up some, but I'm not sure. I think I'll go visit him tomorrow and take him something, some food or something.

While the passage required no specific response from the ninth-grader, the older student did share an important experience with that younger student and showed how he dealt with a friend being in the hospital.

After several months we (Heath and I) shifted the ninth-graders from a personal one-to-one writing task to a group task in which Heath wrote the group and they responded as individuals to her letters. When she wrote, she discussed information about her travels, her work, and tasks she wanted them to help her do.

Since you will not be writing letters [to your pals] this semester, I had hoped to ask you to help collect fieldnotes for me. Fieldnotes are the records anthropologists make of what happens in life around them in the place they are living. I have lived and written fieldnotes in many parts of the world. Some of you may want to look at the map and see where these places are, since I had not heard of many of these places until I was much older than you are. I worked first in Guatemala and Mexico, living among Indian groups there and studying their children at home and at school. Then I went to Japan and went to the most northern island—Hokkaido—where I studied the rural people and their ways of coping with modern life—cars, televisions, roads, and tape recorders. . . .

The students responded to her letters by asking questions and telling her about themselves.

. . . Shirley I've gotten to know you more than I thought I did. You're very sweet. I think that you would go out of your way to help us as much as possible, and anyone else. [The following questions are with reference to a tote bag that Shirley sent to Cassandra when she returned from her trip to Brazil.] Shirley I would like to ask you a question or 2. What does Chemin de Fer, means? Does it mean that thats the name of the company that manufacted it? [The tote bag] Or it's the name of a building.

The letter exchange with the researcher, like the first exchange, took one class period a week and was voluntary.

Heath served as a new, impersonal audience who had a "felt need" for the work the ninth-graders produced. She and I made the class shift from writing the individuals to writing the researcher before the end of the school's semester, but we had them continue writing their pals. In preparation for the shift, I showed a filmstrip about an anthropologist who was working in Central America. She was using the Central American Indians both as informants and assistants. As the students viewed the filmstrip, one of the fellows said, "We was informants. Now we going to be assistants like that man but do we have to wear them funny looking clothes to be assistants?" I assured him that he would not have to wear strange clothes to write an anthropologist or help her with her tasks. The fellow with a somewhat relieved look on his face said, "Okay, then I'll help her."

In addition to that filmstrip, I showed the students similar films about an anthropologist at work. The students also wrote autobiographies which used a series of questions to guide them through that activity. My purpose was to have the students begin recording who they were, where they were from, and what they wanted for themselves (as far as goals, a future career, and a family). After they wrote the autobiographies, we videotaped the students presenting those to their fellow classmates and then mailed copies of their papers to Heath.

Heath responded asking the group to become researchers on the uses of reading and writing in their own communities, school, and classroom. The purpose for this was to enlist them as coresearchers with her in learning about the patterns of using reading and writing across communities of the United States. This task was more specific than her earlier request for fieldnotes. Her recently completed study of language uses in communities in another region was sent to the students, and I read portions of it to them in order for them to understand what the completed results of a research project looked like.

As the year progressed, more tasks evolved around Heath's requests for data and my ideas about the students' activities that might be of interest to her. Those tasks also expanded as she wrote critical comments on the students' fieldnotes, reports, and letters describing their communities.

The students continued their personal letters to Heath, but expanded their writings to include fieldnotes, interviews, observation, and timed writings. They taped oral histories of older people in the community and young children learning to talk. The following is a sample of the reading that one of the students observed:

Reading
Friday After School

My neaighbor was reading the *O-A* News. (A local newspaper)
My aunt look at the mail when she got home and read the HBO
book to see what was coming on TV. My uncle looked in the
phonebook for a number.

Saturday

I read a record cover and looked at a magazine. I read a candy
lable (Sneaker). I also read the names on the T.V. screen when
a movie came on. I read a Kodak film box. . . .

The students could decide on their own format for fieldnotes
as long as they observed Heath's rule for using detailed descriptions.
Write as much description as you can. Remember, paint a picture or take a photograph for me through your words. . . .

The following shows another student's approach and style for taking
fieldnotes.
On the night of 4/13/82 I went over on campus to go to the
movie which was at the War Eagle. When a friend and I got
there and got our money out the lady said that a parent had
to be there in order for us to see it. My uncle got us in. The
movie's name was up on a side wall. It read "Grow Up at
Party." After that a friend and I went to McDonald's. I ordered
a Big-Mack, small fries, and a large order coke.

Heath gave the students comments on these tasks rather than
grades. Her comments were extensive, specific, and always demanding of more and more attention to detail, care in observation, and
coverage in writing. The following excerpt shows a typical set of
comments which also served as instructions.
When you write down the kinds of questions, you will need
also to write down what happened around the question. Did
the people look at each other? Did one person do what the
other asked? Did anyone ask a question to try to figure out
what the first question meant? . . .

In late spring, Heath came to the class and talked with them
about their final tasks as a group and as individuals. She divided the
class into smaller groups for those tasks. One group interviewed people about language used in sports. While she gave them a task sheet
describing the kinds of information she needed, they developed their
own format for obtaining this information. Another group directed
the class in administering a sample community reading inventory

215

and then tabulated the inventories' results when the students returned their copies. Some of the students continued their fieldnotes about the questions they heard outside school and the occasions for writing, reading, and conversations.

One student who had been in the class from September until she dropped out in November, continued to write her writing pal, the researcher, and me during the winter. In response to the researcher's request (in a letter), she taped a history of her first child's language development and agreed to begin reading with her toddler thirty minutes each day and taping this reading. She continues to collect tapes and communicate with the researcher, who sends her letters commenting on ways in which the toddler is increasingly responding to the reading.

Another student with severe learning disabilities had not written over a half page at a single setting by late fall. By November, he occasionally wrote two pages for his letter writing pal. During a timed writing contest in early spring, he wrote nine pages during one class. He later completed the story which totaled sixteen pages.

A young girl who loved to write poetry, wrote poems on scraps of paper and did not try to compile them or read other poems. The researcher wanted her to continue writing poems during the summer and to start reading poetry. Now, the girl is writing on a regular basis, keeping her poems in a journal, and reading poetry along with her escape fiction.

All of the students experienced growth in developing a positive self-image, writing on a regular basis, interacting and functioning as a working group, reading a variety of materials, and functioning as researchers. They passed their Basic Competency Test for Alabama's ninth-graders and realized that literacy functioned in their lives both in and out of school. One young fellow described the project in the following way:

> Well as we reach to the end of this school year I think of all the work that we have did to creat this book even though I have wrote a few stupid things I had to write something good so I will take the good and forget about the bad because we as a class did that. Well I hate writing just to be writing but this is a book so I wish I could work more on it next year because I have already planned my summer and I am looking forward to enjoying it. If I had my way I would not wish to go on back in school but for Mrs. Branscombe to teach us next year this same class and we continue well I believe I would enjoy it if it went on to our senior year to show that we achieved something at Auburn High School besides a diploma so I must leave my end.

Another student wrote the following about the class.

> At the beginning of the year I though these English class would be the same as the others but it turend out to be different. I though all of the wrighting would be a wast of time to the 11th grader and the wrighting to Mrs. Heath but as we got to know each other I began to like it. These was more than a English class it was a beging a begining to a career these class has taught me so much about me and others how to see a problem and know how to solve it with out harm done. I have just come to reality to see what I would do and doing it.
>
> Know I have to move on and keep in mine what I have learned and use it to the best of my ability.

Because the work was voluntary and did not receive a grade, students were asked at the end of the year to respond to doing the work without grades. One wrote:
6/1/82

> It was not a big issue to me not having a grade on my paper. I feel it you've done well a person's grattitude can be appreciated just as much as an perfect 100. It seems as if you don't have a grade on your paper then it's not telling you what your work is worth. But I'd rather have Shirley say, "Loretta's work was extremely good." Then I can sit back and say "You know what can I "Say". Instead of having a number at the top of my paper giving me a total of what my work was worth.

Another student wrote:

> I like working without a grade because I thought I was getting a and wasn't. I guess I am like Shirley. She likes her work and so do I. Since I like my work I didn't really care about a grade. My work with me cousin is really great. While I am working with him I am not concerned about any grade. I just want to make you and Shirley happy with me and my work. The grade is not so important. Our work is.

I, too, experienced personal and professional growth while working with the researcher and the students. At the beginning of the project I was the typical classroom teacher who felt that my role was to stand in front of the room and *pour knowledge* into the students, while they sat at their desks and *learned*. As the year progressed, I gave up that role and became a co-learner with my students. I no longer stood in front of them. In fact, I gave up my classroom and changed it into a learning lab in which the students and I equally focused on gathering the data that we needed.

Heath helped bring about this shift. She encouraged the students by broadening their worlds through her letters about her travels, and gave them a real audience who needed their data. She also helped me to make a shift from a teacher who imparted skills and knowledge to a person who was a co-learner and who started telling my own story as well as helping my students tell theirs. She also helped me by allowing me to call her once a week. These calls to Heath added new ideas to my approaches, and acted as my sounding board. Because she was so positive in her attitude about us and with us and because she let us share her work and her tasks as researcher, we made our classroom functional. Our work, added to hers, created a cooperative learning environment for all concerned.

We had become co-producers of knowledge with other researchers in other areas of the country. We became researchers who would take our data and release it through analysis so that other teachers and researchers could use it in the larger body of knowledge about students' learning patterns, teachers' patterns, and classroom activities.

The students and I felt that we were in a real work setting, doing something that mattered. Our activities generated work in the traditional classroom sense and also created more writing and reading for other students and for Heath. Attendance improved, students became monitors for each other's classroom behavior, individual students improved their academic skills, and everyone had fun learning.

Any teacher who sets out to do classroom research will encounter many totally different problems from the ones she faced in her traditional classroom setting. I would be dishonest if I did not mention some of the ones I faced. Our research project had no financial assistance other than my pocketbook, and a $250 research grant from Bread Loaf School of English, so I always needed money. I often had difficulty keeping up with the research project and my other four writing classes (whose sizes ranged from twenty-four to twenty-eight students per class). Because I had no secretary or aide, I photocopied and mailed everything to Heath, which took hours to do. Finally, I experienced my students' anger when they did not understand why the researcher did not write them individually but continued to treat them as co-workers expected to accomplish tasks. None of these problems caused me to avoid doing other research projects in which my students and I could play major decision-making and learning roles.

I will not try to duplicate this project; too much of it came from love, intuition, and classroom magic. Only now that we have finished can Heath and I look back and say that certain activities made sense according to a certain "theory."

While I do not advocate that every teacher attempt formal research in her classroom, I do suggest that they look at what is happening in those classrooms. When they start looking, they may shift to interactive learning activities, which will cause them to become interested in research and producing information with their students that can contribute to the larger body of knowledge about students' and teachers' learning habits in those classrooms. In other words, I agree with Ann Berthoff, who states in "The Teacher as REsearcher":

> My spies tell me that it's becoming harder and harder for researchers to get into the schools; I rejoice in that news because I think it might encourage teachers to become researchers themselves, and once that happens, the character of research is bound to change.

Reflections on Classroom Research

LUCINDA C. RAY
with the 11–3 ENGLISH CLASS OF 1982–1983
Pioneer Valley Regional School, Northfield, Massachusetts

What's the purpose of classroom research? Why in the world would anyone study writing in a bottom-track eleventh-grade English class when Mina Shaughnessy and Sondra Perl have already cornered the market on research among basic writers? Here are some of my initial reasons for undertaking such a project.

1. I was frustrated and dissatisfied with the lack of success I had in talking with my students about their writing.
2. I wanted to apply what I was learning about the writing process in summer courses, workshops, and reading.
3. I was tired of September enthusiasm fading by December. I thought an ongoing project might help keep me mentally alive and consistent.
4. A professor and several fellow teachers encouraged me to try it.
5. Bread Loaf School of English offered me one of several very small research grants, which dignified, though did not really compensate me for, my efforts.

In September of 1982, when I began a year-long study of what happens when I talk with my students about their writing, I chose

The 11–3 English class of 1982–1983 included Todd Ackermann, David Adams, Roger Doiron, Mary Hogan, Tina Holton, Kevin Olson, Kellie Singley, Brandon Staiger, Chris Staiger, and Nancy Walker.

my 11-3 English class, rather than my college prep 11-1 section. It is these students who have become my coauthors in this project. I teach at a rural, regional high school in Western Massachusetts. The class vacillated between ten and thirteen members, with nine students consistently enrolled. Of these nine, six had failed the state-mandated Basic Skills test in Writing in both ninth and tenth grades. They were to take the test, for the third time, in November.

Now, in June of 1983, I sit down to reflect on what we have learned, taught each other, written, read, discovered. *Reflect* is a multifaceted term. It includes remembering, thinking, mirroring, creating images, changing perspectives. All of these connotations apply to the research project of the last school year.

Perhaps the most significant finding is that the very act of undertaking and continuing a classroom research project forced me to take time to reflect upon what was happening in my classroom. After teaching for seventeen years, it is no small thing to admit that I am usually too busy grading and evaluating to pay very much attention to learning in June. However, this year, as I went back to my initial research proposal, I was struck by its aptness:

"Research is not a process of proving something, but a process of discovering and learning." This was one of the summarizing points made by James Britton in his course, "Studying Writing: Approaches to Research" (Bread Loaf School of English, Middlebury, VT, Summer 1982). This view of research is tremendously liberating, for it allows classroom teachers to take seriously the ordinary business of their lives as teachers. Britton emphasized that teachers need to theorize from their own experience, to develop a rationale for what they do which is based on both knowledge of theory and on their own experience.

Within my classroom, important thinking, talking, reading, and writing go on during writing conferences. My research proposal, then, is to keep track of these conversations so that I may learn more about what actually takes place, what effects become evident in the students' continuing writing, and what changes I might make to make this conference time more effective for writing and learning.

Britton (1970) advocates the importance of:
. . . the role of teacher as a sympathetic reader: with the least articulate writers it may well be that all progress depends upon such a relationship. (p. 257)

Nancy Martin (1976) offers another evaluation of the teacher's role:
It can make a crucial difference when the teacher is prepared to be a good listener as well as a fluent talker. By definition

almost, where this is the case the learning context becomes more cooperative because there is scope in it for pupils to make genuine contributions of their own and to follow the thread of their own thoughts. (pp. 38–39)

Further, I believe that the talk of students among themselves is equally important as they explore ideas and try to establish a clear sense of audience in their writing. This cannot happen if I am the only audience.

Therefore, I propose to listen carefully to my students as they talk with me and with each other about their writing. I will tape-record conferences and enlist my students in transcribing the tapes. Nancy Martin (1976) documents "how valuable it can be to preserve talk so that it can be talked about further." (p. 51) The tapes and transcripts, then, will not only provide me with information about my part in the conferences, but they will legitimize for the students the value of their own talk about their writing. Martin reports:

The teacher had handed out copies of the transcript . . . gradually the fact that it was *their own talk* that they were reading dawned on them and a further interesting discussion about the differences between spoken and written language took place. (p. 51)

It is the relationship of the talk with the writing which is my primary interest. Therefore, I will be looking at the drafts and further writings which relate to these conferences. Once I begin to discover more clearly what takes place, I will begin to focus the conversations more helpfully so that students can learn from their own writing. My assumption is that increasing awareness of the importance of the talk which takes place will enable students to clarify their thinking and their writing. As they internalize slowly the real audiences our talk has provided, an increased awareness of audience will emerge in their writing. Here, then, are the details of my proposed inquiry:

Research Questions

1. What does the actual conversation consist of during a writing conference?
2. What effects does the conference have on subsequent drafts and other pieces of writing?
3. What differences in conversation and effects are evident if the conference is between student/student or teacher/student?
4. Can I modify the conference pattern to make learning and writing more effective?

I learned some answers to these questions. I modified my original design. I learned to ask some new questions which I hadn't anticipated. I made discoveries about my students as writers that I would not have known enough to question at the beginning.

Reflection, as remembering, thinking about, and seeing from a new perspective, describes the impact of the study on me as a researcher and learner. Reflection as a way of talking with students about their writing describes the impact of the study on me as a teacher of writing. That is, I helped students to see their writing by reflecting its effect on me as a reader.

Probably the most important tool of the project was the tape recorder. It helped me hear what I really said, not what I planned to say, or hoped I'd said, or wished I'd said, or intended to say. It helped me listen to what my students said, didn't say, ignored, picked up on. We English teachers are highly verbal. The tape recorder reflected the power of this verbal dominance over students. At the beginning of the study, I hoped it would help me recognize and redirect that power. At the end of the year I believe the tape recorder accomplished that goal. It was able to capture talk, that fleeting tone or barely heard comment. It helped me recognize the cumulative effect of my presence as I listened to myself, five or six conferences in a row.

First, I could consider what we had said together and what kinds of writing had prompted the talk and resulted from it. This opportunity to learn about my own teaching style was sometimes painful, but definitely worthwhile. It had a far different impact on my practices than workshops or academic readings.

Second, as Nancy Martin suggested, using the tape recorder lent weight and dignity to the talk. Its presence demonstrated that what we said was worthwhile. This is an indefinable feeling, but talk did become an increasingly important and even essential phase of the writing process in this class.

I taped conferences throughout the year. I transcribed and categorized a set of conferences in September, February, and May. The results of this analysis are included here. I saved the drafts and finished pieces which relate to these conferences and have included samples.

I had conducted one previous brief research project in my school, with the enthusiastic approval of my principal, and once again I experienced administrative approval for this project. Several colleagues have similar interests in the writing process and the use of conferences. I also talked with and gained the approval of my eleventh-graders before the project began, so that they were not specimens but participants. I believe this supportive climate was an essential preliminary step.

Table 1. Transcripts Proportion of Words

September	Words	%	February	Words	%	May	Words	%
Student C.	24	6	Student Ke.	218	34	Student K.	63	15
Ms. R.	391	94	Ms. R.	428	66	Ms. R.	375	85
Student A.	139	30	Student D.	154	35	Student To.	118	25
Ms. R.	321	70	Ms. R.	281	65	Ms. R.	362	75
Student K.	42	7	Student R.	151	39	Student D.	229	55
Ms. R.	546	93	Ms. R.	281	61	Ms. R.	281	45
Student T.	184	25				Student N.	212	30
Ms. R.	548	75				Ms. R.	491	70
Student N.	158	24						
Ms. R.	491	76						

The students were cooperative but academically nonverbal. Discussion of any kind was a struggle, as the September writing conferences dramatically demonstrate. Table 1 shows the number of words spoken by teacher and student. In general, I initially outtalked my students 4 to 1, or 80 percent to 20 percent. Clearly, we would have to unlearn a lot of unproductive talk habits for my students to be able to use talking for learning to write.

The following conference transcript and paper drafts of one of those early conferences is typical:

Student C

Draft 1 (September)

The rallie started with people entering the Gym screaming and yelling trying to find a place to sit, there was walls full of poster and signs with the saying vote Kim for Quenn and other one's to. After sitting down, the speaker anounced the 9th grade Queen and escort candidate, with muscic in the background, they walked down the Isle and around, walking between balloons they sat down at the end of Isle, the next couple came the speaker told about them.

Draft 2 (After Conference)

The only reason I like rallies is because the classes are shortened, they are really a pain because one, you never can find a place to sit, two, you never can understand what the is saying, three, if you don't sit in the back you get covered with flying debris, like sawdust and confetti. As you enter the Gym, little kids are running around, other kids are screaming and yelling.

I try to find where the Juniors are sitting, I look to the right, there they are at the very end of the gym. Getting up to the top of the Bleachers is another problem, but I managed to get to the top. I set my stuff down and grab a handfull of confetti from a neighbor and get ready for the Junior Queen and escort to enter, here they come people are screaming and yelling then they appear infront of the Bleachers. In a second they are plastered with confetti.

While this is going on you cannot hear the speaker or the muscic which is the most important part. Then finally the Rallie is over, and you repeat what you just did coming in, you do on the way out.

Conference

MS. R.: Could you hear the speakers?

C.: No.

MS. R.: I've never been about to hear the speakers. That's all there is, is screaming, right? Um. . . . Where did you sit?

C.: uh . . . on this side, corner, by the door.

MS. R.: Not the seventh- and eighth-grade side? The seventh and eighth grade, you know, where the seventh and eighth grades were, across? The locker room side?

C.: Yeah, yeah.

MS. R.: OK, and you were sitting sort of where the teachers were, or all the way on the other side?

C.: Other side.

MS. R.: All the way down. I thought maybe we just couldn't hear at our end. OK, so here's the gym. Here's the locker room. You're sitting here? (drawing diagram)

C.: Right here.

MS. R.: OK. Um . . . I think the information that you couldn't understand, in fact you can't hear the music either—it's supposed to be a song they really think about picking out, right?

C.: Yeah.

MS. R.: They spend some time picking it out. Um . . . might be clearer if you did a kind of description of what you actually *could* see and hear. And contrast it with what you were supposed to be able to see and hear. You were sitting up or down?

C.: Up. Top.

MS. R.: OK. Was that better for seeing, do you think? And that means you could probably see the person speaking right here?

C.: Yeah.

MS. R.: Even though you can't hear what they're saying. (laugh) You hear a lot of screaming. But, you don't get hit with anything, either, right?

C.: No.

MS. R.: That's an advantage! (laugh)

C.: Yeah. (laugh)

MS. R.: OK, so maybe you could just describe one trip around. And what was supposed to be going on and what you could hear. But, make it more descriptive. Like, "As I pushed up to the top row of bleachers, people were pushing me." And somebody was screaming in your ear, and you couldn't hear what they were saying. Where do they do the records from, over here?

C.: Yeah.

MS. R.: Can you see that? From where you were? So describe what you can see and that would make it clearer how confusing and loud and noisy it is, than just saying it was confusing and loud and noisy. Like, if you can see them put the needle on the record, but you don't hear the record. (laugh)

C.: Yeah.

MS. R.: But, you might want to pick just one candidate to do that for. Like one candidate where you know what they should have been saying, but you couldn't hear it or you could only hear part of it. . . . OK? Was that helpful?

C.: Yeah.

	Words	*%*
Ms. R.	391	94
Student C.	24	6

These samples demonstrate that I am primarily probing in an effort to extend student ideas, as a method of pre-writing, rather than restructuring, refining, revising. Much of the second draft incorporates ideas talked about, details. However, the decision to divide into paragraphs was the student's own. So even though I talked too much and took more ownership of the piece than I wish I had, the conference certainly helped the student to extend and to discover an organizational framework for the piece.

Probably the most exciting result of my research is that I can verify the change and development I *feel* has taken place with the hard evidence of the transcripts and drafts. My research may not break new ground in theory of writing process, but it documents how teaching and learning, informed by theory, can be improved even in a potentially discouraging class.

We have made consistent changes in the use of air time. The proportion of the conference talk is now close to 60 percent for the teacher and 40 percent for the student. I am learning to talk less. My students are learning to talk more. They are being allowed to talk more, as I learn to pause and wait. I frequently begin the conference by asking the student to read her piece (not included in the word count). This practice may give students freedom to continue talking.

The content of the talk has changed along with the proportions. Frankly, I regard this as the most significant area of change. As Table 2 shows, we discuss their written text and their plans more. I do less pre-writing or extending talk. I do more questioning or clarifying of ideas they are already working on. I encourage more. The specific instructions I give seem to be in the realm of mechanics, writing technique, to help them clarify their own ideas. Students come to the conference with more questions. They disagree occasionally. The conferences end with energy and optimism rather than deadening silence and directives. Finally, I am learning to use group conferences. Writing groups only began to function well, however, after four or five months of individual conferences.

The following excerpts from a conference about two drafts of a student's January paper illustrate some of these changes.

Student Ti.

"Sorry To See You Go"

Draft 1

A while ago there was this friend of mine during the end of the summer she met this boy and she liked him alot but she didn't know what to do well one night she had a dream that she would take her dog for a walk and pretend that her dog got away well the next day she was taking her dog for a walk she usually takes it for a walk and when she got to the house where the boy lived he was out side with his dog well she was not paying any attention to the dog that it ran write over to the boy or his dog. . . .

Draft 2

You know how it is when you see someone you like but you don't want to go up and say anything to them. Because your afraid he won't like you.

Table 2. Content of Conferences

	SEPTEMBER (5 Transcriptions)	FEBRUARY (3 Transcriptions)
TEACHER		
Focus on Writing—Text		
1. Teacher describing student writing	9	5
2. Asking student to describe writing	0	13
3. Focus on specific sentence in text	5	0
Supporting Writing		
1. Encouraging, approving	10	18
2. Agreeing	1	1
3. Linking with other students	0	6
4. Laughing, joking	5	3
Questions, Student as Expert		
1. Asking for clarification	16	1
2. Asking student for information beyond text	46	3
3. Rephrasing, repeating, checking, understanding	18	11
Questions, Writer's Craft		
1. Composing	0	2
2. Changes in drafts	2	0
3. Focus on structure	3	4
4. Audience	0	5
Clarifying Options, Choices	12	4
Teaching, Instructing	1	5
Specific Suggestions for Changes in Text	30	4
STUDENT		
Focus on Writing—Text		
1. Describing writing	0	14
Answering Teacher Questions		
1. Supplying more information about text	54	9
2. Agreeing	31	13
3. Don't know	6	0
Asking Questions		
1. Asking for clarification	2	3
2. Asking for instruction	0	2
Thinking Out Loud		
1. Telling about composing	0	3
2. Haven't written it yet	0	3
3. Initiating an idea	1	2
Making Choices		
1. Disagreeing with teacher	1	1
2. Choosing from alternatives posed by teacher	3	0
3. Uncertainty, insecurity	0	4

Sandy thought the same thing. During the end of the summer she saw this boy she liked his name was Mich he lived just down the road.

One night Sandy had a dream that she would take her dog Lady for a walk and when she got to Mich's house Sandy would pretend that Lady got away. It would go over to Mich's house.

The next day Sandy was taking Lady for a walk it wasn't unusual for her to take Lady for a walk because she usually takes Lady for a walk. When Sandy got to the house where Mich lived Sandy was so busy looking at Mich that she didn't realize that Lady saw Mich's dog and started after it. . . .

The student who wrote this piece was the class champion writer of run-on sentences. To the best of my recollection, the only conversation we had about the first draft was my traditional recommendation that she check for run-ons. After she had written the second draft, we talked about the differences between the two.

Conference

MS. R.: How do you feel about the difference between the two?

TI.: Well, I like this one (second) a little bit better.

MS. R.: Yeah. I like it a whole lot better. What parts particularly do you like?

TI.: Um. . . . Well, the beginning where I put how you don't want to go talk to somebody but . . .

MS. R.: You mean this section (indicating first paragraph)?

TI.: Yeah.

MS. R.: Somehow that makes it really personal, because now I know who's writing it. And it's not about you, but it kind of establishes that a person is telling a story about these two people, and it's a story about *feelings*. I think that's a really effective way to open. That just really jumped out at me. I looked at it and that was so much more effective than this kind of impersonal . . .

TI.: And then the names helped you understand a little bit better. But I think I used the names *too* much.

MS. R.: So then you could go back and change some of them to "she." Yeah. In here (indicating fourth paragraph).

TI.: Yeah.

MS. R.: The shorter paragraphs seem to work better. Did you find it easier to keep track of reading here (top) than down here?

TI.: Yeah.

MS. R.: You might look at where this breaks into units. . . .

As this transcript shows, I am learning to let the student identify what part of the piece we will talk about. I try to reflect the effect her changes (opening, paragraphing) have on me. I emphasize the parts I think are good. Perhaps this seems obvious. However, when working with a class such as this one, with so many possible writing errors and problems that I *might* focus on, it has taken me a long time to learn to praise. I have a hunch that I'm not much different from many other English teachers.

Conferences take place at many different points in the composing process. My students now expect to write several drafts and usually want to talk before they begin to write. Although I never taped this part of the class time, virtually every new piece of writing began with talk. After giving an assignment and answering immediate questions from the whole class, I'd circulate to each student, pausing for anywhere from five seconds to two or three minutes, talking, questioning, brainstorming. This was very informal. However, I discovered that if I skipped this step, many students did not begin at all. One or two others would dash off a paragraph and then hand it to me, asking if they were "doing it right," but really asking to talk about their piece. "But we haven't had time to *talk* about it!" would be an angry outcry, if a deadline was too close and there hadn't been enough conference time.

Students began to come to conferences with a variety of materials: lists, paragraphs, notes, questions, partial drafts, endings, nothing. I have occasionally distributed a list of questions or concerns we will focus on during the conference. After reading Edith Wharton's *Ethan Frome,* I asked the class to write a narrative using the technique of the flashback, which we had talked about in reading the novel. I used the following list of questions to help structure the conferences about their stories.

1. Describe briefly what you are going to write about.
2. Which part will be included in a flashback?
3. Which part will you work on first?
4. Is any part giving you trouble right now?
5. How do you want your readers to feel when they read the finished piece?
6. Who would you like to help you, read your drafts, offer suggestions?
7. Who in the room would you like to help?

The last two questions were designed to help move the class from individual conferences to writing groups. As the next papers will show, by February we began to use the group in a way which was helpful to the writers.

One of my goals throughout the whole project, indeed one of the reasons I wanted to focus on the conferences I had with students, was to discover ways to move student revision from the editing level to a restructuring or conceptual level. I hoped to help them see the possibilities of change within their writing rather than to view manuscripts as frozen, merely in need of spelling corrections and punctuation. In previous years, most of the revisions had been in response to changes I had specifically suggested. However, as I stopped making marks in the margins and asked questions rather than gave directions, I began to see some independently motivated changes, like the beginning of the story "Sorry To See You Go."

Further, I began assigning assignments which lent themselves to structural changes, such as the flashback assignment. As is evident from the conference questions, I was encouraging students to start writing at any point in the story and then arrange the paper in a later draft.

Following are two drafts of student To.'s flashback story along with the group conference which came in between the drafts.

Student To.
"Flashback"

Draft 1

Intro

Hey Joe, "you want to watch the war movie. "ya sure." This movie reminds me of the war we were in. Ya it dose.

Body

The area is getting bombed. Machine guns are constantly blasting off. The enimy are coming through the woods. It seems like nothing can stop them. The bullets are flying through the branches above me and my buddy's heads. The open area between us and the enimy has just been bombed.

It stopped the enimy for a while. Then we started to retreat. Me and my buddy are trying to get back to the rest of the group. Machine guns are still blasting off. Granads are getting throw around. We start running as fast as we can to get back. We can see our group start getting into the tanks and trucks. The enimy seems to be getting closer.

A couple of tanks start taking off plus a couple of trucks. The rest of the people are getting in the rest of the trucks. All of a sudden I herd a rapid machine gun blasting. Then I realized that my buddy wasn't running next to me any more. I started to turn around, everyone was yelling hurry up, get out. I couldn't keep on going unless I looked back. As I did, the trucks started taking off. I saw that my buddy was dead. I felt like running back to help him. I couldn't believe that he dead. I had to turn and run to the trucks . . . for I could get out of there.

Group Conference

(The group has been describing what they heard when To. read his draft.)

MS. R.: Tina, what strikes you?

TINA: Well, this guy gets killed. (laughter)

MS. R.: OK, well here's one other version. You've decided the guy is killed. The people have decided that he's *not* killed. (pause) Well, that's interesting information for Todd, because he has to decide now as a writer, is that buddy *dead.*

ROGER: He *did* say he was dead.

MS. R.: But, but three people don't believe it here! (laughter)

DAVID: He said he was dead. But just by looking back at . . .

KELLIE: Yeah, but his not saying anything about whether he was dead or alive makes it more interesting. You have to wonder.

DAVID: But if you look back and saw a man blown to bits it's different.

MS. R.: OK. So that's information for Todd to decide. (pause)

(At this point, a long discussion took place about other possible settings for the beginning, such as an arcade, a school yard.)

MS. R.: Any other suggestions about how he could set up the introduction? Mary?

MARY: His introduction . . . I don't know. He doesn't write it right.

MS. R.: Well?

MARY: I know, but I mean like . . .

DAVID: What's wrong with it?

MARY: You can't have it, like, all clumped together.

ROGER: Let's go beat her up! (laughter)

MS. R.: You mean the . . . quotation marks?

MARY: Yeah!

MS. R.: OK. Well, that's secondary, OK? Let's not deal with the sentence structure and things like that. We're just talking about how can you make . . . That's *true,* he's got to move the dialogue in. . . .

ROGER: It's not time to look at *spelling* and stuff. It's time to look at the whole story.

MS. R.: I agree. Not that that's not *important,* but . . .
ROGER: 'Cause you're going to find a *lot* of spelling errors when
    you read mine! (laughter)

*   *   *

MS. R.: I have a question for the thinkers out here. How're you
    going to work him back into the present? What's going to
    happen on the other half of the frame? We've got the be-
    ginning, and flashing back. Now we've got to bring him
    back into the present. What's going to happen there? Todd,
    do you have ideas about what you want to have happen?
TODD: No.
ROGER: Is he thinking about the war while they're watching the
    movie right now? Or is this after they watch the movie?
TODD: During.
ROGER: You could have him go nuts. His friend shake him out
    of it or something.
CHRIS: Then shoot him. (laughter)
DAVID: Somebody knock him out on the floor.
MS. R.: To break him out of it, you mean? Then what?
DAVID: I mean you always have that happen. You're sitting
    there concentrating on something, you start daydream-
    ing. . . .
ROGER: The phone rings.
DAVID: The phone rings and knock on . . .
MS. R.: What would be his condition when he comes back into
    the present?
ROGER: Crazy.
DAVID: Amazed.

Draft 2

"There's a war movie on TV Joe. Do you want to watch it?"
"Yeah sure."
"Sit down. I will turn the TV on."
"Looks like the movie already started."
"Yeah, and that looks like the area of woods we were in, re-
member that?"
The area is getting bombed. Machine guns are blasting off.
The enemy is coming through the woods. It seems like nothing
can stop them. Bullets are flying over our heads, through the
low branches.
The area has just been bombed. We start to retreat. The bomb-
ing slowed down the enimy a little. Then my buddy and I start
to run as fast as we can, to get back to our group. Machine guns
are still blasting off. We finnilly catch up to our group. We all

start to head to the tanks and trucks. Soon I can see the clear-
ing and our camoflage tanks. A couple were all ready full and
taking off.

All of a sudden I hear a rapid machine gun fire. I soon realize
that my buddy isn't running beside me any more. I start to turn
around. Everyone is yelling for me to keep on running and save
my own life. When I turn around, I see him lying there. I don't
know if he is dead or not. I felt my self fall to the ground.

I get up and look around. Everything looks broken or full
of bullet holes. Joe tells me that I ran to the gun cabinet and
started shooting everything in sight. He also says that he had to
lie on the floor so he didn't get shot.

I didn't talk any further with Todd after the group conference,
except for supplying the correct spelling of "yeah." Paragraphing,
handling of dialogue, and the conclusion were completed independently. Obviously, the group helped him expand the introduction and
add the ending. An intermediate draft included the following sentence
at the beginning of the final paragraph: "When I got up I realized
that I tripped over the telephone cord." This sentence was crossed
out in pencil and eliminated in the final draft. When I asked why,
Todd said, "I didn't like it." This seems to me to be evidence of testing and rejecting the group's suggestion in this case. However, he accepted and expanded their ambiguity about the buddy's death, plac-
ing Joe on the floor in the buddy's place in his concluding paragraph.

Noteworthy in the group conference is their recognition that
their purpose is to work on ideas rather than mechanics. Todd made
good use of the ideas which were suggested. He also heeded Mary's
concern about the arrangement of sentences in the opening section.
However, the mechanical corrections were done on his own. In this
class, I virtually never marked errors on drafts. Initially, there were
just too many. I noticed that they asked for correct spelling when
I had made it clear that I would give free information. We spent
other class time doing drills on fragments and run-ons, on sentence
combining. I told them that final drafts should be as error free as
possible. When they had as much investment in the piece of writing
as they often developed, they did mechanical corrections as well as
did other classes for whom I had marked every single "frag" and
"sp" in the margin.

It is important to remember that this group conference took
place in February, after the class had had extensive experience in
individual conferences with me and with each other. Initially, the
student-with-student conferences were fifteen-second-long silences.
Even here I did a lot of directing of conversation, because although
we were talking specifically about Todd's paper, all the other mem-

bers of the class were dealing with similar issues in their own papers. Initially, my proposal had envisioned taping regular student-student conferences and students transcribing their own tapes. I abandoned both of these ideas almost immediately, although I believe they might work with more sophisticated students. Informal but stable support groups among students did form, however, and pairs or trios of students regularly read each other's work without my intervention.

The last sample of writing and conferences demonstrates the increased connections between student talk and writing. The assignment was to write about a single event from three different points of view. Students were asked to write one point of view each day. Then we would talk about them so that they could unify the sections in some way to create a continuous piece. The stages in Nancy's composing of "Softball Game" illustrate remarkably clearly the progress we all made in using talking for learning and writing.

"Softball Game"

Draft 1

Hitter's Point

Well I'm almost up, oh no. She just made the 2nd out and the tying run is on 3rd. Winning run is me. Oh no, I've never made it out of this situation before. Oh please stop cheering me on, boy are they making me nervous. We need this game so bad in order to make it to the state finals. "Batter up" yells the base ump. Well here goes nothing, maybe she'll walk me, boy if the coach ever heard me saying that he kicked me off the team for two weeks. Here comes her wind up oh no here comes the ball. "Strike," Strike no way. That was down at my ankles. This ump is going to make this tough, I knew he was for the other team. Here it comes again Strike two, well that one was close. Boy is everyone getting nervous, what am I saying so am I. Here it comes again it's mine. Wow I hit it everyone keeps hollering go, wait a minute I'm rounding 3rd I couldn't of hit a home run. Slide everyone yells, slide. Oh no that means the ball's close, it't the ump's call. He looks at me. I look at him, then I hear safe. I think I died and went to heaven Yahoo! Yahoo! Here comes the team. Some are crying some are laughing and a few are stunned. They carry me off and the coach comes over and says Honestly Walker, I didn't think you could do it.

(Coach's and pitcher's points of view have been omitted.)

234

Conference

MS. R.: OK. What are you working on right now?

N.: What do you mean, what am I working on?

MS. R.: You finished the three pieces, right?

N.: Yep.

MS. R.: What are you doing, what have you decided to do? Or have you decided . . .

N.: Well, you told me about the state finals not being in all of them except for this one (hitter), so I took it and connected it here (last sentence after hitter). This one is the coach talking here and then here is his point of view and at the end of this one I've got the pitcher talking here. So I'll hitch it to this one.

MS. R.: Read me how that happens.

N.: Well, let's see . . . . OK, it goes: "The state finals are in great jeopardy, especially knowing that Walker's up."

MS. R.: Now that's just inside, though. He's not saying that out loud. OK.

N.: Yeah. "Oh I hope she makes it. Great hit." And then he yells it out like that. Then it goes: "State finals look like they're going to be ours. With this girl up next we've got it."

MS. R.: OK. So you're going to . . . What form is the whole thing going to take? You're just going to then switch back, go back in time, and start with the pitcher?

N.: Yep.

MS. R.: OK. And where does, which order is Walker going to be? Going to start with the coach?

N.: No. With the hitter, the coach, the pitcher.

MS. R.: OK. (pause) Um. Yeah, OK, that makes sense because you need that first "I honestly didn't think you could do it" in reality before you hear the coach think about it.

N.: Yeah.

MS. R.: Um. . . . I really *like* this. (pause) I think the thing you need to work on when you put it all together is how to do . . . you have it all in one great big paragraph . . . how to divide it up so that it makes sense. Because you don't have anyone saying anything out loud except . . .

N.: The coach when he says I honestly didn't think you'd make it.

MS. R.: Right.

N.: And then the sliding and the ump hollering safe.

MS. R.: Yeah. (pause) Do you know how to do . . . dialogue?

N.: Well . . . sort of . . . .

MS. R.: Every time . . . like right here. (indicating "batter up")
That *has* to begin a new paragraph, every time someone
new speaks, no matter where you are. Now this is . . . then
you have to go . . . (writing it out) "Batter up, comma,"
yells the ump, the base ump.

Now you have a decision at this point. Now this (indicating) is back to you thinking, Walker thinking. If you were
to continue: Well here goes nothing, it kind of connects it
with the base ump, so you probably want to start a new
paragraph: Well here goes nothing, to let us know we've
switched back to your point of view.

N.: There's a "strike" somewhere. Right there. (pointing)

MS. R.: Is that the ump hollering "strike"? OK. So, then you
probably want to end the paragraph here. Start a new
paragraph with "Strike." And then again go back to your
own train of thought inside.

N.: OK.

MS. R.: I think that will divide up the paragraphs for you.

N.: Then at "everyone's hollering slide."

MS. R.: "Slide," everyone yells. I think that will be the vehicle
for dividing into paragraphs.

N.: OK.

MS. R.: Just every time there's a voice from outside, you start
a new paragraph and just have that voice from outside.

N.: OK.

MS. R.: Then you start another new paragraph with what you
think. Now is this part of . . . ?

N.: The coach.

MS. R.: The coach. I think you might want to double space between the coach and Walker.

N.: OK. So like here, where I put this here? I should double
space, between them. This is the pitcher and this is the
coach. (indicating another section of the paper)

MS. R.: I think so. I think otherwise it might be confusing because you're going inside of each one of those heads. And
the double space . . . sometimes in books you see dot dot
dot in between to let you know it's a new section. (pause)
I really liked it. I thought is was nice. That's called internal
monologue. You did a good job with that. And they each
end with this nice (laugh) this nice little . . . It's kind of a
different version of the same thought. It's good.

OK. Why don't you put it all together and see what it
looks like?

Draft 2

Well, I'm almost up. Oh no. She just made the second out, tying run is on third, winning run is me. Oh no, I've never made it out of this situation before. Oh, please stop cheering me on, boy are they making me nervous. We need this game so bad in order to make it to the State Finals.

"Batter up," yells the base ump.

Well here goes nothing. Maybe she'll walk me. Boy if the coach ever heard me saying that he'd kick me off the team for two weeks. Here comes the wind up. Oh no, here comes the ball.

"Strike."

Strike, no way that was down at my ankles. This ump is going to make this tough. I knew he was for the other team. Here it comes again.

"Strike two."

Well, that one was close. Boy everyone's getting nervous. What am I saying, so am I. Here comes the pitch, it's mine. Wow, I hit it, everyone keeps yelling go. Wait a minute I'm rounding third, I couldn't have hit a home run.

"Slide," everyone yells.

Slide, oh no, that means the balls close. It's the umps call. He looks at me; I look at him. Then I hear;

"Safe."

I think I died and went to heaven.

Yahoo! Yahoo!

Here comes the team, some are crying, some are laughing, some are stunned. They carry me off. The coach comes over, looks at me and says,

"Walker, honestly I didn't think you could do it."

Group Conference

(I had duplicated both draft 1 and 2.)

MS. R.: This one . . . the one that's in paragraphs, is the second version of the hitter's point of view. Somebody just want to describe for Nancy what they see the differences are between the first draft and the second draft, so she can understand what she's done? I gave her some suggestions, and she's made some changes. And it would be helpful if she could hear how *you* see the differences between the first and second draft.

DAVID: It's in paragraphs. That's better.

MS. R.: Why?

ROGER: You can tell what's happening better. It sections it off.

MS. R.: OK. Anything else you could tell her about that? Or what else she might do to it?

DAVID: More vocabulary.

MS. R.: Like where? Like what? Who?

DAVID: You could have more people talking.

MS. R.: Like where?

DAVID: You could have somebody yell from the bench.

ROGER: Pitcher saying something to her.

MS. R.: Is that helpful? (to Nancy) I hadn't thought of that.

NANCY: Well . . . It's just me right there . . . what I'm thinking of, not someone outside.

MS. R.: We do also have the pitcher's point of view, which is *his* interior monologue.

When I was talking to Nancy yesterday, I wasn't sure how to help her get the pitcher's point of view in. If we're going to make this into one long story, where, how can we get that coach in there? That's basically why I gave it to you. See if you have some suggestions. How do we get the coach into the story? You can see how here the second draft is starting. Where could the . . .

DAVID: You could have her glance back every once in a while. Looking at the coach or something.

KEVIN: Having the coach thinking something.

MS. R.: Could you give some suggestions about that?

KEVIN: I don't know.

MS. R.: Anybody have any ideas for how to move from inside Walker's head?

KELLIE: Dialogue?

MS. R.: She doesn't say anything.

DAVID: You could *make* her say something.

ROGER: You could have her say something . . . encourage her and stuff.

DAVID: They have signs. Have her glance over for signs.

MS. R.: And then glance over for signs and that being a way to get inside the coach's head as she's giving signs, maybe?

In the final version, Nancy decided to interweave the points of view rather than telling them one after another. She chose to use the suggestion about signals, about looking at the coach, and about adding dialogue. Once again, this final version emerged independently, with no further help in the area of mechanics or content from me.

Final Draft

Well, I'm almost up, oh no she just made the second out. The tying run is on third, winning run is me. I wonder what the coach is thinking right now, with the State Finals in jeopardy.

Oh, I hope she makes a great hit, homerun would be excellent. If she doesn't get a hit we won't win. Just look at Walker over there, she's so scared she'll never get a hit. "Damn it," she just struck out, we blew the state finals. I might as well go sit on the bench. But, look at those faces, they're still praying. I better stay here. If I go and sit down, Walker will just get more nervous. I wonder how the pitcher must feel knowing she's the key to the State Finals.

Well, it looks like the State Finals are ours. This one's just standing there for the count, like she's dead. Look at that girl that's up next, she's so scared she'll never hit it.

"Strike three," yells the base ump.

"Yahoo, Yahoo," yells the opposing team.

Hee, hee. I knew I'd get her. Here comes my next and last batter. If I can strike her out and the girl on third doesn't come home, we're home free. Huh, look at her. She's so scared, if I remember correctly she sat there the last two times for strikes. If she couldn't hit it then she'll certainly not hit it now. I can imagine how she must feel.

"Batter up," yells the base ump.

Well, here goes nothing, maybe she'll walk me, boy if the coach ever heard me say that he'd kick me off the team for two weeks. I better look for signals, boy he looks real nervous. Here comes the pitcher's wind up. Ohhh here comes the ball.

"Strike one," yells the ump.

"Strike, no way, that was down at my ankles." This ump is going to make this tough, I knew he was for the other team. Here comes her pitch again.

"Strike two," yells the ump once again.

Well that was a little close. Boy is everyone getting nervous, wait, what am I saying, so am I. Here it comes again, it's mine. The coach must be shocked.

Here comes the pitch. God, Nancy, *hit* it! Strike, well that was a little low. Here comes the second pitch. I'll never understand why she did that. Well maybe now the pitcher will walk her. Wait, what am I saying, that's just the attitude I told my players to forget. Here comes the third pitch, she hit it. Yahoo! The pitcher must be mad.

Well, here goes my best pitch.

"Strike one," yells the ump.

Wow, this is easier than I thought it would be. Here goes my second pitch.

"Strike two," yells the ump.

Here goes my last pitch. Oh my God she hit it. Noooo, not past center. Oh no, she's rounding third. What the hell is she standing there holding the ball for. "Throw it you jerk!" Wow, what a great throw. Look at the runner, she must be wondering what's going on.

Wow, I hit it. Everyone keeps yelling go, wait, I'm rounding third. I couldn't of hit a home run.

"Slide," everyone yells.

Slide, oh no, that means the ball is close. I slid under the pitcher, she never hit me. It's the ump's call. He looks at me, I look at him. Then I hear.

"Safe."

I think I died and went to heaven.

"Yahoo, Yahoo," yells the team.

Here comes the team, some are laughing, some are crying, some are just stunned. Boy this pitcher must be ripped. But I honestly didn't think I could do it.

Here she comes, boy she's daring, I've got her I just know it. Oh, no, she's going to slide under me, I had to hit her. The ump has to call her out. Come on ump, call it.

"Safe," yells the ump.

"No way," yells the pitcher's team.

Honestly I didn't think she could do it. I wonder how their coach must feel.

"Go," yells the coach. Wow at least now we're tied. Wait, Walker's still running, she's turning third. "Go, you can make it." Wait, what am I saying, she's not that fast of a runner. "Slide!" Oh please let her be safe. Ump, call it.

"Safe," yells the ump.

"Safe! Yay! We won," yells the coach. I can't believe she did it. Boy, she'll play more often. Look at her sitting there glowing with pride and satisfaction. What should I say to her, well the truth would do. Boy is she going to get a write up on this.

"Honestly, Walker, I didn't think you could do it."

James Britton was right when he said research is not so much a matter of proving something as a quiet form of discovering and learning. Like Walker, I honestly didn't think I could do it sometimes. But, like Walker, I surprised myself. What have I learned? I have new expectations and understandings of the function of the writing conference. I have a different definition of what revision means for these student writers.

As I reflect upon the tapes, I hear myself repeatedly using the conference time for exploring ideas. My role is most often the preliminary audience. I hear myself ask questions which will help the writer to see gaps in what has been written, to elaborate, to add detail that hasn't been included in the draft. I try to help the writer hear the effect the piece has on the reader.

I have learned to give positive support. My students' ability to make their own editing corrections reveals that they could see what was wrong with their writing. They needed also to see what was right. I am certain that this change in my approach to their writing contributed as much as any other factor to their willingness to continue writing.

Perhaps the most surprising discovery was a new habit I developed. I found myself describing each of my student writers to themselves and to each other in terms of their particular strengths or typical styles: Mary does dialogue and thinks up great character names, Roger is funny, Kevin is gruesome and ends his pieces with odd twists, David would rather write than read, Brandon prefers exposition to narrative, Kellie writes great description. In this way, I taught them to see themselves and each other as writers. Don't forget, half of them saw themselves as two-time losers in the Basic Skills in Writing test at the beginning of the year, including the author of "Softball Game." All six passed the test in November. By June, I believe each of us had discovered abilities and identities as writers, rather than merely learned how to correct errors and make the changes the teacher insisted on.

I learned to focus much more on the content of their writing. Frankly, I became interested in their stories. As the transcripts show, I did spend a lot of time on mechanics, punctuation, paragraphing. However, this kind of instruction resulted from the need to make what the writer was saying more understandable in the next draft. I'm sure my interest helped them to attempt another draft.

I discovered that if I wanted students to revise their writing, they needed to write something *worth revising*. I dealt with this issue in two ways. First, I designed assignments (flashback, multiple narrator) which students wrote a section at a time, then decided how to combine, order, organize at a later stage in the process. Since these students had some difficulty maintaining long pieces, this was a way of creating manageable units. Rereading, changing, working on transitions, altering point of view, shifting time and verb tense, all became possible because we could save it for later. Revision wasn't just recopying but the next step of assembling the parts. Revision was getting the story to work, getting it to be good.

Second, at least half of the writing in this class has been either expressive or poetic, to borrow Britton's terminology. This was a practical necessity at first, to get the class writing. However, they are now clearly interested in narrative writing, either personal memory or fiction. Two of the samples I have included here are memory, two fiction. This focus of the class wasn't intentional; I've never included much narrative writing in my classes before. Three or four class members write extended stories in their journals. They report that they have never been asked to do much narrative writing in school, but when I give a choice of assignments most of the class chooses to write stories.

The conferences about more traditional expository writing are much less satisfactory than the ones I've transcribed and categorized about expressive writing. I have much more difficulty keeping quiet, because I have "ownership" of the knowledge: the content of *The Crucible* or *Ethan Frome,* the techniques of writing about books, the organizational strategies of expository writing. And it must be admitted that these are students who feel no guilt at refusing to do a distasteful assignment.

On the other hand, when the content is the student's experience, memory, or imagination, I can be a reader, a legitimate audience, rather than an evaluator, a judge. There is no question that these students write more fluently, at greater length, with more willingness, in expressive or poetic modes. Stories were frequently two to six pages. Exposition was usually two to four paragraphs. At least four students report that they prefer writing to reading as a class assignment. Three of these four say they didn't know they liked to write before this year. In other words, if one of my goals was to help them improve the quality of their writing through conferences and revision, it became obvious that it was expressive or poetic writing which engaged their interest and provided the motivation to revise.

As I reflect on my initial reasons for undertaking this research project, I have a revised set of reasons for studying the writing in my own classroom.

1. The project taught me more than any single course I've taken, though the courses and workshops and conferences were important preliminary and supporting steps.
2. My students benefited *far* more directly and continually. They were not guinea pigs or subjects, as in some kinds of research, but beneficiaries, and teachers.
3. I learned new and unexpected directions, rather than merely verified ideas gleaned from readings.
4. I'm confident that it improved my teaching in a permanent way.

References

Britton, J. (1970). *Language and learning.* Harmondsworth: Penguin.
Martin, N., D'Arcy, P., Newton, B., & Parker, R. (1976). *Writing and learning across the curriculum 11–16.* London: Ward Lock.